Sacred Scripture

Also by Richard N. Soulen and R. Kendall Soulen:
A Handbook of Biblical Criticism, 3rd edition

Sacred Scripture

A Short History of Interpretation

RICHARD N. SOULEN

WESTMINSTER
JOHN KNOX PRESS
LOUISVILLE · KENTUCKY

First edition
Published by Westminster John Knox Press
Louisville, Kentucky

10 11 12 13 14 15 16 17 18 19—10 9 8 7 6 5 4 3 2 1

Book design by Drew Stevens
Cover design by Lisa Buckley
*Cover art: Jordaens, Jacob/*The Four Evangelists/*Louvre, Paris, France*
Photo: Erich Lessing/Art Resource, NY

Library of Congress Cataloging-in-Publication Data

Soulen, Richard N., 1933–
   Sacred Scripture : a short history of interpretation / Richard N. Soulen.
     p. cm.
   Includes bibliographical references and index.
   ISBN 978-0-664-23246-7 (alk. paper)
   1. Bible—Criticism, interpretation, etc.—History.   I. Title.
   BS500.S57   2010
   220.609—dc22
                       2009028362

For My Children and Grandchildren

Contents

Preface and Acknowledgments   xi

Introduction   xiii

Chapter One: What Is Sacred Scripture?   1

  The Old Testament as Sacred Scripture   1

  The New Testament as Sacred Scripture   9

Chapter Two: Which Scripture Is Sacred?   17

  The Sacred Scripture of Judaism   18

  The Sacred Scriptures of the Early Church   22

  Summary   27

Chapter Three: Which Manuscripts?   29

  What's the Problem?   29

  The Reformation and the Beginnings of a Critical Text
    of the New Testament   33

  Recent Discoveries   36

  The Development of the Critical Text   39

  Summary   43

Chapter Four: Which Translation?   45

  The Blessing of Translation   45

  The Challenge of Translation   46

  Translation: From the Septuagint
    to the King James Version   48

  The Aims of Modern Translation   52

  The Geneva Bible Redivivus   58

Chapter Five: How Does Scripture Interpret Itself?   61

   Introduction   61

   Scripture Interpreting Scripture in the Hebrew Bible   62

   Typology in the New Testament   70

   Conclusion   75

Chapter Six: What Did the Early Church Leaders Say?   77

   Change and Continuity   77

   Irenaeus, Bishop of Lyon   78

   Origen   80

   Augustine, Bishop of Hippo   86

   Conclusion   94

Chapter Seven: How Many Senses Does Scripture Have?   97

   The Quadriga   97

   Abbot Suger and the Anagogical Sense   100

   Bernard of Clairvaux and the Tropological Sense   102

   Peter Abelard and the Allegorical Sense   105

   Conclusion   112

Chapter Eight: What Is the Center of Scripture?   113

   The Center of Scripture and Luther's Reformation   114

   The Center of Scripture and Protestant Scholasticism   120

   The Center of Scripture and Pietism   121

   Conclusion   129

Chapter Nine: What Is the Literal Sense of Scripture?   131

   Introduction   131

   The Historical Event behind the Text: Reimarus   132

   Authorial Mind or Intent: Schleiermacher   138

   Ideas or Concepts Independent of Either History
      or Intent: Jefferson   147

   Summary   153

Chapter Ten: What Is Modern Biblical Interpretation?   155
   Modern and Postmodern   155
   Source Criticism   158
   Form Criticism   161
   Redaction Criticism   164
   Summary   169

Chapter Eleven: What Is Contemporary
Biblical Interpretation?   171
   A Postmodern Analogy: On Playing Ball with the Text   172
   Postmodern Biblical Interpretation: John Frank Kermode   173
   Liberation Biblical Interpretation: Jon Sobrino   176
   Postcritical Biblical Interpretation: Hans Frei   183

Epilogue   191
Bibliography   197
Index   207

Preface and Acknowledgments

For two millennia, hundreds of millions of people of every race and nation have held the Bible sacred for telling "the greatest story ever told" and for revealing to those "who have ears to hear" the nature and will of God. I am one of those people. Raised in a Methodist parsonage in a small town on the Plains during a time of economic scarcity and national peril, that is, during the Depression and World War II, it is perhaps not surprising that the life of the family and the life of the worshiping community were for me essentially one and the same. Expressed in the captivating language and imagery of the Bible and the liturgical seasons of the church, Christian faith was the needle that threaded all the experiences of life into an unbroken and cherished whole. The rhythm of life was set by morning worship and vespers on Sundays and prayer service on Wednesday nights, with the festivals of Christmas and Easter serving as the recurring joys that kept sacred time and sacred place fresh in memory and in anticipation. Over against this world so full of joy and purpose was another, and being a pre-teen with a vivid imagination this other world was all too threateningly present, like the acrid smell of an approaching fire. It was the world of man's inhumanity to man, the world of unfaith, of unremitting cruelty and fear. In that world nothing was sacred and nothing holy. I did not doubt then, nor have I doubted since, which of these worlds was true and which was false; which led to life abundant and which to meaninglessness and death. I knew as well that the first world was built by men and women devoted to the world envisioned and proclaimed by sacred Scripture, and that the Scriptures were sacred for that very reason.

What I did not know was how the Bible related to that second world, to the world of disinterest and disbelief, to secularism and materialism—to the profane world of man's inhumanity to man (an old phrase, pithy and inclusive). The more I was convinced of the truth of the biblical story, from the moment of creation to creation's telos in time, the more I wanted to discover the essential nature of that truth. Fortunately for me, no one ever suggested that religious faith and critical reason were incompatible. Both were a part of God's created order. The challenge lay in finding out in what way that was true. That quest began well over a half century ago and joyously continues still.

The following essays, some of which owe their origin to classroom handouts, address but a few of these questions and those I have repeatedly heard in my twenty years in the pastorate and thirty years teaching in seminaries and colleges. The questions are introductory and illustrative. Many more questions could be asked, and should be asked, were a larger work possible, such as John Calvin's inquiry into the relationship of Scripture to church doctrine, or the place of Scripture in Roman Catholicism and in Eastern Orthodoxy. Other questions would be equally relevant, but then the book would neither be "short" nor in accordance with the publisher's requirements.

I welcome here the opportunity to thank those who have encouraged me in this endeavor, not least my students at the Samuel DeWitt Proctor School of Theology at Virginia Union University in Richmond, VA, and at the Course of Study School for Local Pastors of the United Methodist Church held at Wesley Theological Seminary in Washington, D.C. Were it not for Dean John W. Kinney's kind invitation to return to Virginia Union in 1996 after years in the pastorate, this book would have been unthinkable. It is to him, in admiration of his inspired leadership of the School of Theology and in gratitude for his friendship, that I give my heartfelt thanks. I also want happily to thank Dr. Patrick Miller of Princeton Theological Seminary (emeritus) and Dr. Richard A. Ray, former editor of John Knox Press, for reading the manuscript at various stages in its writing, and for their friendship. Over the years both have been trusted mentor and friend to literally hundreds of scholars seeking guidance and advice. Most especially I must record my deep gratitude to my son, R. Kendall Soulen, Professor of Systematic Theology at Wesley Theological Seminary. His skill in editing an overwrought manuscript into one more focused, as well as his wise and perceptive counsel throughout, has been invaluable. Special thanks go to Jon Berquist and Dan Braden of Westminster John Knox for their expert care in preparing the manuscript for publication, and to Erika Lundbom for her technical assistance. Finally, I must thank my wife, Peggy, for her constant encouragement and support; we both have found joy in this adventure and in more than fifty years of life together.

Introduction

The following chapters focus on some of the major theological issues the church has faced through the centuries in the interpretation of sacred Scripture. What follows is obviously not a complete history—even of the issues considered. It is, rather, a basic discussion—at times somewhat narrowly focused—of topics that bear on scriptural interpretation.

The key rubric used in the chapters is a very simple one: *a question.* What is sacred Scripture? Which Scripture is sacred? Which manuscripts? Which translation? These and other questions have been chosen because they illuminate the task of scriptural interpretation from a distinct vantage point.

Chapters 1 through 3 are preliminary to the more chronologically ordered topics that follow. Chapter 1 asks the question, "What is sacred Scripture?" In the experience of Israel and the church, it is argued, Scripture arose out of the common need to pass on in writing the experience of the Divine within the secular, the holy amid the mundane. Chapter 2 asks the question, "Which Scripture is sacred?" Here we get an overview of the struggle in the first and second centuries between Judaism and Christianity, as well as between emergent Catholicism and heterodox Christian communities, to define which writings were to be regarded as sacred and which were not. Out of this struggle came not only the Christian canon known as the New Testament, but the Hebrew canon as well.

Chapters 3 and 4 ("Which Manuscripts? and "Which Translation?") find their place among these essays because it is too often assumed by laity and seminary students alike that the Bible is like any other book in print, that the English copy in hand reads as Mark, Paul, or Isaiah intended it to read, without slippage of any kind. To ask which manuscript is "sacred," or at least "the best," is not an idle question. Much doctrinaire foolishness results from not being humbled by the lack of certainty about the biblical text. Chapter 4 extends this caution to translations of the Bible. Here too stumbling stones exist when, without stated criteria of judgment, all translations are treated equally without cognizance of the nature and purpose of a specific translation.

With chapter 5, the book begins to take a more conventionally chronological shape. The questions we examine provide the opportunity to view some of the major developments in the history of Christian biblical interpretation.

Chapter 5 asks, "How does Scripture interpret itself?" and in some respects it is the heart of the matter. It tries to show, in a limited way, how the interpretation of sacred traditions began with the appearance of the traditions themselves. The phrase, "I mean—" is an overused contemporary colloquialism, a space-filler to steal time for the mind to organize its thoughts. But it expresses the human proclivity to seek meaning and to reexamine old assumptions and valuations about what is thought to be known. So ancient authors boldly reexamined claims about the nature and will of God, the nature of sin and salvation, of justice and injustice, and so on. From the Christian perspective, Jesus of Nazareth posited a radical reinterpretation of normative Judaism in his day, just as the early church cherished not one but four Gospels, each offering a different interpretation of the message and meaning of Jesus. Cognizance of how Scripture interprets Scripture is itself a liberating and cautionary tale, and so we devote time to it here.

Chapter 6 ("What Did the Early Church Leaders Say?") begins an illustrative (not exhaustive) account of how the church of the second to the fifth century interpreted the story of Jesus to a non-Jewish culture by appealing on the one hand to the thought-forms of Hellenism, while on the other hand acknowledging the church's roots in Judaism. We turn to the foremost thinkers of the three centuries: Irenaeus (second century), Origen (third century), and Augustine (fourth-fifth centuries) in order to show the power of Scripture to captivate three of the greatest minds of their day on behalf of the Christian faith.

Chapter 7 ("How Many Senses Does Scripture Have?") is a bit more playful in that it focuses a thousand years on the lives of three twelfth-century contemporaries as different as life permits and yet equally devoted to the Christ of Scripture. The three abbots (Suger of St.-Denis, Bernard of Clairvaux, and Peter Abelard) each ascribed to the multiple senses of Scripture but in fascinatingly divergent ways. To our abbots, as we shall see, a literalist, univocal view of Scripture in the modern fundamentalist sense would have been unimaginable.

In chapter 8 ("What Is the Center of Scripture?") we turn to Luther (1483–1546) to the exclusion of John Calvin (1509–1564) because it is Luther who sought to get behind the encrustations of church doctrine and the patristic tradition of multiple senses to the center of Scripture itself: Jesus Christ. While Protestant Scholastics sought to defend the objective truth of that claim, the Pietists argued that until scriptural truth was subjectively appropriated it remained ineffectual. One Lutheran follower of a pietistic bent put it this way: "Were Jesus born a thousand times in Bethlehem and not in me, I would still be lost."

With chapter 9 we turn to "one of the most perplexing yet important" questions in the history of biblical interpretation: "What is the literal sense of Scripture?" To illustrate the problem we turn to three "misinterpretations" of the question that come from the latter days of the Enlightenment: H. S. Reimarus, F. D. E. Schleiermacher, and Thomas Jefferson. The rubrics of the chapter are taken from the work by Hans Frei, *The Eclipse of Biblical Narrative: A Study in Eighteenth and Nineteenth Century Hermeneutics* (New Haven: Yale University Press, 1975).

Chapter 10 asks, "What is modern biblical interpretation?" Here the term "modern" refers to the approach to biblical interpretation that dominated the field for well over a hundred years, from the middle of the nineteenth century to the last third of the twentieth. We call it "modern biblical interpretation" because, originating in the Enlightenment, it was sustained by the conviction that, as in science, objectivity in interpretation was not only necessary but possible.

The final chapter ("What Is Contemporary Biblical Interpretation?") looks at three broadly representative perspectives: postmodern, liberation, and postcritical biblical interpretation. Each has experienced numerous permutations and garnered an equal number of advocates, none of which can be discussed here because of space limitations. For the first two perspectives we turn to John Frank Kermode and to Jon Sobrino, SJ. We end with Hans Frei's "postcritical" approach to Scripture, not because his thought is readily accessible to students of Scripture; indeed, it is not. We close with him because of the fecundity of his ideas, and because they most readily explain the experience of the ordinary Christian, like those I have described of myself as a child reared in a family for whom the Scriptures of the Christian church were sacred.

Chapter 1
What Is Sacred Scripture?

Not every religion has sacred Scripture. Even among the three "religions of the book," Judaism, Christianity, and Islam, scripture plays significantly different roles. In Islam, for example, according to tradition the Qur'an was revealed over a period of years to one man in Arabic and is conceived of as the Word of God in itself. The situation is different in Judaism and Christianity. How and why the Scriptures of these two religious faiths came into being as sacred literature, and in what their sacrality lies, is the focus of this chapter.

THE OLD TESTAMENT AS SACRED SCRIPTURE

"Long ago God spoke to our ancestors in many and various ways by the prophets" (Heb. 1:1a). With these words the author of the Epistle to the Hebrews in the New Testament expressed the widely held sentiments of first-century Judaism and Christianity. Recorded in the Scriptures of the Old Testament were accounts of the "many and various ways" by which the ancestors of Judaism experienced the self-revelation of God, first preserved as oral traditions. The most important of these traditions are the divine revelations through which God called the people of Israel into being (Gen. 12), made covenant with them to be God's people (Gen. 15), revealed the law to guide their life (Exod. 19–20, passim) and, finally, blessed, comforted, warned, and chastised them through the generations.

1

These are the ancient traditions that form the core of Israel's Scriptures. The many and various ways by which Scripture said divine self-disclosure took place included visions (e.g., Gen. 15; Isa. 6), dreams (e.g., Num. 12), auditions (e.g., 1 Sam. 3), visitations (e.g., Gen. 12), direct encounters—either with the messengers of God (lit. "angels"; e.g., Gen. 16; 19) or with God himself "face to face" (e.g., Gen. 32; Exod. 33:11)—and, most prominently, the prophetic oracle (Elijah, Elisha, etc.). In time these traditions were inscribed and, since all were considered sacred revelations, all the writings were attributed to inspired "prophets" or *nebiim,* a Hebrew term that designated a variety of religious functionaries, including the role played by Moses, the greatest of all the prophets.[1]

The many and various ways God "spoke" also took on the many and various linguistic forms appropriate to its varied content: narratives, laws, oracles, psalms, and wisdom sayings—to name only the larger genres—all of which became sacred speech in its own way and setting. Of this vast subject, the single point to be illustrated here is that behind the varied forms of sacred literature lie many and varied sacred epiphanies of divine self-disclosure, the greater number of which were perceived linguistically as "Word of God." That *Scripture* should follow upon God's speaking was a matter of course, since Israel conceived its relationship to God as covenantal, that is, as a legal agreement binding to both parties, as *promise* on the one hand and *faithful obedience* on the other. Written codes, cultic and social, set down the commandments, statutes, and ordinances by which the covenant between God and Israel was to be observed (see, e.g., Deut. 4–6; Ps. 119).

On occasion, God himself is said to write the laws of the covenant, as with the Ten Commandments (Exod. 34:1; Deut. 10:2). At other times, God commands his prophet to write (Exod. 34:27; Deut. 6:9). Once written, the resulting inscription on tablet or scroll was to serve as a "memorial" for posterity (e.g., Exod. 17:14). The words were to be read publicly (Exod. 24:7) or privately, for example, by the king (Deut. 17:19).

Creation

The first and inescapable memorial of divine revelation is creation itself, and for that reason the story of creation assumes its rightful place at the beginning of Israel's sacred Scripture (Gen. 1:1–2:4).

---

1. See the classic study that informs this chapter by Samuel Terrien, *The Elusive Presence* (New York: Harper & Row, 1978).

The rhythmic pattern of the opening verses of Genesis is representative of Hebrew poetic speech in general. Poetry not only speaks of the beauty that creation presents to the eye, it re-creates it for the ear. Nevertheless, beauty is finite and transitory; it speaks not of itself but of the transcendent majesty of the Creator upon whom all creation is dependent. This profoundly religious intuition is eventually ineffable, but it springs forth in poetic metaphor. As Michael Fishbane has written, "the poet does not so much imitate the world as remake it."[2]

> The heavens are telling the glory of God;
>   and the firmament proclaims his handiwork.
> Day to day pours forth speech,
>   and night to night declares knowledge.
> There is no speech, nor are their words;
>   their voice is not heard;
> yet their voice goes out through all the earth,
>   and their words to the end of the world.
>   (Ps. 19:1–4)

To the Hebrew mind, nature is revelatory, but insufficient. The proper medium of revelation is not the eye, but the ear.[3] The heavens "tell . . . declare . . . proclaim" the glory of God. One can *see* that creation is good, as the days of creation in the beginning are divinely declared to be; but less susceptible to idolatry as things visible and far more stunning to contemplate is the efficacy of the word that brought creation into being. God says, "Let there be . . ." and it came to be (Gen. 1:3, *et passim*)! It is God's word of power that is sacred, and since God cannot be identified with any created thing, least of all images made by hands (Hab. 2:18–19), divine epiphany occurs only at God's own choosing.[4]

Theophany

Theophany (or divine appearing) is thus another of the "many and various ways" God spoke to the ancestors in addition to creation itself. A theophany can occur at any time and at any place. The Lord's presence

---

2. *Sacred Attunement* (Chicago: University of Chicago Press, 2008), 29.

3. Unlike Hellenism, Judaism bequeathed few aesthetic forms of value whether of pottery, sculpture, bas relief, or architecture until the Hellenistic period.

4. There is nothing in Hebrew thought akin to later mysticism in which by stages of psychic preparation and skill one ascends into union with God.

is therefore inescapable; as the psalmist says: "If I ascend to heaven, you are there; if I make my bed in Sheol, you are there" (Ps. 139:8).

The two most important theophanies in shaping the self-understanding of Judaism and its Scriptures concern Moses: the calling of Moses, in which God's name is revealed (Exod. 3), and the giving of the Ten Commandments (Exod. 19–20), by which God's ethical will is made known. Each has its own special role in the sacred narrative that the Scriptures tell.

The Divine Name

The calling of Moses and the revealing of the divine name occur on Mount Sinai/Horeb in a moment of divine self-disclosure: Moses, herding sheep after fleeing slavery in Egypt, comes upon a burning bush that is not consumed. It is a natural wonder—not a dream, as when Jacob envisions angels descending and ascending a ladder leading to the exalted Lord (Gen. 28:1–17). Like fire, the bush is not to be approached, nor can it be adequately described. The visual experience is ineffable. With Moses made attentive by the miracle, the eye gives way to the ear as a divine-human dialogue ensues. Moses removes his sandals, because the ground on which he stands is holy, made holy by the divine self-disclosure itself. He is given a commission by a voice from the burning bush: he who fled Egypt is now commanded to be an actor in the flow of history. He must return to Egypt to set the enslaved people free. The commission is curious. Moses is to be the representative of the one who speaks, but who is he? Who shall Moses say sent him? It is then that the Lord reveals his name. It is a name holier than any other name. It will become known simply as a name of four letters: *YHWH*, the Tetragrammaton. It is so holy that it is not to be pronounced, nor can it be written with a defiled pen. It can be referred to only by its surrogate, "*Adonai*, Lord."

The significance of the revelation is clear: Only those who know the name of the Lord belong to him. To deny the name is to be denied by the name (Hos. 1:8). When, centuries later, Jesus proffers the model prayer, it is the hallowing of this name that forms the prayer's first petition (Matt. 6:9–13 par.). Further, as the name is holy and mysterious, so is the story of how it was revealed to Moses. There is disclosure, but there is also concealment. The identity behind the name is not disclosed, only the enigmatic response, "I am who I am," is given (Exod. 3:14). Little wonder, then, that the narrative of the burning bush should be written on a scroll to become sacred Scripture, as sacred as the name it contained; and that the story be told within the context of a people set free from bondage by "the mighty hand and the outstretched arm" of the Lord (Deut. 4:34). The identity of the Lord is to be known by his deeds of salvation and by his law.

Sacred Narrative

Although world history is conveyed in the Genesis stories of Adam and Eve, Cain and Abel, Noah's ark, and the tower of Babel, with which both Jews and Gentiles may identify, it is the stories of Abraham, Isaac, and Jacob and the many generations of "ancestors" (Heb. 1:1) that constitute the history of salvation for the people of Israel. What is thought to be the oldest formulation of that story, stated in the form of an affirmation of faith, is found in Deuteronomy, thought by some to be perhaps a later form of the scroll found in the temple of Jerusalem in the days of Josiah the king (ca. 639–608 BCE). The creed (Deut. 26:5–9) alludes to the patriarchs, but the central affirmation is that the very Lord who revealed his name to Moses is the same Lord whose mighty acts, hundreds of years earlier, had freed the people of Israel from slavery in Egypt and led them into the promised land. The creed, couched in the mysterious holiness of a sacred festival, is placed in the first person. It speaks of "my" Aramean ancestors who went down to Egypt and became a mighty nation, how the Egyptians treated "us" harshly, how "we" cried to the Lord, how the Lord heard "our" voice, saw "our" toil and affliction, and how the Lord with signs and wonders brought "us" into a land flowing with milk and honey. For these great and ancient acts of divine blessing the people are now to place the offering of the firstfruits of the harvest before the Lord and to bow down in reverence before him. It is rightly suggested that the whole of the Old Testament (apart perhaps from Job and Ecclesiastes) is an explication of this creed. As such, the Old Testament (as narratives, genealogies, laws, psalms, proverbs, wisdom sayings, and oracles of warning and comfort) is the sacred canopy under which the whole of life is blessed and given meaning, to the Jew first, but also to the Christian (Rom. 1–2). For those who affirm, in whatever way it may entail, the "my," "we," "our," and "us" of these verses, the Old Testament is sacred Scripture.[5]

---

5. On this theme, see chap. 5, "How Does Scripture Interpret Itself?"

Such an affirmation, however, involves responsibility. What one notes about the creed is that there is no reference to Sinai/Horeb as the holy mountain on which the commandments were given to seal Israel's part in being "the people of God." To reclaim that side of the covenant with God is the task of the writer (or writers) of the book of Deuteronomy.

The Ten Commandments

A dominant genre (or way) of divine revelation in the Pentateuch is that of legal sayings. Law is of primary importance because it is the articulation of God's righteous and holy will for the whole of Jewish life. Nevertheless, covenantal law[6] is a two-way street. It is the standard by which God's faithfulness and justice as well as that of Israel is to be measured, for nothing is truly holy that is not also at least ethical.[7] In the Hebrew language, the Ten Commandments are called the ten "words" (Exod. 34:28). Written by the finger of God, they may be thought of as Judaism's first holy scripture (Exod. 31:18). By their observance Israel is to become "a kingdom of priests and a holy nation" (Exod. 19:6; see especially Leviticus, passim). Because of the law's centrality, the term *Torah*, which in its first meaning is "teaching" or "instruction," came to refer not only to "the five books of Moses" in which the law is found (the Pentateuch—including Deuteronomy!), but to the whole of the Hebrew Bible, and later also to the Oral Torah (set down in the Mishnah and commented upon in the Gemara, the two sections comprising both the Palestinian and Babylonian Talmud[8]) as well. This suggests that Torah, whether narrowly or broadly defined, is sacred not only because of its divine origin as revealed law, but because of its efficacy as teaching to create, order, and explain life, even to preserve and defend it.

---

6. Usually divided into the Covenant Code (Exod. 21–23), the Priestly Code (the rest of Exodus, Leviticus, and Numbers), and Deuteronomy.

7. The classic discussion of the holy is that of Rudolf Otto, *The Idea of the Holy*, trans. John W. Harvey (Oxford: Oxford University Press, 1923; 2nd ed. 1950). Otto argues that the experience of the Holy is more than of pure goodness or the ethical, to which he gives the name "the numinous" and equates with the feeling of awe before tremendous and ineffable mystery. Of course, the intellectual history of Israel is marked by a constant reevaluation of "what the Lord requires" (Mic. 6:8).

8. Dates for the two Talmudic traditions created in Palestine and Babylon are debated, the former generally placed in the mid-fifth century, the latter in the mid-sixth century, although the Mishnah, upon which the Gemara is commentary, was written down around 200 CE under the guidance of rabbi Judah ha-Nasi. For brief definitions, see Richard N. Soulen and R. Kendall Soulen, *Handbook of Biblical Criticism* (Louisville: Westminster John Knox, 2001).

Psalm 19, quoted above, continues by suggesting that what the heavens are *telling* is not only the glory of the Lord but also the wisdom of God's handiwork as revealed in the law:

> The law of the Lord is perfect, reviving the soul;
> The decrees of the Lord are sure, making wise the simple;
> The precepts of the Lord are right, rejoicing the heart;
> The commandment of the Lord is clear, enlightening the eyes.
> (Ps. 19:7–8)

Like the encounter with the burning bush, the theophany accompanying the giving of the Ten Commandments is also shrouded in mystery. Mystery is the essence of sacred narrative. There is earthquake, fire, smoke, thick clouds, thunder, and the sound of trumpets—all of which symbolize the enormity of what is about to be written on tablets of stone: "The tablets were the work of God, and the writing was the writing of God, engraved upon the tablets" (Exod. 32:16). Enunciating God's holy will for all who would be the people of God, the commandments become the centerpiece of the covenantal law binding God with Israel. Thus called to be holy, the law by which Israel's holiness is defined must a posteriori be sacred and holy. Hence the warning: "You shall not add to the word which I command you, nor take from it" (Deut. 4:2 RSV). The holiness of Scripture is inseparable from the holiness of the Law; Scripture is to be handled with the deference holy things acquire.

The Prophetic Oracle

By the first century, all the writings of the Hebrew Bible, from Genesis through 2 Chronicles,[9] were attributed to prophets, including Job, the Psalms (David), Proverbs, and the Song of Songs (Solomon). This conviction arose from the high esteem accorded not only to Moses but to the great "writing prophets," Isaiah, Jeremiah, Ezekiel, Hosea, Amos, and so on. Only in a few instances do we have an account of the moment when the great prophets received the divine calling that gave legitimacy and authority to their words. The most vivid is that of Isaiah (chap. 6). His revelation occurred in the temple of Jerusalem "in the

---

9. Second Chronicles is placed at the end of the Hebrew Bible, with its eschatological exhortation for the gathering of the people and the restoration of Jerusalem, whereas the Christian Old Testament concludes with the twelve minor prophets, ending with Malachi.

year that king Uzziah died." In a dazzling ecstatic vision, Isaiah sees the Lord seated on a high throne, attended by spectacular seraphs in flight. The seraphs hover in adoration about the throne and proclaim in a loud voice, "Holy, holy, holy is the LORD of hosts. . . ." Terrified by what he is allowed to see, Isaiah cries out, overcome by his own unworthiness: "Woe is me! I am lost, for I am a man of unclean lips, and I live among a people of unclean lips, yet my eyes have seen the King, the LORD of hosts!" Then, with a live coal from the altar, a seraph touches Isaiah's lips, the symbol of his inmost being. His sin is cauterized, his guilt removed. Thus purified, he hears the voice of the LORD: "Whom shall I send [to the people of Israel]?" And Isaiah answers, "Here I am! Send me!" (6:8).

Jeremiah is but a boy when he is confronted by the Lord. The Lord tells Jeremiah that he had been chosen to be the Lord's spokesman even before he was born. The terrified Jeremiah protests: he is too young to be a mouthpiece for the Lord. "Then the LORD put out his hand and touched my mouth; and the LORD said to me, 'Now I have put my words in your mouth. See, today I appoint you over nations and over kingdoms, to pluck up and to pull down, to destroy and to overthrow, to build and to plant" (1:9–10). Here it is the hand of the Lord that is the agent of inspiration.[10]

Although in most instances we are not told how individual prophets received their divine commission, the symbolism present here in both Isaiah and Jeremiah suggests a common idiom: the symbolic purification of the mouth, to enable the prophet to declare boldly the word of the Lord. "Thus says the LORD" is a phrase used over 160 times in the oracles of Jeremiah alone. Made holy, the prophetic oracle is holy, and as Scripture written down by Jeremiah's scribe Baruch, it is sacred Scripture. In Ezekiel the prophet eats the heavenly scroll handed to him by one described with reverent circumlocution as "the appearance of the likeness of the glory of the LORD" (Ezek. 1:28b). Having consumed the scroll he may now speak "the word of the Lord."

According to first-century Jewish tradition, well known to the author of the Epistle to the Hebrews in the New Testament, prophecy had ceased in the fifth century BCE shortly after the exile in Babylon. This is the contrast the author draws in the first sentence of his epistle between God's speaking "long ago" and the revelation of his Son "in

---

10. On "the hand of the Lord," see "Life in the Present and Hope for the Future" by Werner E. Lemke in *Interpreting the Prophets*, edited by James Luther Mays and Paul J. Achtemeier (Philadelphia: Fortress, 1987), 200.

these last days." Herein also lies the significance of Jesus' question to the Pharisees: Is John the Baptist a prophet as the people say he is, or had prophecy ceased centuries before, as both the Sadducees and the Pharisees claim (Luke 20:3–8; cf. Matt. 11:7–15 par.)? If prophecy has not ceased and John is truly a prophet, then perhaps a new revelation is unfolding, not just spoken but lived—a Word made flesh! This was the Christian claim.

THE NEW TESTAMENT AS SACRED SCRIPTURE

"Long ago God spoke to our ancestors in many and various ways by the prophets, but in these last days he has spoken to us by a Son" (Heb. 1:1–2). With words such as these, the followers of Jesus differentiated themselves from the rest of contemporary Judaism. The difference between Jews and Christians in these early days lay not in what constituted sacred Scripture or in the identity of the God of Abraham, Isaac, and Jacob, whose name Christians continued to hallow. The difference lay in the identity of Jesus of Nazareth and how the Scriptures, on which that identity was based, were to be interpreted. Who was Jesus? By whose authority did he speak? To orthodox Judaism, Jesus was not, as his followers claimed, God's Messiah of whom the prophets had spoken: To the Sadducees, he was a troublemaker who had violently disrupted temple order. To the Pharisees, he was a lawbreaker and blasphemer for reasons beyond number. But to others, this Jesus was the Messiah, the Christ; he was the Suffering Servant, the Son of God, the Redeemer, the Lord of life, the Lamb who was slain, attested to and prophesied by Scripture itself. By way of various titles and ascriptions, Jesus was identified as the one through whom God had revealed his saving love by raising him from the dead. This is the good news "handed on . . . by those who from the beginning were eyewitnesses and servants of *the word*" (Luke 1:2–4).

If "Torah" as instruction is the appropriate way to refer to the sacred Scriptures of Judaism, and the heart of that instruction is the Law, then "the Word" as good news is the appropriate way to refer to the sacred Scriptures of Christianity, and the heart of that "news" is the forgiveness of sins brought about by Jesus' death and resurrection.

According to the Synoptic Gospels, however, the identification of Jesus with the forgiveness of sins and a new law began during his own lifetime.

Sayings of Jesus as "Sacred Scripture"

The earliest identity given to Jesus is that of "teacher" (*didaskalos;* Mark 1:22; 4:8, *et passim*).[11] It is little wonder then that the oldest "scripture" in the New Testament (other than Old Testament quotations) is a collection of Jesus' sayings, now incorporated in the Gospels of both Matthew and Luke. For convenience' sake, scholars refer to this collection of sayings as "Q" (from the German *Quelle*, meaning "source"). Although the exact wording of verses comprising this body of sayings is disputed, as well as its role in the theology of the early church,[12] it is clear that the sayings were treated as authoritative: "For he taught them as one having authority and not as the scribes" (Mark 1:22). These sayings include the injunction to love one's enemy (Matt. 5:43–48 par.), to lay up treasures in heaven (Matt. 6:19–21 par.), not to serve two masters (Matt. 6:24 par.), and to build one's house (faith) on rock (Matt. 7:24–27 par.); it includes as well beatitudes and woes, the Lord's Prayer (Matt. 6:9–13 par.), the Golden Rule (Matt. 7:12 par.), and so on.

Many of these sayings differentiated Jesus and his disciples from the practices that characterized the scribes and Pharisees—laws concerning Sabbath observance, for example (cf. Matt. 12:1–8 par.). One may think of Q as the "torah" (or teachings/instructions) of Jesus. It acquired a degree of sacrality during his ministry for that reason. But, following his crucifixion and in a manner not completely paralleled by the Law in the Old Testament, the teachings of Jesus are made subordinate to the *story* of Jesus, most notably his passion. This is partly the case because all the teachings of Jesus are subsumed by him under one commandment: to love God with one's total being, and one's neighbor as one's self, for it is the sum of the Law and the Prophets (Matt. 22:36–40). But it is also the case that laws are by nature finite and transitory, whereas love is infinite and eternal in its reach.

Were the sayings of Jesus all that was known of him, Jesus would at most have been considered a peripatetic teacher of wisdom, and perhaps an eschatological prophet in the manner of John the Baptist. It is not likely that the sayings themselves would either have been preserved or considered sacred by anyone had the speaker of the sayings not had the fate of being crucified as a common criminal, and then been pro-

---

11. Jesus is not called "rabbi" in the Synoptic Gospels; in Matthew Jesus warns his disciples not to be called "rabbi" (23:8).

12. For a proposal concerning the place of Q in the development of the early church, see John S. Kloppenborg, *Q, the Earliest Gospel: An Introduction to the Original Stories and Sayings of Jesus* (Louisville: Westminster John Knox, 2008).

claimed as raised from the dead "in accordance with scripture" (1 Cor. 15:4)—though no such explicit reference is to be found in the Old Testament.

The *sayings* of Jesus, however, are equaled in antiquity with *stories* about Jesus that arose during his ministry in Galilee and its environs. They too undoubtedly began as oral traditions and, whether oral or written, served in addition to the Gospel of Mark as another source for Luke in setting down his own account (Luke 1:1–4). Such stories were passed down as epiphanies of an ordinary kind. They too revealed who Jesus is, filling out the identity of the one crucified, and like his sayings became sacred stories and sacred Scripture for that reason.

Epiphanies of an Ordinary Kind

As with figures in the Old Testament who had an encounter with God, so also in the Gospel story those who encountered Jesus "in many and various ways" experienced the transformation of their lives. The stories of these encounters are of an ordinary kind, but they are also demonstrations of Jesus' spiritual power (Greek *dynamis*). The call of the disciples is stark and simple. Simon and Andrew, like James and John, make their livelihood by fishing on the Sea of Galilee, but confronted by Jesus they abandon their nets to follow him (Mark 1:16–20). The same happens to Levi, a tax collector (2:13–17). Once encountered, these men cannot go back to life as it had been. One may suppose that some of the miracles (*dynamis*) of healing are in their brevity parables of these sudden transformations of a psychic nature: so a fever is healed by a touch, as is a withered hand; sight is given to the blind, the lame are made to walk, the deranged are made whole, the dead are brought back to life. However miraculous in themselves, and whatever their historicity, physical wonders in the Gospels are often subsumed under a more telling narrative, for example, concerning the authority of Jesus to forgive sins or the power of faith to bring about wholeness, as in the story of a paralytic (Mark 2:1–12 par.), and the woman with a hemorrhage (Mark 5:25–34). What is being asserted is that only the presence of transcendent holiness can make one whole or holy: recognizing Jesus' holiness to be of that nature, a harlot washes his feet with her tears and anoints them with costly ointment. Her deeds are received as acts of repentance to the one who is holy, and she is forgiven (Luke 7:36–50). In all such instances in the Gospels the narrative conveys an awareness of divine presence, of something that interfuses the ordinary with the extraordinary, the human with the Divine. Not everyone who knew Jesus experienced this presence; and of those who did it was not always in the same way or to the same degree. Those closest to Jesus (and therefore principals in the Gospel story) are Peter, James, and John, and also the sisters Mary and Martha, and Mary Magdalene. Peter, James, and John are the first to be called by Jesus, the last to be with him in the Garden of Gethsemane. It is they who are chosen to ascend a "high mountain" where Jesus is transfigured before them in an epiphany of a special kind. These life-transforming epiphanies are experienced by ordinary men and women.

What proved to be universally appealing about the narratives of the Gospels is that they are about ordinary people—among whom Jesus himself was counted (cf. "Can anything good come out of Nazareth?" [John 1:46]). Such lives are the *subject* of sacred Scripture. It is a hallmark of the Jesus movement that this is so (cf. 1 Cor. 1:26–31); and it largely remained so for the subsequent three centuries, that is, throughout the period during which the canon of sacred Scripture was being formed. Chapter 16 of Paul's Letter to the Romans captures this phenomenon in a remarkable way. By sending greetings, Paul blesses and immortalizes twenty-seven persons by name, from Andronicus to Tryphosa. He greets them in the Lord's name, calling them all "saints," not because they are holy, but because they have been made righteous in Jesus Christ (Rom. 3:21–26) and because they are *called* to be holy. The ordinary people who later made Paul's letters "canonical" and therefore authoritative did so because they could identify with their predecessors in faith. Like the Deuteronomist's personal identification with his Hebrew ancestors in Egypt, readers of Paul's letters decades and centuries later recognized *themselves* as those who were being "greeted in the name of the Lord" and blessed thereby. This power of *the word* to incorporate the believer into the body of Christ, like the sacrament of baptism, lies also at the root of what makes Scripture sacred. Hearing in faith is an epiphany of an ordinary kind (Rom. 10:14–17).

Epiphanies of an Extraordinary Kind

Had the story of Jesus ended with his crucifixion, there would be no Christian church. The experience of the risen Lord, and the stories that related that experience, brought the church into being and formed the core of its Scriptures. The Gospels do not describe the resurrection, and what is said about the resurrected body by the Gospel writers and Paul is contradictory (cf. Luke 24:39 with 1 Cor. 15:50). What the New Testament does describe are encounters with the risen Lord. Even here, however, such encounters remain largely mysterious and ineffable. Luke's account of Paul's conversion, for example, is told three times in three different ways (see Acts 12; 22; 26). His story of Cleopas and his companion is no less elusive, yet it is telling.

The Road to Emmaus

An encounter with the risen Christ is called a christophany (cf. Matt. 28:16–20; John 20–21). The most compelling of the Gospel christophanies, and the most illuminative as theological reflection, is told by Luke as taking place on the road to Emmaus (Luke 24:13–35). Two disciples are walking together engaged in a theological discussion concerning the events they have witnessed when, unrecognized, the risen Christ meets them along the way. What are you discussing? the stranger asks. Surprised that the stranger does not know what has happened, one of the disciples, Cleopas, tells him of Jesus' crucifixion at the hands of the high priests and the rulers of Jerusalem, how certain women that very morning had discovered his tomb empty, and how in a vision angels had told them Jesus was alive. Then the Lord chides the disciples. Did they not know what the prophets foretold, that it was necessary for the Christ to suffer and be exalted? Then, "beginning with Moses and all the prophets, he interpreted to them in all the scriptures the things concerning himself" (Luke 24:27).

Still there is no recognition. The idea that the Christ had to suffer was too unexpected and unwanted to connect the crucified Jesus with the Anointed One (Messiah) of God. Being near to the village, they ask the stranger to join them for the evening. At supper, he takes bread, blesses it, and shares it with them. Through these words and the breaking of bread (the Eucharist) the companions recall Jesus' living presence. Then "their eyes were opened and they recognize him," and he "vanishes out of their sight." As with Old Testament theophanies, the presence of the Divine is elusive, even ephemeral. Astonished at what they have experienced, they reflect on the course of the day. They say to each other, "Were not our hearts burning within us while he was talking to us on the road, while he was opening the scriptures to us?" Reversing their course, they return to the disciples in Jerusalem, where the risen Lord instructs them all concerning his identity: "Then he opened their minds to understand the scriptures, and said to them, 'Thus it is written, that the Christ should suffer and on the third day rise from the dead, and that repentance and forgiveness of sins should be preached in his name to all the nations" (Luke 24:45–47).

Here understanding who Jesus is by way of sacred Scripture and table fellowship is itself an epiphany apart from which the encounter would remain mysterious and ambiguous. Given clarity by Scripture and experience, their own story takes on sacrality as part of the "good news." "The Lord is risen," they say; "the Lord is risen indeed! And he has become known to *us* in the breaking of bread" (Luke 24:34–35). The story becomes both Scripture and sacrament.

The Road to Damascus

The most dramatic christophany in the New Testament concerns the apostle Paul (1 Cor. 15:8–9). As the story is told by Luke, the event occurred as Paul was on his way to Damascus to arrest followers of "the Way," having been sent by the high priest to bring Christians back to Jerusalem for trial (see Acts 9; 22; 26; 1 Cor. 15). As Paul approaches the city, he is confronted by the risen Christ, and though all he sees is a blinding light, Paul hears Christ's voice, which, in Luke's third account, commissions Paul to preach the forgiveness of sins and the sanctification that comes through faith in Jesus (Acts 26:18).[13]

Writing of the event in his Letter to the Galatians and in a manner fully commensurate with the great prophets of the Old Testament, Paul tells his readers that his calling into the ministry of Christ was something God had destined for him even before he was born. Thus called by grace, he recalls, "God was pleased to reveal his Son to me so that I might proclaim him among the Gentiles" (Gal. 1:15–16).

From Paul's letters we know that by this encounter with Christ, Paul believed that he had been reconciled to God through Christ Jesus, that *faith* in Christ's death as a divine sacrifice of love and not *works* of the Law had set him right with God, and that this good news pertained to all the world, to the Jew first but also to the Greek (i.e., Gentiles; Rom. 1–2). To come to faith in Jesus' death and resurrection as some-

---

13. This third rendition of Paul's conversion conflates into one experience what the earlier accounts suggest occurred over a period of time; see Acts 12 and 22.

thing God had done for the salvation of the world, Paul argued, meant to follow Jesus, to enter into his death through baptism so that the old self might die to sin, and the new self might rise a new being reconciled to God. Through this sacrament of baptism, through dying and rising with Christ in faith, the believer became part of the body of Christ, the church. Thus reconciled with God and made righteous through faith, the believer was called to become an ambassador for Christ in the continuing ministry of reconciling the world to God (2 Cor. 5:18).

Paul's epiphany is thus understood as a calling into the ministry of reconciliation. Hearing with faith is thus a common theme in his letters: "Everyone who calls on the name of the Lord will be saved. But how are they to call on one in whom they have not believed? And how are they to believe in one of whom they have never heard? And how are they to hear without someone to proclaim him? . . . Faith comes from what is heard, and what is heard comes through the word of Christ" (Rom. 10:13b–17). In the first century, even reading in private was done aloud.

As noted above, the Christian tradition presents its Scriptures as the *Word* of God. The good news is something *proclaimed*. News is something to be heard, that is, what is proclaimed has to be appropriated person by person, by the individual who has the ears to hear. The most personal form of written communication is the letter, and for this reason the greater portion of the New Testament is made up of letters. Form fits content. Of course, more personal than the letter is the person. The Christian claim, spelled out most distinctly by the Gospel of John, is that the Word, in the beginning with God (1:1), has become flesh in Jesus (1:14) that in *him* God, whom "no one has ever seen," might be made known (1:18).

Because of this belief the words of Jesus and the word about Jesus became sacred to the *community* of faith, the church. Scripture not only identified the Lord, it also identified the church as the body of Christ in the world, and gave practical guidance for its ministry of reconciliation: "All scripture," writes the author of 2 Timothy, "is inspired by God and is useful for teaching, for reproof, for correction, and for training in righteousness, so that everyone who belongs to God may be proficient, equipped for every good work" (3:16–17). In short, Scripture is the Logos become *logoi* (the Word become words), containing all that is sufficient "for faith and practice." In sum, what had been seen became something heard, so that what had been heard might become seen again (cf. 1 John 1:1–4).

Chapter 2
Which Scripture Is Sacred?

Which Scripture is sacred? Today many people (encouraged by popular books and films) imagine that the decision about which Scriptures are sacred, and which are not, has been made by secretive and sinister cabals of religious leaders eager to foist their own interests on the unsuspecting. But the historical record suggests a very different story. The formation of a canon of sacred Scripture grows for the most part from below, indigenously, as writings receive recognition as efficacious of the holy by a community of faith.

From time to time, action by religious leaders (both orthodox and heterodox!) is part of the story, often in response to major urgent challenges. At other times, changes in the nature of writing and its dissemination have played a role. But all of these factors have usually confirmed intuitions that are largely already in place on the ground.

The process of discerning which Scripture is sacred took place gradually, over decades and even centuries, whether one is thinking of Judaism or Christianity, and never in complete uniformity among believers everywhere. The canons (or lists of sacred writings) of the two faith communities share a common source and are therefore partly overlapping, with the Hebrew Bible being an inextricable part of Christian Scripture. On the other hand, Jews and Christians define their canons in part over against each other, in part in light of each other. This chapter seeks to clarify that relationship and the process of canon formation.

THE SACRED SCRIPTURE OF JUDAISM

The Jewish canon of Scripture formed over many generations. The scholarly analysis of that formation is extensive, complex, and contentious. A review of that analysis is not within the purview of this short work. Two illustrations of the evolution of the Hebrew Bible will suffice.[1] The first centers on the book of Psalms. Any reader of the Psalms will quickly note that it is not one book, but a composite of books made, in its present form, to model the first five books of the Old Testament: book 1, Psalms 1–41; book 2, 2–72; book 3, 73–89; book 4, 90–106; book 5, 107–150. The reader will also note that within these five books are smaller collections from obviously earlier times, such as Psalms 120–134. (See also 72:20, which at one time ended a collection of psalms.) That Psalms 1–150 was not an immutable collection held to be sacrosanct is further evidenced by the acceptance of other psalms by the Jews of the Qumran community (ca. 160 BCE to 70 CE).[2] The Greek psalter, in the translation known as the Septuagint, contains 151 psalms.

A second illustration relates to the first. The Psalms are traditionally referred to as "The Psalms of David," to whom their composition, in part at least, is attributed. In the tenth century BCE, when David was king, the Pentateuch as we know it did not yet exist. The book of Deuteronomy, the last of the five books making up the Torah, was not written (or at least not "discovered"; see 2 Kgs. 22) until the reign of Josiah in the latter half of the seventh century BCE. Deuteronomy, scholars believe, underwent further editing at a later date. This means that our present book of Psalms took shape only after Deuteronomy had become equal in dignity and sacrality with older traditions found in Genesis–Numbers, and that means most likely after the exile in Babylon (587–539 BCE).

The Torah, the Prophets, and the Writings

By the beginning of the first century CE, Judaism had become notably diverse. Divergent groups or sects were identified in part by the different centers around which their devotion was oriented. The life of the Sadducees focused on the temple, the Pharisees on the synagogue, while the Essenes, disillusioned by the religious establishment, withdrew to

---

1. The formation of Old Testament traditions over time is discussed further in chap. 9.
2. See the *Thanksgiving Psalms*, or *Hodayot*, of the Dead Sea Scrolls (1QH).

isolated communities, such as the Qumran community beside the Dead Sea.[3] Yet despite this diversity these sects held to a common core of beliefs and sacred Scripture: the Law, the Prophets, and the Writings (often called the Tanak: the *Torah, Nebiim,* and *Kitubim,* respectively). Strictly speaking, "the Law" (or Torah) referred to the Pentateuch, but in common parlance it could refer to all the scrolls of the Hebrew Bible, or (later) to both the written and the oral law, that is, to the Mishnah and Gemara. The term *prophets* was not so malleable, since prophecy was thought to have ended with the deaths of Haggai, Zechariah (note 13:6), and Malachi and, with their deaths, the departure of the Holy Spirit (1 Macc. 4:46; 14:41). But the term was broadly conceived. Since all Scripture was inspired, all the authors of the sacred books were considered prophets, not only Moses, deemed the author of the Pentateuch, but also the authors of Joshua, Judges, and the other works now considered histories as well. The book of Psalms, clearly inspired by the Holy Spirit, cast their author David into the same mold. For this reason the psalms could be read as prophetic oracles. This was especially true of that messianic sect within first-century Judaism known as "Christians" (Acts 26:28; 1 Pet. 4:16), for whom Psalms 2 and 110 were particularly important (see, e.g., Heb. 1:5–13). Among the Essenes of Qumran, the canon of sacred Scripture developed in opposition to the Sadducees and the temple of Jerusalem as well as to the Pharisees. Nevertheless, the Qumran community valued all the books of the Hebrew Bible except Esther, plus writings composed in Greek, and works indigenous to their own community, such as *The Manual of Discipline, The Rule of the Congregation, The Temple Scroll,* and *The War of the Sons of Light against the Sons of Darkness.* So isolated from mainstream Judaism was the community that, like the Sadducees and the temple in Jerusalem, the Essenes of Qumran disappeared following the community's destruction during the Jewish revolt against Rome in 66–70 CE.

The books least agreed upon as sacred by the three dominant sects of first-century Judaism were referred to collectively simply as "the Writings" (or Hagiographa, meaning "sacred writings"). In the Hebrew Bible they now comprise Psalms, Proverbs, and Job, and a later collection of five scrolls: the Song of Solomon (Song of Songs), Ruth, Lamentations, Ecclesiastes, and Esther; to which are added the historical works, Daniel, Ezra–Nehemiah, and 1–2 Chronicles. In the first century the two works

---

3. A brief discussion of the Qumran community and a listing of the sacred writings is found in Richard N. Soulen and R. Kendall Soulen, *Handbook of Biblical Criticism,* 3rd ed. (Louisville: Westminster John Knox, 2001), 43–44, "Dead Sea Scrolls."

most in dispute among Jews were the Song of Songs and Ecclesiastes. The argument for both was that if Solomon wrote them, they must be inspired because, like all the authors of the Old Testament, Solomon was a prophet. By the beginning of the second century its inclusion was settled, with Rabbi Akiba one of its strongest supporters. The argument for the canonicity of Ecclesiastes is found in a gloss at the end of the book itself (see Eccl. 12:9–13). However, since the Hagiographa were not used in the Jewish liturgy, the term was simply not defined; it commonly included writings other than those that ended up in the Hebrew Bible, some of which were present in the Greek translation of Jewish Scriptures known as the Septuagint.

The Septuagint (LXX) and Greek Wisdom Writings

The dispersion of the Jews into the Hellenistic world made important contributions to the canon, although, as it would ultimately turn out, ones more influential among Christians than Jews. As Hebrew and Aramaic faded from common use following the conquest of the Near East by Alexander the Great, the exiled Jews of Alexandria, Egypt, called for the translation of their sacred Scriptures into the language they knew best: Greek. The resulting translation was called the *Septuagint* (meaning "Seventy") because, according to a legend found in the spurious but influential *Letter of Aristeas*, that was the number of days it took the appointed seventy (or seventy-two) Jewish scholars to complete their task. The Septuagint, not the Old Testament in Hebrew, was the Bible of the early church.

The Septuagint encompassed not only the traditional Scriptures composed in Hebrew and Aramaic (the thirty-nine books of the Old Testament), but also fifteen additional writings composed in Greek. These fifteen books are today called the Apocrypha and appear only in select editions of the Bible. In addition to the Apocrypha, there were other writings composed in Greek that were never part of the Septuagint, although they also circulated among Greek-speaking Jews as sacred. These writings, some of which are quoted directly or indirectly in the New Testament, such as *1 Enoch* (Jude 9) and the *Assumption of Moses* (Jude 6, 14–15), are now commonly referred to as "Pseudepigrapha" (or "falsely titled writings").[4]

---

4. For a listing and bibliography, see ibid., 147–49, "Pseudepigrapha."

The Emergence of Judaism

After the fall of Jerusalem in 70 CE, the Scriptures in Hebrew came to be ever more central to the life of the remnant Jewish community. Scholars have believed that emergent rabbinic Judaism set limits to its canon of sacred writings at the so-called Council of Javneh (or Jamnia) at the end of the first century. While this picture is no longer certain, it is clear that rabbinic Judaism, with its roots in Pharisaism, ultimately endorsed a canon of Hebrew texts more limited in number than the canon then in use by Greek-speaking Jews and Christians. Greek writings fell outside the Hebrew canon of rabbinic Judaism in part because of the esteem with which Christians regarded them. This included the Greek translation of the Hebrew Bible itself. The issue was in large measure doctrinal. The most contentious point was the Septuagint's rendition of Isaiah 7:14, which referred to a "virgin" (Greek *parthenos*) who would conceive and bear a son. The more ancient Hebrew version of Isaiah reads "young woman" (Hebrew *alma*), not "virgin." By rejecting the Septuagint and reverting to the Hebrew texts of Judaism's sacred Scripture, the rabbinic movement sought to counter the scriptural proofs Christians employed to defend Jesus' messiahship as prophetically foretold. That is, the Hebrew Bible came into being in part as a defensive reaction to the rise of Christianity and its preference for Judaism's Scriptures in Greek. Under the leadership of Rabbi Akiba, the Jews condemned the Septuagint for this and other reasons in 130 CE.

The writings of the Qumran community were excluded by mainstream Judaism as too sectarian and novel, if indeed they even came into consideration. As one Jewish scholar has written, it was the Hebrew Bible that "constituted the very protoplasm of Jewish existence, the matrix out of which emerged all subsequent development"—not the numerous and diverse body of "writings" in Greek or the sectarian writings of the Essenes.[5]

Yet this act of delimitation, by which only writings in Hebrew were accepted as inspired, went hand in hand with the expansion of sacred writings in new directions. The Mishnah is a vast body of rabbinic oral and written traditions that developed from the late second century BCE to the end of the second century CE. The Mishnah comprises commentary on the written and oral law. The two Talmuds, the Palestinian and

---

5. Clemens Thoma and Michael Wyschogrod, eds., *Understanding Scripture: Explorations of Jewish and Christian Traditions of Interpretation* (New York: Paulist Press, 1987), 9.

the Babylonian, are but commentaries on the Mishnah. It is a common observation, but a helpful one, to note that the Mishnah is to Judaism what the New Testament is to Christianity.

THE SACRED SCRIPTURES OF THE EARLY CHURCH

For the first decades of the church's life, the church's only sacred Scriptures were the Scriptures of Judaism—in Greek. The gospel circulated originally in oral form, as witness to the resurrection, as commentary on Scripture, and as remembrances of Jesus' life and teachings.

Like Judaism itself, the early church lived happily with an expansive and fluid sense of its sacred canon. The core was the Torah and the Prophets (cf. Luke 24:27). Reference is made to "the law," meaning the *Torah,* or "the book of Moses" (Mark 12:26; or simply "Moses"), or "the book of the law," or to "the law and the prophets" (*Nebiim*; e.g., Matt. 5:17; 7:12; Luke 16:16; Acts 13:15), or to specific books, such as "the book of the prophet Isaiah" (e.g., Luke 4:17) or "the book of the prophets" (Acts 7:42). However, there is no collective reference in the New Testament to what the Jews called "the Writings"—although some scholars believe Luke's reference to "the psalms" (24:44) is a catchword inclusive of all the writings.

Gradually, the Christian movement began to produce its own literature, such as the letters of Paul, and pseudonymous letters attributed to Paul (such as Ephesians and the Pastoral Epistles), as well as the four Gospels and Acts, all appearing in the first century. In most instances we know little about their specific origins, but it is clear that before long Christian congregations treasured collections of these writings alongside the sacred scrolls of Jewish tradition (see 2 Pet. 3:15–16). The terms *Old Testament* and *New Testament* were not yet current, nor is it even certain that Christians would have applied the term *scripture* (lit. writings) to both sets of literature. It is evident that the Christian movement treasured both, but the list of those treasured varied from church to church across the broad reaches of the empire.

The innovation introduced by Christians was the codex (or bound book). Now for the first time collections of texts could circulate as a single volume, not a bundle of scrolls. Even so, the "Bible" in our sense was not known. The library of sacred literature was far too vast and differently valued to be enclosed within two covers at this stage in the life of the church or in manuscript production.

Diverse Christianities and the Formation of the Canon

An important stimulus for a clearer demarcation of the Christian canon resulted from the emergence of profoundly different forms of Christianity, each holding a very different conception of the true nature of the gospel. The appearance of heterodoxy forced orthodoxy to set limits to what was acceptable (see, e.g., 2 Tim. 3:10–17; 2 Pet. 2), just as the appearance of Hellenistic Christianity forced rabbinic Judaism to revert to their Scriptures in Hebrew.

Marcion

So far as we know, the first Christian to draw up a firm canon (or list) of Scripture was a Christian named Marcion (fl. 140). We are interested in Marcion because he shows that the impulse to draw the line between what was sacred and what was not did not originate only from the side of what was to become orthodoxy. Such a desire was equally at work among streams of Christians now known as heterodox or heretical.

A native of Sinope on the Black Sea, Marcion believed that the "pure" gospel stood in unrelieved opposition to Judaism. He believed that the God of the Old Testament was a vengeful, deceitful, and evil god, and that he was the ultimate cause of the world's suffering. In Marcion's mind there was a second or higher God who had remained hidden and unknown until he revealed himself in Jesus Christ as the God of love. By faith in Christ, the believer shared in Christ's victory, escaped the remnant power of evil in the world, and entered into the kingdom of God. As a sign of this faith, Marcion advocated a severe asceticism, including celibacy for the married and chastity for the unmarried. The material world, as the product of the evil creator god, was to be rejected.

The letters of Paul provided Marcion with what he believed to be the true essence of the gospel: a sharp distinction between law and grace, that is, between the legal requirements of Judaism on the one hand and the unmerited love of God given in Christ Jesus on the other. In the language of hermeneutics, this distinction became the interpretive key by which Marcion cut and pasted his way through traditional Christian Scriptures in his effort to establish what he claimed had once been the original form of the gospel. So desirous was he of expunging from Christianity any hint of Judaism that he rejected all the Gospels except the Gospel of Luke, which he then heavily edited, as he did the letters of Paul, deleting texts he believed had been corrupted by later, judaizing accretions.

Marcion is significant for our study because in the second century it is he, more than any other single figure within the broader religious phenomenon known as Gnosticism, who forced the early church to consider the formation of a canon of sacred writings acceptable to the whole church. Marcion was soon banned from the church; his view of the Old Testament and the apostolic writings was also rejected. But his wide appeal (in spite of his stringent sexual mores) is illustrated by the fact that Marcionite churches continued to exist for more than two centuries after his death.

Irenaeus and the Canon of Two Testaments

In response to Marcion, church fathers such as Irenaeus (ca. 135–200) argued in behalf of a Christian canon consisting of two parts, the Old Testament and the New. The Marcionite heresy wanted to sever Christian faith from its roots in historical Judaism, turning it into a suprahistorical cosmic drama divorced from life in the world. Ultimately neither Judaism nor Christianity would have any part of that.

The church's New Testament, which Irenaeus was among the first to treat as sacred, also had no strict limits observed everywhere. A library of scrolls could contain what was sacred and what was not. It is not until the early fourth century that we find collections of sacred writings bound together with pages of durable parchment (sheep- or calfskin), although bound papyrus volumes begin to appear early in the second century. The introduction of the codex had a clear impact on the formation of the canonical tradition. As long as Scriptures existed as separate scrolls rather than in codex form, there was less urgency for deciding which books were in and which were out. Bound volumes made a true canon possible. In the early decades of the fourth century, when the first Christian emperor, Constantine (ca. 288–337), commanded Eusebius (ca. 263–340), the first great historian of the Christian church, to prepare fifty copies of the Bible, a selection had to be made. Eusebius had to decide which writings to include and which to exclude, since the individual writings were going to be sewn together into a single volume. Whatever decision Eusebius made (no extant copies of his Bible remain), regional church traditions, with their own collections of writings, kept the issue open.

The criterion of canonicity was whether the writing in question had been authored by an apostle of Jesus, or by someone who had known the apostles. Paul was not an apostle, but he came to know some of the apostles well, and the power of his letters were enough to cause them to be treasured. Ephesians, Colossians, 1 and 2 Timothy, and Titus were, scholars suggest, probably not written by Paul, but by his adherents. The authorship of other works, such as Hebrews, is unknown, while the identity of the authors of books such as James and the letters of John is disputed.

For the first four centuries and more, the number and selection of books within the canon of sacred Scripture varied from one part of the empire to another. Some books were favored by the Eastern or Byzantine (Greek) church, others by the Western or Latin church. Among the Eastern churches, a New Testament of twenty-two books was common, omitting 1 and 2 John, 2 Peter, Jude, and the Apocalypse. Even as late as the Quinisextine Council of Constantinople in 692, a canon was ratified that excluded the Apocalypse but included *1* and *2 Clement.*

The Apocryphal New Testament

Only in recent decades, dating from the discovery of the Nag Hammadi manuscripts in the mid-twentieth century, has the general public become aware of the vast array of Christian writings produced in the early centuries of the church and ultimately excluded from the canon. Today these writings are collectively known as the Apocryphal New Testament, a name given to them by a modern editor, M. R. James.[6]

An idea of their scope and content can be gained from the titles themselves: *The Gospel according to the Egyptians, The Birth of Mary, The History of Joseph the Carpenter, Letter of Pilate to Tiberius, The Assumption of the Virgin, The Acts of John* (also *Paul, Andrew, Peter, Thomas,* etc.), *The Apocalypse of Peter* (also of *Paul* and of *Thomas*). They came into being out of the simple human desire to clarify the unknown and to enhance the mystery of an already mysterious story. It was a desire that resulted in the writing of Gospels, acts, apocalypses, and letters to fill in the gaps of knowledge concerning the missing years of Jesus' life, or those of his parents, or of Peter and Paul and other Christians not recorded in the Acts of the Apostles. Although of no historical value

---

6. *The Apocryphal New Testament* (Oxford: Clarendon, 1955).

in reconstructing the early life of Jesus or the apostolic period, they do reflect the diversity within Christendom and the fluidity of the canon during the second to fourth centuries.[7]

Many of these writings show the influence of Gnosticism. Like Marcion, the Gnostics were dualists, dividing reality into two distinct and opposing forces. Gnostics believed all matter to be evil. Salvation was seen as a process of liberating the spirit from the delusive and deadly power of materiality. An important Gnostic text called the *Gospel of Thomas* was discovered in the mid-twentieth century near Nag Hammadi, Egypt, though known of earlier from papyrus fragments at the turn of the century. Rather than being a true Gospel, the document is a collection of sayings, comparable to those found in the Sermon on the Mount in Matthew's Gospel (chaps. 5–7). A few of the sayings are essentially identical to those found in the Gospels; others markedly embody the worldview from which Gnosticism comes. One example will suffice:

> Simon Peter said to them: "Let Mary go out from among us, because women are not worthy of the Life."
>
> Jesus said: "See I shall lead her, so that I will make her male, that she too may become a living spirit, resembling you males. For every woman who makes herself male will enter the Kingdom of Heaven."
>
> (Saying 114)[8]

Although this saying was unknown to M. R. James in the early 1920s, the manuscript discovery having yet to be made, his observation concerning the whole corpus of apocryphal writings applies aptly here as well: "It will very quickly be seen that there is no question of anyone's having excluded [these writings] from the New Testament: they have done that for themselves."[9] Surely James speaks for the modern reader and arguably for early Christians as well.

The Unresolved Canon

By the end of the fourth century, there was a great deal of consensus concerning the limits of the canon. True, there were at least nominal

---

7. See Edgar Hennecke, *New Testament Apocrypha*, vol. 1: *Gospels and Related Writings*; ed. Wilhelm Schneemelcher, Eng. trans. ed. R. McL. Wilson (Philadelphia: Westminster, 1964).

8. For this translation, see *The Gospel According to Thomas*: Coptic Text Established and Translated by A. Guillaumont, H.-CH Peruch, G. Quispel, W. Till and Yassah 'Abd al Masîh (New York: Harper & Brothers, 1959), 57.

9. *The Apocryphal New Testament* (Oxford: Clarendon, 1955), xi–xii.

Christian congregations within the empire during the second to the fifth centuries for whom writings such as the *Gospel of Thomas* and the *Gospel of Judas* (rediscovered in the twentieth century) were sacred Scripture. Moreover, even as late as the sixth century, extracanonical works were found in codices of the church, especially in Africa and Asia (such as the epistles of *Clement,* the *Epistle of Barnabas,* the *Shepherd of Hermas,* and the *Revelation of Peter*). Nevertheless, the main contours of the canon were set, and would remain set for centuries.

There was, however, already contained in the canon itself seeds of future contention. Jerome (ca. 340/350–420) turned to the Masoretic (Hebrew) texts to translate the Old Testament into Latin, having concluded that they were superior to the Septuagint. On similar grounds, the Protestant Reformation would ultimately come to limit its Old Testament canon to books originally written in Hebrew, while relegating the other books to a secondary status, calling them, after Jerome, "Apocrypha." For this reason, Protestant Bibles, following Luther, are usually printed without the Apocrypha, while Roman Catholic Bibles, following the Latin Vulgate, include the Apocrypha.

SUMMARY

Contrary to popular and secular perception, the formation of the Christian canon is not the product of a single act of hierarchical power, but one of gradual development influenced by multiple forces. In some cases, the impulse to draw boundaries of what is sacred and what is not has come from outside the faith, not from within. Even changes in the technology of writing have played a role. But the dominant role in the case of the church has been played by the memory of the God of Israel and of Jesus Christ.

Chapter 3
Which Manuscripts?

Once, perhaps, there was only one copy of Paul's letter to the Philippians: the one committed to writing by Paul's amanuensis and delivered to the congregation in Philippi. It is possible, however, that Paul kept a copy for himself, in which case there was more than one "original" manuscript from the beginning. In any case, we can be sure the original manuscript (or manuscripts) was copied, and then the copies were copied, and so on through the centuries. From the beginning, we may assume, small differences began to appear among the copies, mostly of negligible importance, but occasionally touching on significant points. When one considers that this same process of copying copies pertains to the entirety of the canon, both Old and New Testaments, one quickly sees that the question, Which manuscripts? acquires great importance.

To illustrate the practical differences this makes, consider the following illustration from the last century.

WHAT'S THE PROBLEM?

In 1946 the National Council of Churches of the United States published the Revised Standard Version (RSV) of the New Testament. The Old Testament was published in 1952. The RSV was immediately attacked as "Communist inspired," the "Bible of the Anti-Christ," the "new blasphemous Bible," and so on.[1] In some instances criticisms had to do with specific translations of the text, as when the RSV substituted the words "young woman" in Isaiah 7:14 for the King James Version's (KJV) "virgin." More alarming to the conservative branch of the church (made up largely but by no means wholly of evangelical and Reformed denominations in the United States not belonging to the National Council of Churches and therefore not members of the RSV translation committee) was the disappearance of blocks of text, familiar and beloved, into notes at the bottom of the page or simply missing altogether. The demoted texts included the resurrection appearances in Mark's Gospel (16:9–20), the universally appealing story of the woman caught in adultery in John (7:53–8:11), the institution of the cup at the Last Supper in Luke (22:19b–20), the brief benediction at the close of Paul's Letter to the Romans (16:24), and the reference to Ephesus in the salutation of the Letter to the Ephesians (1:1). While no comparably large sections of the Old Testament were subject to the same fate as passages in the New, the recurring footnoted use of "The Hebrew term is unknown," or "The meaning of the Hebrew is uncertain," or the "Hebrew lacks . . ." was equally disturbing to this group of conservative and evangelical churches, as were notations indicating that the Hebrew did not conform to traditional readings, as when Isaiah's prophecy speaks of a young woman who "is with child" rather than of one "who shall conceive" as in the KJV.

Collectively, these opponents of the RSV responded by commissioning the translation of a more doctrinally friendly rendering of the Word of God. It was to be a "completely new translation" while preserving "some measure of continuity with the long tradition of translating the Scriptures into English." In other words, it was to conform more closely to the familiar and beloved KJV. But when the new translation, called the New International Version of the Holy Bible (NIV), finally appeared more than twenty years later, it did not differ radically from the RSV. Passages such as Mark 16:9–20, John 7:53–8:11, Acts 8:37, and Romans 16:24 were set apart by a line and provided footnoted explanations, such as, "The most reliable early MSS [manuscripts] omit . . ." or "Some MSS add. . . ." This is not to say that the NIV accepted all the textual decisions of the RSV. It did not. But all in all, the judgment was clear (and it became increasingly so as the remain-

1. See, e.g., the article by Oswald T. Allis, former biblical professor at Princeton and Westminster theological seminaries, "Revised Standard Version of the Old Testament," *Eternity* 3 (November 1952): 5–7, 44–46.

ing decades of the century passed and new translations and versions appeared at every hand): the NIV had more in common with the RSV, and perhaps differed less, than any current or subsequent version of the Bible published in America in the twentieth century.

What had occurred in the intervening years to account for such a change of heart and mind? While many factors were involved, we wish to focus on but one: the mid-century discovery of manuscripts pertaining both to the Hebrew Scriptures and to the New Testament, as well as the collation of information from manuscript discoveries earlier in the twentieth century. These newly discovered manuscripts all antedated the two great biblical codices, Sinaiticus and Vaticanus, discovered in the nineteenth century, on which were based the Revised Version (1881–1885) and the American Standard Version (1901), both of which were revisions of the KJV. Despite theological differences, in the end both the progressive and the conservative branches of the church reached similar conclusions about the task of translation, because they had come to see eye to eye on a prior question: Of all the manuscripts of the Bible available, which are the best?

The Best Manuscripts and Early Christian Tradition

The desire to work with the best manuscripts available is an ancient one that has played a role in Christian life from early times.

The two great biblical scholars of the early centuries of the church, Origen (185–254) and Jerome (ca. 345–420), may properly be described as textual critics, for they both knew manuscripts differed from one another and that some were better than others, because certain texts could be shown to possess more original and therefore more "authentic" readings of the text. Origen's massive Hexapla of sixty-five hundred pages placed six versions of the Old Testament in parallel columns, noting differences from the Hebrew text. Not surprisingly, the Hexapla exists today only in fragments.

Jerome versus Augustine and the Choice of the Hebrew Text

In Eastern Christendom, centering in Constantinople (modern Istanbul), where Greek continued to be spoken, the Septuagint remained the version of the Old Testament most acceptable to the church. In the

Latin West the situation was different. As knowledge of Greek declined among the general populace, Latin translations of the Bible began to appear, none of which achieved a status worthy of official recognition. In 382 CE Pope Damasus sought to remedy the situation. He commissioned his new scriptural advisor, Eusebius Hieronymous (Jerome), to replace the existing Latin versions of the Gospels with a superior translation. Whether commissioned or not (the full extent of the commission is not known), Jerome extended his work to include the whole of the Septuagint. It was this task that occupied Jerome for the next twenty years in his monastic retreat in Bethlehem of Judea. It was a task left incomplete at the time of his death.[2]

Being aware that the Latin translations at hand were inadequate, Jerome set about systematically constructing the best possible Greek text upon which a new translation could be based. In time, however, Jerome recognized the futility of his labor; he was simply translating a translation. Influenced by his Jewish mentors to turn to the Scriptures in Hebrew, Jerome came to believe the Septuagint not only mistranslated the Hebrew but also included writings of questionable merit, writings the Jews themselves did not consider sacred, in part because some did not exist in the ancient Hebrew language and in part because in rabbinic opinion prophecy had ended with Ezra. These writings were 1 and 2 Esdras, Tobit, Judith, Additions to Esther, the Wisdom of Solomon, Ecclesiasticus (or the Wisdom of Jesus the Son of Sirach), Baruch, the Letter of Jeremiah, the Prayer of Azariah and the Song of the Three Young Men, Susanna, Bel and the Dragon, the Prayer of Manasseh, 1 and 2 Maccabees. All of these works Jerome treated as secondary, calling them Apocrypha (Greek "unknown" or "spurious").

Augustine (356–430), the great bishop of Hippo in North Africa and Jerome's junior by ten or more years (Jerome's date of birth is unknown), was deeply distressed by Jerome's reversion to the Hebrew texts and encouraged him simply to retranslate the Septuagint to correct the "terrible defects" of Old Latin versions. By Augustine's reasoning the Septuagint had been good enough for the evangelists and the apostles and therefore it should be good enough for Jerome (*Epistle* 71).[3] If the Septuagint differed from the Hebrew Bible, Augustine

---

2. Jerome, under the pressure of certain bishops, unwillingly continued to translate books of the LXX not in the Hebrew Bible. See H. F. D. Sparks, "Jerome as Biblical Scholar," in *The Cambridge History of the Bible*, Vol. 1: *From the Beginnings to Jerome*, ed. P. R. Ackroyd and C. F. Evans (Cambridge: Cambridge University Press, 1970), 510–41.

3. *The Works of Saint Augustine: A Translation for the 21st Century*, II/1: Letters 1–99, trans. Roland Teske, S.J. (Hyde Park, N.Y.: New City, 2001).

averred, then it must do so "with good reason." In Augustine's mind, the Septuagint translators were no less inspired by the Holy Spirit than the original Hebrew writers had been.

What finally, centuries later, came to be known as the Latin Vulgate was only in part, though in major part, the work of Jerome. There is no evidence that he ever translated any writings of the New Testament other than the Gospels. In spite of its composite origin, the Vulgate came to be treated in the Latin West as entirely the work of Jerome; and though Jerome himself considered translation an almost impossible art to master, as attested by his own inconsistency in translation,[4] the Vulgate came to be regarded as superior to both the Hebrew Old Testament and the Greek New Testament. At the Council of Trent (1545–1563), in response to Protestant interest in vernacular translations of the original texts, the Vulgate was declared the "repository of orthodox Christian biblical doctrine."[5] To make the point graphic, the great Catholic Complutensian Polyglot Bible (1514–1517) places the Vulgate in the center of the folio, with the Septuagint version to the left, and the Hebrew to the right, "placing them," as the "Prologue to the Reader" says, "like the two thieves one on each side, and Jesus, that is, the Roman or Latin Church, between them."[6]

THE REFORMATION AND THE BEGINNINGS OF A CRITICAL TEXT OF THE NEW TESTAMENT

The textual basis of Martin Luther's 1522 translation of the New Testament, and William Tyndale's English translation of 1534, was a Greek text prepared by Erasmus of Rotterdam in 1516 and revised several times over the next half century. This revised Erasmus text came to be known as the Textus Receptus (TR), or the Received Text. It was the textual basis of the KJV of 1611 and remained the official Greek text of the New Testament until the latter part of the nineteenth century. Understandably, the Textus Receptus was based on manuscripts most

4. See H. F. D. Sparks, "Jerome as Biblical Scholar," and Gerald Bonner, "Augustine as Biblical Scholar," in *From the Beginnings to Jerome*, ed. P. R. Ackroyd and C. F. Evans (vol. 1 of *The Cambridge History of the Bible*; Cambridge: Cambridge University Press, 1970), chaps. 16–17.

5. See Raphael Loewe, "The Medieval History of the Latin Vulgate," in *The West from the Fathers to the Reformation*, ed. G. W. H. Lampe (vol. 2 of *The Cambridge History of the Bible*; Cambridge: Cambridge University Press, 1969), chap. 5, esp. 108.

6. See Basil Hall, "Biblical Scholarship: Editions and Commentaries," in *The West from the Reformation to the Present Day*, ed. S. L. Greenslade (vol. 3 of *The Cambridge History of the Bible*; Cambridge: Cambridge University Press, 1963), 51.

readily available to Erasmus in Basel, Switzerland, where it was published, not on manuscripts that careful study had shown to be the most ancient. Manuscripts of the text type underlying the Textus Receptus primarily date from the tenth century and later, that is, from the height of the Byzantine Empire. For this reason, the text type found in the Textus Receptus is called a Byzantine text.

The Emergence of Textual Criticism

The corrupt state of the Byzantine text, and therefore the Textus Receptus, although analyzed in the eighteenth century, did not truly become widely apparent until Constantin von Tischendorf's discovery and publication of the two great fourth-century codices, Codex Sinaiticus (siglum ℵ) and Codex Vaticanus (siglum B). They are the best preserved and most complete ancient manuscripts of the New Testament, but as scholars in the twentieth century discovered, they are not the oldest. Tischendorf's *Editio octava critica maior*, being a critical Greek text of the New Testament based on Codex Sinaiticus, was published in 1869–1872. In 1881 B. F. Westcott and F. J. A. Hort published their *New Testament in the Original Greek* based on Codex Vaticanus and Codex Bezae Cantabrigiensis (siglum D), which they thought contained readings of the Gospels and Acts dating from the third and "probably" the second century. In this conjecture they have been proved wrong by the papyri. Nevertheless, these two critical texts provided translators with a text of the New Testament that was at least two hundred years closer to the original than the Byzantine text employed by the translators of the KJV.

It is really not until the nineteenth century, with the work of Tischendorf, Westcott, and Hort, that the principles of textual criticism were laid down in detail, principles that, though expanded, have guided all subsequent work in the field. Again, because our purpose is quite limited here, we shall not be concerned with all the details of the emergence and development of textual criticism, which can be said to have begun in the eighteenth century by J. Semler and J. J. Griesbach—with precursors even in the seventeenth century. Rather, I want to emphasize that the cumulative effect of textual discoveries between 1860 and 1960, coupled with the publication of increasingly comprehensive critical texts of the New Testament, had by the end of that period ushered in a whole new era of Bible translation. According to Harry Orlinsky and Robert Bratcher, who have sketched the history of biblical translation from the first century onward, the fourth great epoch of Bible translation began in 1960, that is, after the release of the RSV, which we have been using as a benchmark of advance and ecumenicity in biblical studies.[7]

The analysis of manuscripts, comparing and contrasting them with one another, collating the differences among them, and making conjectures concerning their relationship to one another as well as to the hypothetical original autograph is the province of that discipline within the domain of biblical studies known as textual criticism.[8] The term *hypothetical* is used here because in every case the original manuscript of the individual books of the Bible has been lost and can be reconstructed *only on the basis of conjecture.* The product of this reconstruction is called a "critical text."

Textual Criticism Today

Thanks in large measure to the textual discoveries of the twentieth century, great progress was made in improving the Greek text of the New Testament. Of equal importance, however, was the employment of immense and meticulous human labor in collating the thousands of manuscripts made increasingly accessible as the decades passed, and now enhanced by computer technology. Today there are in existence almost thirty-three hundred New Testament manuscripts and twenty-four hundred lectionaries, as well as numerous versions from the second and later centuries in Latin, Syriac, and Coptic, in addition to citations of the New Testament in the writings of the early church fathers. It is easy to see why the differences among these many texts number in the hundreds of thousands, from variations in spelling to the omission of whole blocks of text, such as John 7:53–8:11. Of these manuscripts, the majority, almost two thousand manuscripts dating from the ninth century and later, belong to what J. J. Griesbach in the eighteenth century identified as the Byzantine family of text types. Because of its ubiquity it is also called the *Koine* (or Common) text. As an imperial text, the Byzantine text includes what have been referred to as "edifying

7. For a history of Bible translation, see Harry M. Orlinsky and Robert G. Bratcher, *A History of Bible Translation and the North American Contribution* (Atlanta: Scholars Press, 1991).

8. For a definition of textual criticism, related terms, and bibliography, see Richard N. Soulen and R. Kendall Soulen, *Handbook of Biblical Criticism*, 3rd ed. (Louisville: Westminster John Knox, 2001).

additions." These were the very class of additions that the RSV foot-noted or dropped altogether from its version of the New Testament. In the last half of the twentieth century, textual criticism generally and the understanding of first-century Judaism and fourth-century Christian-ity were greatly enhanced by the two factors mentioned above: textual discoveries and human labor.

RECENT DISCOVERIES

We can list these discoveries as three:

The Dead Sea Scrolls

Parallel in time to the release of the RSV in the late 1940s and early 1950s, many thousands of miles away, were other events, far more dramatic and transformative in their intellectual and historical con-sequences for understanding the Bible than the American debate sur-rounding the new translation. That was the discovery in Palestine, over more than a full decade (1947–1960), of scrolls hidden away in the caves of Wadi Qumran along the shores of the Dead Sea.[9] In addition to writings unique to the Jewish sectarian community to which the scrolls belonged, now known by its place name as the Qumran com-munity, were copies, in whole or in part, of every book in the Hebrew Scriptures, except Esther. More significantly, the scrolls were invariably acknowledged by scholars to be one thousand years and more older than any other manuscript of the Old Testament previously known to exist, or to have been available to editors of Hebrew manuscripts employed in biblical translation in the sixteenth or any subsequent century. The discovery of the Dead Sea Scrolls (DSS), nineteen hundred years after their deposition in the caves, was like a miracle to anyone interested in the Bible or in the history of Judaism in late antiquity, including the rise of the Jewish sect first simply known as "the Way." The impact of the Dead Sea Scrolls on scholarship, both Jewish and Christian, was broad and deep, and it continues.

One effect was essentially to create for the first time the possibility of a textual criticism of the Old Testament in a manner comparable to

---

9. For a listing of the scrolls and bibliography, see ibid., 43–44, "Dead Sea Scrolls."

manuscript analysis of the New Testament, at least in terms of antiquity, since heretofore Hebrew manuscript witnesses had been too meager and too late in origin to be of significant usefulness. The antiquity of the scrolls, dating from the second century BCE to 70 CE, changed all that. It is not that the textual history of the various books of the Hebrew Bible is now easily delineable; it is rather that the complexity of that textual history is clearer, and with it, perhaps, some understanding of the freedom by which ancient traditionists viewed the written text. The Dead Sea Scrolls predate the establishment of the Masoretic Text (MT) by Jewish rabbis from the seventh to the tenth centuries, though the consonants differ little from wording established in the second century. The Masoretic Text, which added vowel signs to what had been only consonantal texts, is the received, authoritative text of Judaism. The freedom in the transmission of texts witnessed to by the Dead Sea Scrolls is understandable when one also remembers that during the time of the Qumran community's existence, the central canon in Judaism pertained to the Pentateuch, less to the Prophets and to the Writings, although the idea of canon existed more in practice than in theory. Even then, the text of the Pentateuch was not literally sacrosanct. This is shown by the fact that some Torah texts conform to the Samaritan Pentateuch, which arose in the fifth century BCE when Samaritans and Jews went their separate ways. Other readings in the Dead Sea Scrolls conform to the Old Greek (proto-Septuagint) texts, while others still are closer to what became the Masoretic Text. The Targums, or Aramaic translations of the Hebrew Scriptures, also show that there was less concern for literal accuracy than there was for the appropriateness of the translation (comparable, for example, to the difference between the American Standard Version of 1901 and the Revised Standard Version of 1946–1952). Archaisms were altered for the sake of clarity.

The discovery of the Dead Sea Scrolls also fleshed out the known diversity of first-century Judaism. By the time of the destruction of Jerusalem in 70 CE, Pharisaic or proto-rabbinic Judaism, the Essenes of Qumran, the Sadducees of the temple, and the messianic movement known as Christianity all possessed, or were in the process of forming, distinctive though largely overlapping canons of Scripture. Differences in beliefs and practices gave rise to differences in canons, which in turn shaped the communities that held them sacred. The canon of the highly structured Qumran community included such works as *The Manual of Discipline, The Zadokite Document, The War of the Sons of Light and the Sons of Darkness,* and *The Psalms of Thanksgiving* in addition to the

Hebrew Scriptures. Sadducaic Judaism and the Essenes of Qumran disappeared following the fall of Jerusalem. Diaspora Judaism of the synagogue with its Hebrew texts and Aramaic translations (Targums), and
the Christian church with its Septuagint and New Testament survived.

The Nag Hammadi Library

The ongoing discovery of scrolls along the Dead Sea, which as noted
took place over a period of years, overshadowed a contemporaneous
find related to the New Testament. This was the discovery in 1946 of
a whole library of writings belonging to a quasi-Christian gnostic sect
of the fourth century. The volumes were reportedly found buried in a
cave tomb near a village of the Upper Nile known as Nag Hammadi,
from which they get their name, the Nag Hammadi Library.[10] The
document of greatest allure among the numerous texts discovered is the
Gospel of Thomas, whose use by New Testament scholars made a profound (though perhaps not permanent) impact on Jesus studies during
the last decades of the twentieth century. For those persuaded by the
authenticity of the sayings attributed to Jesus in the *Gospel of Thomas*,
the extracanonical character of the source further threw into question the notion of the literal authority of the New Testament text. In
Roman Catholic tradition, that assurance of authority lay with ecclesial
pronouncements undergirded by apostolic succession and tradition;
but in conservative and fundamentalist circles, that assurance lay in the
doctrine of verbal inspiration and verbal inerrancy. But all the traditions, not just the Catholics and evangelical conservatives, found the
Nag Hammadi discoveries, largely gnostic in character, something to
reckon with. Again the truth was underscored that an interpretive circle
exists between a canon of Scripture and the community that holds them
sacred. Gnostic Christianity existed for more than two centuries.

The Beatty and Bodmer Papyri

As far as New Testament textual criticism is concerned, however, neither the Dead Sea Scrolls nor the Nag Hammadi Library, as extremely
important as they were, equaled the much less heralded appearance of

---

10. For a listing of the codices, see ibid., 116–17, "Nag Hammadi Codices."

papyrus manuscripts of the New Testament that came to light in the
1930s and the 1950s. They are known respectively by the names of
their acquirers, the Chester A. Beatty papyri, most of which are cur-
rently in Dublin, and the Bodmer papyri, housed in Cologny, Switzerland. These papyrus manuscripts comprise almost the whole of the
New Testament and date from the first half of the second century to
the beginning of the fourth century. In other words these manuscripts
are in the main a full century older (and therefore closer to the original autographs) than the two great codices so dramatically discovered
and heralded in the nineteenth century by the foremost textual critic
of that century, Tischendorf: Codex Sinaiticus, first discovered in
the library of Saint Catherine's monastery on Mount Sinai in 1844
(though not made accessible until 1869), and Codex Vaticanus, present in the library of the Vatican in Rome since at least 1475 but not
photographed and released for common use until 1889/1890. Sinaiticus contains the whole of the Old Testament and New Testament plus
the *Epistle of Barnabas* and the *Shepherd of Hermas*; Vaticanus is incomplete, with part of Hebrews, the Pastoral Epistles, Philemon, and the
book of Revelation missing. The Beatty and Bodmer papyri have made
an invaluable contribution to the creation of a critical text.

THE DEVELOPMENT OF THE CRITICAL TEXT

Critical texts of the New Testament in Greek as developed by the
United Bible Societies enable readers to decide whether to agree with
the hypothetical text as reconstructed by the societies' scholars or side
with an alternate reading found in some other ancient manuscripts and
provided to the reader in footnotes. To compare a few problems in the
Greek text with their modern translations is informative. The illustrations are from the first chapter of the Gospel of John.

John 1:3–4

These verses present the textual critic with a problem in punctuation
for sentence division, not a problem in wording. In the first century the
Greek language was written without punctuation and without spaces
between words or sentences, leaving it to the reader, including monks
of the early Middle Ages as well as the modern editors of the critical

text, to decide where to add periods, commas, question marks, and so on. In the opening verses of the prologue to John's Gospel, one must decide whether to place a period before or after two Greek words, *ho gegonen* ("which was made"), thus interpreting them as belonging either with the words immediately before or after. Words in **bold type** indicate the decisions of modern editors/translators of the Gospel.

1. Tischendorf, *Novum Testamentum Graece* (1869; in English translation), reads, "And without him was not anything made **which was made**. In him is life. . . ."

2. Westcott and Hort's *New Testament in the Original Greek* (1881, in English translation) reads, "And without him was not anything made. **That which has been made** in him was life. . . ."

3. *Novum Testamentum Graece* (21st ed., 1952) reads (in English translation), "and without him was not anything made **that was made**. In him was life. . . ."

4. *Novum Testamentum Graece* (25th ed., 1968) and *The Greek New Testament* (2nd ed., 1968) revert back to the reading of Westcott and Hort: "And without him was not anything made. **That which has been made** in him was life." The third edition (1971) and fourth edition (1983, repr. 1994) of the latter remained the same following the majority opinion led by Kurt Aland. However, Bruce Metzger, in his *Textual Commentary on the Greek New Testament* (second edition, 1994), offered his dissenting opinion (pp. 167–68), citing John's fondness for beginning a sentence or clause with the preposition "in" (Greek *en*), his repetitive style, his doctrine (cf. 5:26, 39; 6:53) "to say nothing concerning the sense of the passage." Metzger notes that the majority opinion was made in concert with "the ante-Nicene writers (orthodox and heretical alike) who took *ho gegonen* with what follows." He then offers this historical observation: "When, however, in the fourth century Arians and the Macedonian heretics began to appeal to the passage to prove that the Holy Spirit is to be regarded as one of the created things, orthodox writers preferred to take *ho gegonen* with the preceding sentence, thus removing the possibility of heretical use of the passage" (p. 195).

5. The KJV (1611) and the RSV (1947) read, "and without him was not any thing made **that was made**. In him was life. . . ."

6. The NRSV (1990), however, reads, "and without him not one thing came into being. **What has come into being** in him was life. . . ."

7.a. The New English Bible (1961; principally the work of British scholars for use where British English is spoken) reads, "no single thing was created without him. **All that came to be** was alive with his life. . . ."

b. The Revised English Bible (1989) reads, "without him no created thing came into being. In him was life. . . ." Here the two Greek words, *ho gegonen*, are either left untranslated or are to be inferred as present in the former clause.

8.a. The Jerusalem Bible (1966; Roman Catholic translation of the Bible that follows textual and interpretive decisions of *La Bible de Jérusalem*) reads, "not one thing had its being but through him. **All that came to be** had life in him. . . ."

b. The New Jerusalem Bible (1984) reads, "not one thing came into being except through him. **What has come into being** in him was life. . . ."

9. Today's English Version (Good News Bible; New Testament 1967, prepared by the American Bible Society for persons who speak English as a second language as well as native English speakers) reads, "not one thing in all creation was made without him. **The Word had** life in himself. . . ." Here too it is not clear how the Greek words *ho gegonen* are being translated, if at all.

10. The NIV (1973, 1984; published by the International Bible Society) reads, "Without him nothing was made **that has been made.** In him was life. . . ."

John 1:18

The prologue to the Gospel of John reaches its climactic conclusion in verse 18. The KJV, following the Greek text of the Textus Receptus, reads: "No one has ever seen God, **the only begotten Son**, who is in the bosom of the Father, he has made him known." The bold type indicates the problematic text. The question is whether the text should read here "Son" or "God." There are several textual variants: *monogenēs theos* (lit. "only begotten God") is supported by P66 (dated ca. 200), Vaticanus, Sinaiticus, Irenaeus, and so on; without a definite article it gives *theos* the meaning of "divine." *Ho monogenēs theos*, containing the article, is supported by P75 (dated early third century), Sinaiticus (editor's hand), among others, and must be translated "the only begotten God." *Ho monogenēs huios*, supported by fifth-century manuscripts, is to be translated "the only begotten Son." *Monogenēs huios theou*, supported by early Latin manuscripts, is to be translated "the only begotten Son of God."

In this textual problem there are three kinds of considerations: external, internal, and translational. External witness has to do with the weight of the manuscript evidence. Internal considerations have to do with John's theology, the consistency and coherence of his language. The final consideration is how these words are to be translated. James Moffatt, in his translation, resorts to what he calls a periphrastic rendering of the phrase ("the divine One, the only Son") in order, he says, "to bring out its full meaning here." J. B. Phillips (1958, rev. ed. 1972) solves the translational problem similarly: "Yet the divine and only Son. . . ."

In the following examples no notice of footnoted remarks concerning the passage is indicated.

1. Tischendorf (1869), in English translation, reads "**the only begotten Son**" (*ho monogenēs theos*).

2. *Novum Testamentum Graece* (Stuttgart, 21st ed., 1952; 26th ed., 1983; identical with *The Greek New Testament*, 4th ed., 1983) reads, *monogenēs theos*, which can be variously translated, as seen below.

3.a. The RSV (1946) reads, "**the only Son.**"

b. The NRSV (1990) reads, "**It is God the only Son.**"

4.a. The New English Bible (1961) reads, "**but God's only Son.**"

b. The Revised English Bible (1989) reads, "**God's only Son.**"

5.a. The Jerusalem Bible (1966) reads, "**it is the only Son.**"

b. The New Jerusalem Bible (1989) reads, "**it is the only Son.**"

6. Today's English Version (1966) reads, "**The only One, who is the same as God.**"

7. The NIV (1973, 1984) reads, "**but God the One and Only.**"

What these translations show is that just as the early transmitters of the text in the first few centuries of the church tried to understand what the evangelist meant by *monogenēs theos*, substituting for it the variants listed above, so too are modern translators faced with the inescapable necessity of interpreting the text. Translation is not simply a matter of writing down the words of one language into the equivalent words in another.

John 1:34

This verse presents a textual problem of a different sort. Some ancient manuscripts support the reading, "This is the Son of God." They include papyri P66 and P75 as well as Codex Vaticanus. Other, almost equally ancient manuscripts support the reading, "This is the elect of God." They include P5 and Codex Sinaiticus. Whereas a scribal change from "the elect of God" to "the Son of God" is understandable, reflecting the general movement of thought within the church from a lower to a higher Christology, the reverse is less explainable. Why, a number of scholars ask, would a copyist, finding "the Son" in the text in front of him, change the reading to "the elect"? This is the position taken by a number of leading twentieth-century Roman Catholic scholars, such as M. Boismard, Rudolf Schnackenburg, and Raymond Brown, as well as the British Johannine scholar C. K. Barrett; their choice may account for this reading being chosen by the New English Bible and the Jerusalem Bible and being retained in their revisions as noted below. Some Old Latin manuscripts as well as some Syriac and Coptic versions read, "the elect Son." The textual critic, and therefore the modern translator, must consider both the external facts (the manuscript witnesses, their age, provenance, etc.) as well as internal factors (the Gospel's theology and theological vocabulary). In a number of instances the alternative reading is footnoted in the editions listed below but is not noted here.

1. The KJV (reflecting the Greek text of the Textus Receptus of 1550) reads, **"the Son of God,"** as does Luther's German translation (based on Erasmus's 1516 text).

2.a. The RSV reads, **"the Son of God."**

b. The NRSV reads, **"the Son of God."**

3.a. The New English Bible reads, **"God's chosen One."**

b. The Revised English Bible reads, **"God's chosen One."**

4. The Living Bible reads, **"the Son of God."**

5.a. The Jerusalem Bible reads, **"the Chosen One of God."**

b. The New Jerusalem Bible reads, **"the Chosen One of God."**

6. Today's English Version reads, **"the Son of God."**

7. The NIV reads, **"the Son of God."**

SUMMARY

In this chapter I have tried to show why and how it is the case that recent twentieth-century translations and versions of the Bible are closer to the original autographs than those of any previous century. This is because the manuscripts now available are older and the techniques of analysis better than those employed in previous centuries. I have also sought to demonstrate that even so basic a task as punctuating the originally unpunctuated Greek texts is an unavoidable and indispensable act of interpretation, however hidden that fact may be from the modern reader. It is the wide recognition of this fact that has narrowed the divide that once existed between the so-called liberals on the left (read: RSV) and conservatives on the right (read: NIV).

Chapter 4
Which Translation?

THE BLESSING OF TRANSLATION

From the earliest days of the church, the gospel has been proclaimed and heard in a variety of languages. This is one meaning of the day of Pentecost recorded in the Acts of the Apostles. On that day there were "Parthians, Medes, Elamites, and residents of Mesopotamia, Judea, and Cappadocia, Pontus and Asia, Phrygia and Pamphylia, Egypt and the parts of Libya belong to Cyrene, and visitors from Rome, both Jews and proselytes, Cretans and Arabs," yet each one heard the story of God's deeds of power *in their own tongue* (Acts 2:1–13).

By the fourth century, the church's Scriptures had been translated into a variety of languages such as Coptic, Armenian, Syriac, and Latin. Today, the Bible, in whole or in part, has been translated into over 2,230 different languages and dialects of the world, from Anuak to Zulu. More than 3,000 translations of the New Testament exist in English alone. The total number of translations worldwide over the past two thousand years is simply inestimable, and it continues unabated. Yet each of these, despite varying degrees of popular recognition, may properly lay claim to being the Word of God and therefore sacred Scripture of the Christian church.

That the church should regard its Scriptures as translatable may seem self-evident, but it is not. One may compare the church's view of the Bible to Islam's understanding of the Holy Qur'an. The Qur'an exists in various languages for the benefit of those who do not know Arabic, but it exists as *sacred* Scripture only in the language of the original revelation. Orthodox Judaism's reverence for the Hebrew text is comparable. By contrast Christianity has no sacred language. Jesus was a Palestinian Jew who spoke Aramaic; yet both his words and the stories about him were passed down in the language of the dominant Hellenistic culture: Koine Greek. Moreover, the Gospels, in whatever language they may appear, are but translated versions of the message *of* Jesus, and the message *about* Jesus is no less interpreted, narrated in four alternative readings of the one life. As Lamin Sanneh notes, "we come upon a remarkable point with respect to the history of religions. Christianity seems unique in being the only world religion that is transmitted without the language or originating culture of its founder."[1] That from its earliest beginnings Christianity has been "*a translated religion without a revealed language*," as Sanneh notes, is a fact whose significance has not always been given its due.[2] Christians pray to God in more languages than any other religion in the world.

THE CHALLENGE OF TRANSLATION

While the church has regarded the translatability of the gospel as a blessing, it has also had to deal with the task of translation as a challenge. An old Italian proverb ironically laments: *traduttore traditore*, "the translator is a traitor."[3] The same point is made in a less cynical but still pointed way in Sirach or Ecclesiasticus (a deuterocanonical or apocryphal book):

> You are urged . . . to read with good will and attention. . . . For what was originally expressed in Hebrew does not have exactly the same sense when translated into another language. *Not only this work, but even the law itself, the prophecies, and the rest of the books* [of the Septuagint] *differ not a little as originally expressed* [in Hebrew].
>
> ("The Prologue to Ecclesiasticus," RSV; italics added)

1. Lamin Sanneh, *Whose Religion Is Christianity?* (Grand Rapids: Eerdmans, 2003), 97. Sanneh notes, "More people pray and worship in more languages in Christianity than in any other religion in the world. Moreover, Christianity has been the impulse behind the creation of more dictionaries and grammars of the world's languages than any other force in history" (69).

2. Cf., for example, the fourth goal chosen by the translators of the Holman Christian Standard Bible as stated in their introduction: "to affirm the authority of Scripture as God's inerrant word and to champion its absolutes against social or cultural agendas that would compromise its accuracy."

3. David Daniell, *The Bible in English* (New Haven: Yale University Press, 2003), 774. This work has been an indispensable resource for much of this chapter.

The translator was cognizant of the transformations that unavoidably occur when the words and meanings of one time and place are translated (literally "carried across") into the language and thought forms of another. As has been said, "translation both interprets and recreates the text it addresses."[4]

The translators of the Septuagint certainly "interpreted" the centuries-old Hebrew texts of their sacred traditions and re-created something more suitable to the Hellenistic world in which they lived. Although we have no copies of the Hebrew texts on which their translations are based, a comparison of the Septuagint with the Hebrew texts of the Dead Sea Scrolls and with the later Masoretic Text (MT) is illuminating. For example, just in terms of the physical texts themselves, Septuagint (LXX) Jeremiah is shorter than MT Jeremiah by one-eighth, and the order of chapters is quite different; LXX Job is shorter than MT Job by one-sixth, and it includes an ending not found in the Hebrew; LXX Esther is almost twice as long as MT Esther; and LXX Exodus and MT Exodus differ in the order of verses and in the inclusion and exclusion of both words and material. Whether any of these textual differences can be attributed to the translators themselves cannot be known, although it has been argued with good reason that, in some instances at least, the translators simply omitted what they found too difficult to translate.[5] In other instances, scholars contend, they arbitrarily altered the Hebrew text, or gave an erroneous interpretation due to lack of understanding.[6] What can be known with certainty is that some effort was made to contemporize the text. This can be seen in occasional glosses to the text, that is, the addition of single words or phrases to qualify something more neutrally stated in the Hebrew, as when the translator of Proverbs adds moralizing conditions, such as poor/rich, good/bad, just/unjust, to the translation (as at 16:7; 15:28a; 19:22); or when embarrassing anthropomorphisms are eliminated, such as references to "the mouth of the Lord" (Josh. 9:14); or, again, when reference is made to Moses speaking to the Lord "face to face," Moses is said to behold not God's "form," as in the Hebrew text, but rather "the glory of the Lord" (LXX Num. 12:8). In like manner it apparently seemed good to the LXX translator of Exodus 4:24 not to say

---

4. See, "English Translations of the Bible" in *The Literary Guide to the Bible*, ed. Robert Alter and Frank Kermode (Cambridge: Harvard University Press, 1987), 647–66, esp., 649.

5. So, e.g., Marvin H. Pope, *Job: Translated with an Introduction and Notes*, Anchor Bible 15 (Garden City, N.Y.: Doubleday, 1965), xl. See also Augustine's complaint, *De doctrina Christiana* 2.12.

6. See Isaac Leo Seeligmann, *The Septuagint Version of Isaiah and Cognate Studies* (Forschungen zum Alten Testament 40; Tübingen: Mohr Siebeck, 2004), 259.

God sought to kill Moses, as the Hebrew says, but that it was (no less inexplicably) "an *angel of the Lord*"; and at 15:3 the translator prefers not to say, "The LORD is a warrior," but rather, "The LORD is one who crushes wars." A final and most intriguing illustration is the translation given to Exodus 3:14. The enigmatic "I am who I am" (as the Hebrew is most often translated in English) becomes in Greek the philosophically laden *ho ōn,* or "He who is," or "the Existent One."[7]

TRANSLATION: FROM THE SEPTUAGINT
TO THE KING JAMES VERSION

In the days of Jerome and Augustine, Latin was the language of the people. Centuries later, Latin was the language of high learning; it was unintelligible to the common people. In Western Europe for almost a thousand years, following the fall of Rome in 405, the Bible was not translated into a vernacular version (it was translated into a Slavic language, although not without great resistance). Nevertheless, biblical stories took hold in the imagination of people everywhere as the Christian faith spread throughout the Continent. So much was this the case, writes the medievalist Geoffrey Shepherd, that even indigenous myths were retold so as to weave the legends of ethnic origin into the great biblical stories, connecting the lineage of tribal chieftains to the offspring of Adam, thereby immersing group identity into a palpably old and universal sacred history (cf., e.g., *Parzival,* ca. 1200, or, in modern times, *The Book of Mormon*).[8] Enculturalization was the linguistic continuation of the miracle of Pentecost, and in time this gave rise to the desire for a vernacular translation.

The road to vernacular translations of the Bible was a long and occasionally bloody one. Although no pope or council had ever absolutely and universally prohibited the translation of Scripture into vernacular tongues, ecclesiastical authorities in England looked upon early English translations by John Wyclif (d. 1384), William Tyndale (1494–1536), and Miles Coverdale (1488–1569) as invitations to heresy. The English statute of 1401, *De heretico comburendo,* introduced the death penalty by burning for the heretical act of seeking to translate the Vulgate into English.

---

7. See Paul Lamarche, S.J., "The Septuagint: Bible of the Earliest Christians," in *The Bible in Greek Christian Antiquity,* ed. and trans. Paul M. Blowers (Notre Dame: University of Notre Dame Press, 1997), 15–33, especially 24.

8. See Geoffrey Shepherd, "English Versions of the Scriptures before Wyclif," in *The West from the Fathers to the Reformation,* ed. G. W. H. Lampe (vol. 2 of *The Cambridge History of the Bible*; Cambridge: Cambridge University Press, 1969), 362–87.

Nevertheless, by the start of the sixteenth century, the several conditions necessary for a new vernacular translation of the Bible were at hand: (1) humanistic interest in returning to the Scriptures in Hebrew and Greek and setting aside the Vulgate; (2) the development of biblical knowledge upon which moral reform and scriptural theology could be based; (3) the maturation of indigenous languages, particularly of German and English; (4) the rise of national pride and identity; (5) the development of the printing press for the dissemination of knowledge and propaganda; and (6) the widespread conviction that moral decay within the Roman Church called for reform. To put the matter briefly, the first of these coalesced in the person of Erasmus of Rotterdam; the second in Luther, Zwingli, Bucer, and Calvin on the Continent, and Tyndale, Coverdale, and John Knox in Britain; the third in Bible translation itself (which force-fed vernacular tongues with a vast array of biblical idioms and vocabulary, and its own concept-creating power), and in such secular literary figures as Spenser and Shakespeare; the fourth in Henry VIII in England, and Luther's protector, Elector Frederick of Saxony in Germany; the fifth in the courageous printers of Antwerp, Worms, Wittenburg, and elsewhere who risked persecution; and the last to the rise of literacy and of cultural standards generally throughout England and the Continent, the fruit of the great urban universities founded from the late twelfth century onward.

Ultimately, the success of the Reformation meant that the Bible was available in English in *more than one translation*. But this very success created a new issue: which translation was to be preferred, and why?

The ramifications of this new question can be illustrated by a brief comparison of the Geneva Bible and the King James Version.

The King James Version and the Geneva Bible

Today the King James Version (KJV) of the Bible of 1611 is well known even among the biblically illiterate, while the Geneva Bible of 1560 is all but forgotten. Yet the Geneva Bible was the one brought to America's shores by the (Calvinistic) Pilgrims of Massachusetts and was soon to be found in the Virginia Colony.[9] Had the Geneva Bible prevailed instead

---

9. That colonists willing to leave England included those of a dissenting spirit is attested by the prevalence of the Geneva Bible among the early settlers of Bermuda, copies of which are still preserved in St. Peter's church in St. George (Bermuda). Bermuda was settled as a British colony in 1612, following the wreck of the *Sea Venture*, the supply vessel bound for Jamestown in 1609, and immortalized in Shakespeare's last play, *The Tempest*.

of the (Anglican) KJV, the church's intellectual history in English-speaking lands might have unfolded quite differently.

The Geneva Bible was the product of English Reformers who took refuge in Geneva in the mid-1550s. With Edward's death and the coronation of his Catholic sister Mary in 1553, many leading Protestant churchmen and scholars fled (again) to the Continent. Some went to Geneva, attracted there by the person and writings of John Calvin (1509–1564). The assembly of reform-minded scholars, though comparatively short-lived, was almost without parallel. Among these learned men were John Knox of Scotland, Miles Coverdale, and Theodore Beza (a prominent Greek scholar). The new translation they produced followed Tyndale. The New Testament was released in 1557, the whole Bible, called the Geneva Bible, in 1560—barely two years after Protestant-leaning Elizabeth I ascended to the throne as Queen of England. The Geneva Bible is the first English edition to use eye-saving roman font instead of heavy gothic letters, the first to use verse divisions, and the first to use italic type for words not found in the original sources. It includes prefatory summaries of books, maps, illustrative woodcuts, chronological tables, and tables "of the Principal things that are contained in the Bible." There is, as the title page of the 1560 Bible notes, marginal commentary, both textual and explanatory, "upon all the hard places." And it was printed in quarto (making the New Testament at least, a "pocketable" book). The Geneva Bible is the Bible of Shakespeare, Spenser, Bunyan, and Milton. As the eminent sixteenth-century scholar and historian of the English Bible David Daniell observes, the Geneva New Testament of 1557, "with its elaborate apparatus of arguments, notes, and tables, . . . forms the first critical edition of the New Testament in English."[10] In time the marginal notations, which originally were almost entirely elucidative and innocuous, were by various editors given an increasingly Calvinist slant. This caused the more conservative bishops of the realm, already dissatisfied with the Great Bible of 1539, to publish their own, unsuccessful translation in 1568, called the Bishops' Bible; it ceased being reprinted after 1606.

The King James Version

Not all the annotations in the Geneva Bible were innocuous. James I, successor to Queen Elizabeth, found "some notes very partiall,

10. Daniell, *Bible in English*, 184.

vntrue, seditious, and sauouring too much of daugerous and trayterous conceites."[11] Little wonder, then, that King James chose the safest possible course for his translation by prohibiting marginal annotations of any kind. Similarly, the king prohibited summaries, introductions, and prefaces, admitting only cross-references. The King's Printer then found it expedient to block the printing and importation of all competing Bibles, especially the Geneva, for which no one held exclusive publication rights. By 1660, fifty years after the appearance of the KJV, the Geneva Bible had been effectively forced from public view, the victim not of merit but of crass commercialism.

In the opinion of David Daniell, the triumph of the KJV over the Geneva Bible was a cultural tragedy. Whereas the Geneva Bible was a "masterpiece of Renaissance scholarship and printing and Reformation Bible thoroughness," amounting to "an encyclopedia of Bible information," the KJV was a throwback to an earlier, restrictive, and elitist time.[12] By giving to all who could read the tools to interpret for themselves the text of Holy Scripture, the Geneva Bible had given practical expression to the Reformation doctrine of the priesthood of all believers. The population that had been lifted up by the scholarship and openness of the Geneva Bible and invited to share in the interpretation of Scripture in "all its hard places" was now disenfranchised and put back in a position of subordination and dependence. As the status of the laity was diminished, the elitist role of Scripture and the clergy was elevated. In the absence of critical notes admitting to uncertainty in the text, or explaining what otherwise could be known only by experts, laypeople in time only naturally fell victim to biblical literalism and charlatanism, finding comfort in believing that what was there in the KJV was none other than the "inerrant and literal word of God."

Biblical fundamentalism, Daniell implies, would not likely have come about had the church been permitted to read, and revise, the Geneva Bible. In its place was "the Bible without notes," "the backward-looking, increasingly Latinist, often baldly unhelpful KJV."[13] For example, the KJV translators "make the one word 'trouble' serve for a dozen different Greek words; one word 'bring' to represent thirty-nine Hebrew words; one word 'destroy' to represent forty-nine Hebrew

---

11. *The Geneva Bible*: A facsimile of the 1560 edition, with an introduction by Lloyd E. Berry (Madison: University of Wisconsin Press, 1969), 15. The quoted text continues: "As for example, *Exod.* 1,19 where the marginal note alloweth *disobedience to kings*. And *2. Chron.* 15,16, the note taxeth Asa for deposing his mother, *onely*, and *not killing her*" (15–16).
12. Daniell, *Bible in English*, 291.
13. Ibid., 617, also 347.

words."[14] Nevertheless, swept along by the Great Awakening and the inherent and undeniable overall beauty of its language, the KJV in the United States alone went through fourteen hundred different editions between 1777 and 1850, with printings in the untold millions. The observation is probably true that, in America particularly, the KJV provided a vital and unparalleled sense of cultural stability in the midst of rapid change. Rare was the home without a King James Bible, whether it was read or not.

THE AIMS OF MODERN TRANSLATION

Today the question, Which translation? presses itself on the reader of the Bible as never before. The challenge today for the English speaker is not to find an English translation of the Bible, but to decide which among a plethora of translations is best.

But what does "best" mean? Is the process of translation to provide a clear and accurate representation of the source text in the receptor language, so that the reader can enter, as much as possible, into the ancient world of the text? Or is the purpose of translation to erase the cultural and temporal distance between text and reader, so that what was said in the source language can have the same force and effect in the target language?

In fact, both of these are legitimate goals of the translator. But a translator cannot pursue both goals in equal measure at one and the same time. A translator must choose. The former approach is called *formal equivalence* (FE) translation; the latter, *dynamic equivalence* (DE) translation. These names approximate the older terms of common usage: word-for-word translation, and meaning-for-meaning translation. The difference is that DE goes beyond concern for *meaning* to the *effect* upon the hearer of what is being said.

Let us look at an example from the book of Romans. In Romans 12:20b, immediately after the admonition to give food and drink to one's enemies, one reads in the KJV, "for in so doing thou shalt heap coals of fire on his head," and, curiously, absent archaic terms, almost all modern English translations have followed in this example of FE translation, for it follows the words of the ancient Greek text with semantic precision. But Paul is using here an ancient metaphor meaning "to shame" or "embarrass." Modern readers, being unaware

---

14. See Bruce M. Metzger, *The Bible in Translation: Ancient and English Versions* (Grand Rapids: Baker, 2001), 74–75.

of Paul's metaphor, may hear something puzzling if not hateful in the expression. Today's English Version departs from the literal wording of the Greek for the sake of a dynamic equivalent: "for by doing this you will make him burn with shame."

One can justifiably argue that those who wish to enter the ancient world of the biblical text to the degree possible have no alternative but to learn the original languages in which the text was written, since substituting the language of modern culture for the language of an ancient culture inevitably removes the prospect of hearing the text as it was once heard. But learning the original languages of the texts is not without its own limitations. For one may also argue that time itself makes the cultural horizon of the text unattainable even when the language is essentially the same, as with Greek-speaking Christians today. Both are facts that must be granted. Since temporal distance is unalterable, the degree of understanding achieved by those who have knowledge of the original languages is therefore relative and imperfect at best. Take, for example, the words of Marvin Pope, a leading Old Testament scholar of the twentieth century, regarding his translation of the book of Job from the Hebrew: "In fairness to the reader, it should be explained that the translation offered in this volume [of the Anchor Bible]—as with every attempt to translate an ancient text—glosses over a multitude of difficulties and uncertainties."[15] Those "difficulties and uncertainties" exist within the *Hebrew* text. There is no reason, therefore, not to provide the student of Scripture with the next best alternative: a translation that is as clear and true to the culture and language of the original text as possible, as Pope endeavors to do. More importantly, as noted at the opening of this chapter, we dare not make a fetish of the "original" languages since, for Christians today and their counterparts in the first century, no text remains that inscribes Jesus' words in his mother tongue, Aramaic. Even in the best of circumstances we are always one translation removed from the *ipsissma verba Jesu* ("the very words of Jesus"). But then, translation, as noted above, is both the point and the task.

Formal Equivalence versus Dynamic Equivalence

To return to the question at hand: Should the translator seek formal equivalence or dynamic equivalence in carrying out his or her work? In FE translation one endeavors to find in the target language that word

15. *Job*, xxxix.

(or words) which is the formal equivalent of the word (or words) in the source text, matching, as far as reason and good sense allow, the same word with the same English equivalent. The more closely this rule is followed, and applied to sentence structure as well, the more wooden and incomprehensible the end result will be. This criticism is frequently raised against the American Standard Version (1901), for example, in 2 Corinthians 3:10: "For verily that which hath been made glorious hath not been made glorious in this respect, by reason of the glory that surpasseth." This may be compared with the still, though less, formal translation of the New English Bible: "Indeed, the splendour that once was is now no splendour at all; it is outshone by a splendour greater still." Of all FE translations, the most mechanical are interlinear translations, which make no pretense at being other than an aid in learning the source languages of the Bible. Under each Hebrew, Aramaic, or Greek word is its equivalent in English. Most FE translations, however, hold the biblical languages in high regard and have wanted to retain as much of the idiom and the cadence of the original as the receptor language permits. Since all modern Indo-European languages flow from the same linguistic source, and have for two millennia been deeply influenced by the language of the Bible, adhering to the rules of FE translation has not been too difficult to do. Indeed, FE translation was the norm until the last third of the twentieth century. Formal equivalence best describes the philosophy behind the KJV, its revision in the British Revised Version (1885), the American Standard Version (1901), the Revised Standard Version (1952), and the New International Version (1976)—all of which chose to continue in the tradition of the KJV; to these may be added the Catholic New American Bible (1970), which sought "to convey as directly as possible the thought and style of the inspired writers."[16]

In 1969, as reception theory was beginning to emerge, Eugene Nida, the dean of Bible translation in the United States at the time, described FE and the shift in philosophy toward DE:

> The older focus in translating was the form of the message, and translators took particular delight in being able to reproduce stylistic specialties, e.g., rhythms, rhymes, plays on words, chiasmus, parallelism, and unusual grammatical structures. The new focus, however, has shifted from the form of the message to the response of the receptor. Therefore what one must determine is the response of

16. From the preface.

the receptor to the translated message. This response must then be compared with the way in which the original receptors presumably reacted to the message when it was given in its original setting.[17]

It should be clear that the two goals of translation are incompatible in the same translation. Both have a useful and necessary function and are therefore complementary, but as translational goals they are at odds with each other. There is, however, more to translating than deciding whether one wants to preserve the formal characteristics of the source language or to concentrate on how the text is received. Translators must also determine who is being addressed by the translation—the so-called target audience. It is one thing to target the highly educated whose mother tongue is English; it is another to make the Scriptures accessible to those for whom English is a second language or who have attained no more than a sixth-grade education. The latter audience describes the vast majority of Christians around the world. Translating for this group cannot fulfill the needs and expectations of those who study Scripture as a window on ancient cultures or to understand Scripture more fully in its original setting.

The effect on language of these two approaches to translation should be obvious. In formal translations the target language is, on first encounter, enhanced and enriched with the theological and cultural terms of ancient Judaism and first-century Christianity. Scholars have often noted the linguistic impact of the Wyclif, Tyndale, and Coverdale Bibles on fifteenth- and sixteenth-century England and the English language. That same impact has been documented the world over as the Bible, or portions of it, have been translated into the vernacular of relatively small ethnolinguistic groups.[18] This impact has been particularly notable when the indigenous name for the local high god is adopted as the name for God in Scripture.[19] So it was in England as over time the vernacularization of Scripture occurred. Speakers of English forget that "God" is a derivation of Old Gothic Guth (Old English Gode, Gud, Gudde), while "Lord" comes from Old English "hlafweard," literally "loaf-ward/keeper," names adopted by early English translators for the Vulgate's *Deus* and *Dominus* to indigenize the language of the Christian faith.

---

17. Eugene Nida and Charles R. Taber, *The Theory and Practice of Translating* (New York: American Bible Society, 1969), 1.
18. See Sanneh, *Whose Religion Is Christianity?* 25; also Samuel P. Huntington, *The Third Wave: Democratization in the Late Twentieth Century* (Norman: Oklahoma University Press, 2001).
19. See Sanneh, *Whose Religion Is Christianity?* 16.

In the case of dynamic equivalence (DE) translations into contemporary English the opposite effect on the receptor language occurs. When DE is sought, particularly when the target audience is composed of those who speak English as a second language, the theological and culturally specific terms found in Scripture are typically replaced with less technical and more readily familiar words and phrases. In this case the target language is essentially unaltered and unenriched, while the language of the Bible (and therefore the church) is deprived of its diversity and richness and, more particularly, of its strangeness and ambiguity—the very ambiguity Augustine found stimulating. For all its Old and New Testament earthiness, theological language tends toward the abstract, and when the vocabulary of abstraction is removed, the wings of transcendence are clipped and reflection suffers. For example, consider John 1:1 in the original Greek as translated by the New Revised Standard Version (NRSV):

> In the beginning was the Word, and the Word was with God, and the Word was God. He was in the beginning with God.

Here the English is formally correct, following the Greek closely, but obviously, without knowledge of the language, the connotations of the Greek words are lost. Among educated Greeks of the first century, the word *Logos* (Word) embodied a rich philosophical tradition that "Word," in the twenty-first century, does not. In two uses of *theos* (God) the noun is accompanied by an article, but in verse 1b it is used without an article, that is (so it has been argued), predicatively, which cannot be captured simply in English,[20] and so on—all of which provided a degree of abstraction richly mined by the Greek fathers of the church and by theologians ever since. Nevertheless, the translation in English retains enough of the character of the Greek to have been deeply stimulative of theological reflection.

Compare then The Message:

> The Word was first,
>   the Word present to God,
>   God present to the Word.
> The Word was God,
>   in readiness for God from day one.

---

20. Note Rudolf Schnackenberg's discussion in *The Gospel According to St. John*, vol. 1 (New York: Crossroad, 1990), 234–35. Or note Raymond Brown's translation of the preposition *pros* (with) as "in God's presence," in *The Gospel According to John: I–XII* (Anchor Bible 29; Garden City, N.Y.: Doubleday, 1966), 3. For patristic reflection, none excels Origen's *Commentary on the Gospel According to John*; see especially his discussion of *archē* ("Beginning"), 1.90–91.

That John opened his Gospel with the words, "In the beginning," in intentional imitation of the opening words of Genesis is lost here, and with that void any possibility of connecting the two affirmations of God as Creator and God as incarnate Redeemer is lost as well. Moreover, being "ready" from "day one" is simply trite, obscuring John's belief in the preexistence of the *Logos*. These words, one may safely hazard, will not be studied and reflected upon two thousand years hence.

only writer's opinion

In his introduction to the New Testament section of The Message, Eugene H. Peterson notes that his "goal is not to render a word-for-word conversion of Greek into English, but rather to convert the tone, the rhythm, the events, the ideas, into the way we actually think and speak." The result, in Daniell's judgment, has been to "reduce the New Testament to the emotions of television soap operas, mixed with a tone of vacuous uplift." The biblical world becomes "the world of feel-good fiction," of "singalong triteness," and "the bright celebration of the self." And, Daniell continues, though claiming in its half-title to be "from the original languages," the text "totally abandons the Greek" or "distorts the Greek very seriously."[21] One might further compare Peterson's rendition of Jesus' instruction concerning prayer (Matt. 6:5–13; the Lord's Prayer ends, "You can do anything you want! You're ablaze in beauty! Yes. Yes. Yes"), or Paul's meditation on love (1 Cor. 13), or Paul's expression of profound gratitude for the consolation of the spirit (2 Cor. 1:3–7) with the same passages in the New Revised Standard Version or Today's New International Version. One is reminded of Rabbi Judah, who, rebelling against the free translation of the targums in second century CE, uttered the paradoxical warning, "He who translates a biblical verse literally is a liar, but he who elaborates on it is a blasphemer."[22] The point being made here is that when the translator succumbs to "the way we actually think and speak," a fatal diminution of the biblical text occurs to the detriment of theological reflection and the integrity of the gospel.

One must acknowledge, however, that when a translation is undertaken with a special target audience in mind and is successful in its purpose, as only the Spirit can bear witness, then that translation may be considered correct.[23] British English and American English differ sufficiently to warrant targeted versions for each, such as the New English Bible/Revised English Bible and the Revised Standard Version/ New Revised Standard Version, and one is no more or less correct than

whose judgment?

---

21. Daniell, *Bible in English,* 617–18.

22. *Tosephta, Megillah* cf. 3.41, ed. M. S. Zuckermandel (Jerusalem: Bamberger & Wahrmann, 1937).

23. See Nida and Taber, *Theory and Practice of Translation,* 163–73.

the other. And as English is spoken by increasing numbers around the world as a second language, so translations must be targeted for that audience, which Today's English Version/Revised Today's English Version (also appearing as the Good News Bible/Revised Good News Bible), and Contemporary English Version were in part designed to do. This means that there can be any number of "correct" translations, however much they may differ in detail and however much they may differ in purpose.

With the proliferation of translations and versions since the appearance of the Revised Standard Version in 1952, the full spectrum of translation styles has appeared, from very conservative formal equivalence translations to a broad range of dynamic equivalent ones, extending to loosely constructed paraphrases of Scripture. Overly strict formal equivalence on the one hand and unanchored dynamic equivalence on the other present the Scylla and Charybdis of modern translation theory and practice. Somewhere in between lie good exemplars of both, and somewhere as well a happy blending, but which is which among existing translations and versions is a hard call to make, and ultimately perhaps unnecessary. We are reminded of Augustine's observation that it is profitable in any case to read Scripture with multiple translations in hand.[24]

A sampling of translations, from the most formal and traditional to the least, can be arranged as follows:

> American Standard Version, New King James Version, Revised Standard Version, New Revised Standard Version, New International Version, New English Bible, Today's New International Version, Jerusalem Bible, Today's English Version (Good News Bible), Contemporary English Version, New Living Bible, Living Bible, The Message.

THE GENEVA BIBLE REDIVIVUS

We end this chapter returning to Daniell's lament that the KJV was a cultural tragedy. If we grant his premise that, following its revision in 1769, the elevation of the KJV to a status of unreasoned devotion led to biblical literalism and unbridled sectarianism, and delayed the rise of higher criticism, is not that judgment now irrelevant? Or, more

---

24. *De doctrina Christiana* 2.12, 13.

accurately, hasn't that history, as far as Bible translation is concerned, been turned on its head? With the endless proliferation of translations and versions and paraphrases, hasn't Scripture become a custom-made commodity, and isn't The Message the prime example? One wants to say yes. The best course to follow is the one Daniell perhaps intended: Affirm the publishing philosophy of the Geneva Bible, which in modern form is the study Bible, providing the aids necessary to make the rough places plain. The most suitable for students of Scripture are those based on translations guided by the principles of formal equivalence because they preserve as much as possible the thought-forms of antiquity, with their inherent richness and ambiguity, while providing the annotations needed for understanding. To be sure, the evangelist will rightfully prefer to begin with a more vernacular translation because the target audience is different.

In this recommendation we would here be attentive to the counsel of Origen in the third century on the purpose of translation and the necessity of study:

> If a Greek wished by wholesome instruction to benefit people who understood only Egyptian or Syriac, the first thing that he would do would be to learn their language; and he would rather pass for a barbarian among the Greeks, by speaking as the Egyptians or Syrians, in order to be useful to them, than always remain Greek, and be without the means of helping them. In the same way, the divine nature, having the purpose of instructing not only those who are reputed to be learned in the literature of Greece, but also the rest of mankind, accommodated itself to the capacities of the simple multitudes whom it addressed. It seeks to win the attention of the more ignorant by the use of language which is familiar to them, so that they may easily be induced, after their first introduction, to strive after an acquaintance with the deeper truths which lie hidden in Scripture. For even the ordinary reader of Scripture may see that it contains many things which are too deep to be apprehended at first; but these are understood by such as devote themselves to careful study of the divine word, and they become plain to them in proportion to the pains and zeal which they expend upon its investigation.
>
> (*Contra Celsum* 7.60)[25]

---

25. *The Ante-Nicene Fathers*, Vol. 4: *Tertullian, Part Fourth; Minucius Felix; Commodian; Origen, Parts First and Second*, ed. Alexander Roberts and James Donaldson (Peabody, MA: Hendrickson, 1994; reprint of the American edition published by the Christian Literature Publishing Company, 1885), 635.

Chapter 5
How Does Scripture Interpret Itself?

INTRODUCTION

One day in 1953 President Truman visited the Jewish Theological Seminary. In the course of his conversation with members of the faculty, someone gestured toward Truman and proclaimed: "This is the man who helped create the State of Israel!" Without a blink Truman responded, "What do you mean, '*helped create?*' I am Cyrus, I am Cyrus!"[1]

Truman's remark is an example of an interpretive principle called typology. Typology means the interpretation of a person, event, place, or thing in terms of their resemblance or correspondence to prior persons, events, places, or things. By identifying himself with the Persian king Cyrus II, Truman was explaining his understanding of the role he played in establishing the modern state of Israel. Following his victory over Babylon in 539 BCE, Cyrus ended Israel's forty-year exile from the land by permitting the Jews throughout his kingdom to return to Jerusalem to rebuild the temple of the Lord. His words are the last words in the Hebrew Bible: "Let [God's people] go up [to Jerusalem]" (2 Chr. 36:23). By using the power of his office following the defeat of Hitler and the tragedy of the Holocaust to midwife the birth of Israel in 1948, Truman wished to claim he had played a similarly decisive role in modern times.

---

1. Michael J. Pragai, *Faith and Fulfillment: Christians and the Return to the Promised Land* (London: Valentine, Mitchell, 1985), 224.

Down through the centuries, all kinds of people, from common-
ers to kings, have employed typological interpretation of the Bible
to understand themselves and to navigate the challenges of life. By
doing so, people have simply interpreted the Bible in the way the Bible
interprets itself. The Scriptures themselves regularly introduce contemporary events, persons, and circumstances by setting them in typological relation to prior persons, events, and circumstances. Indeed,
the Scriptures employ typology so commonly, at so many levels, with
such richness, sophistication, and variety, that typology amounts to
one of the key ways in which the Bible as a whole may be said to hang
together.

The prominence of typology in Scripture is theologically important,
for it points to something profoundly significant about the portrait of
God we find in Israel's Scriptures. The "God of Abraham, Isaac, and
Jacob" is a God for whom history matters. Had Abraham, Isaac, and
Jacob by some anachronistic miracle been philosophers in the manner
of Socrates, Plato, and Aristotle, we would be as little interested in the
history of Israel as we are presently uninformed of the ancient history
of the Greeks. The ideas of the great philosophers are, in most matters, separable from the secular history in which the philosophers lived
(as opposed to the history of the ideas themselves). Like recipes, their
thoughts could be used to cook up good ideas any time, any place.
By contrast, Scripture is rooted in time and space; its language is not
abstract, but rife with stories and metaphors, parables and puns—and
types—the language of history.

SCRIPTURE INTERPRETING SCRIPTURE
IN THE HEBREW BIBLE

Michael Fishbane's *Biblical Interpretation in Ancient Israel* is a mas-
terful study of how Scripture interprets itself, with a special focus on
typology.[2] Fishbane categorizes these inner-biblical typologies using
the following morphology: (1) cosmological-historical correlations;
(2) historical correlations; (3) spatial correlations; and (4) biographical
correlations.[3] We shall follow him in looking at each of these categories

---

2. Michael Fishbane, *Biblical Interpretation in Ancient Israel* (Oxford: Clarendon, 1985), 353.
3. Ibid., 356.

as we examine what we call Scripture interpreting Scripture. We shall then apply his typology to the New Testament.

Cosmological-Historical Typologies

Cosmological-historical typologies use "a cosmological event as the prototype or warrant for a historical redemption to come."[4] An example is Isaiah 65:17: "For I am about to create new heavens and a new earth; the former things shall not be remembered or come to mind." The passage goes on to relate that Jerusalem itself shall be restored in a new way that parallels but surpasses God's original creation of the world. No more shall weeping or the cry of distress be heard in it. The new earth will be Eden-like: longevity, peace, and productive fields will be the norm; even the wolf and the lamb shall feed together, and the lion shall eat straw like an ox (vv. 18–25). This, says Fishbane, is not to be understood as an apocalyptic vision. Ordinary time does not end. The new creation is not in discontinuity with the past. Rather, the events about to take place constitute the cosmos's reparation, not its dissolution. It will be a reparation so great that the former vicissitudes of human existence will simply be forgotten. But it will happen within time, within history.

Fishbane identifies three important aspects of cosmological-historical typologies. First, from a typological perspective, key events in Israelite history are looked upon as *the reiteration of foundational cosmic patterns* that had occurred in a *pre*historical period.[5] In the mythic imagination still current in the prophetic period, those primordial events were characterized by divine combat with and victory over the powers of chaos, and that pattern of combat and victory provided the prism by which the dynamics latent in subsequent historical events were disclosed. The dividing of the waters at creation provided a correlate to the dividing of waters at the exodus, for example. Such a correlation thus became the basis for the hope in an imminent recurrence. Fishbane argues that it is through this kind of typological thinking, connecting separate events together through a perception of common pattern or type, that the Israelites perceived a deeper unity running through the events of

---

4. Ibid., 354.
5. Ibid., 356.

history. Present and future redemption are possible and hoped for only because of the unity and continuity of the future with the past.

A second aspect of Israelite typological thinking lies in *the historicization of myth*. It is a development, says Fishbane, of major import. By applying the pattern of prehistorical events in later history, "the older mythic structures and their central actors" are transformed. This occurs, for example, when the demonic forces of pre-creation chaos are identified with the historical enemies of Israel, or when the sea is not depicted as a dragon but a historical-geographic entity (Ezek. 29:1–12).[6] In this way the archaic mythic elements still inhabiting Israelite cultural consciousness, like fragments of a dream, were demythologized. Entities of an unseen and mythic realm are substituted with real ones in this world. Equally important, a reverse process also occurs. The contents of history are themselves remythicized in a unique way. As Fishbane explains, "to the degree that the routing of the enemies and evil ones of Israel's history is typologically presented as a reactualization of a primordial cosmic event, historical redemption becomes a species of world restoration and the dynamics of history reiterate creative acts of divine power."[7] The result is a profound reconsideration of the status of the historical. Events do not lose their "concrete historical facticity." But a whole new dimension is given to them when they are correlated with the prototypes of divine activity. God and history are thus joined.

The third aspect of typological thinking is the importance of *repetition and reiteration*. Contrary to a common misconception, Fishbane maintains, biblical thinking is not only and completely linear and historical. It is also cyclical, at least in the sense of the iteration of a prototypical pattern. Events are always unique, but at the same time specific events may be understood as an(other) occurrence of what is perceived as fundamental or prototypical. When, for example, Isaiah employs the mythic imagery of God in combat with the forces of chaos (depicted as beasts, dragons, creatures of the sea, etc.) to describe the watery struggles accompanying the Hebrews' escape from Egypt (as in Isa. 51 noted above), the exodus, perceived as a historical event, is itself elevated above history into a metahistorical level. A given historical event is placed on the same plane as its prehistorical prototype. To quote Fishbane again, "History is thus transformed just where it uti-

---

6. Ibid., 357.
7. Ibid.

lizes non-historical models, just where temporal events are correlated with pretemporal ones—typologically."[8] Creation explains the exodus, the exodus explains creation. Out of chaos comes order.

Typologies of a Historical Nature

Fishbane distinguishes two kinds of historical typology: those that find the prototype reiterated in a later event, and those that employ the prototype to configure a hoped-for future event.[9] Fishbane calls these *retrojective* typology and *projective* typology respectively.

Retrojective Typologies

An example of retrojective typology for Fishbane is Joshua 3–5. Here one historical event, the exodus, is used to explain the metahistorical meaning and character of the crossing of the Jordan River, a crossing that led to the conquest of the promised land. In Joshua 3:7 the Lord addresses Joshua, telling him, "as I was with Moses" so "I will be with you." Joshua is further informed that he is to tell the Israelites that when the priests, bearing the ark of the covenant, proceed into the Jordan the waters flowing from above "shall be cut off" and "stand in a single heap" (NRSV; cf. Exod. 15:8). When events transpire as foretold, "all Israel" "stood in awe of [Joshua], as they had stood in awe of Moses" (Josh. 4:14). To commemorate the event stelae were erected so that when the children in future generations ask, "What do these stones mean?" the elders could explain: "Israel crossed over the Jordan here on dry ground" because the Lord God had "dried up the waters of the Jordan for you until you crossed over, as the Lord your God did to the Red Sea" (4:22–23).

The correlation between the two events is also evident in the details. But there are other parallels as well. Both events take place during the Passover season, that is, on the tenth day of the first month (cf. Exod. 12:6). Just prior to the siege of Jericho, Joshua is instructed: "Remove the sandals from your feet, for the place where you stand is holy" (Josh. 5:15). Details such as these have two aspects: their surface manifestation and their deeper, hidden signification. The power of the typological identification is to be found in its ability to reveal the deeper

8. Ibid.
9. Ibid., 358.

meaning of historical events in a way accessible to the cultural imagination. The remembered or recent past is rendered luminous to faith by its correlation with a more distant, prototypical, event. In Fishbane's words again, "By means of retrojective typologies, events are removed from the neutral cascade of historical occurrences and embellished as modalities of foundational moments in Israelite history."[10]

Let us cite another modern example to clarify what is being said. It comes from the life of Martin Luther King Jr., the foremost leader in the African American struggle for civil rights in America. On the eve of his assassination in Memphis, Tennessee, in the midst of a strike by city sanitation workers whom he had come to support, King delivered a sermon at the Mason Temple in which he likened himself to a type of Moses. Ranging back and forth between biblical imagery and contemporary events, King spoke of slavery in Egypt, of crossing the Red Sea, of going through the wilderness, equating the struggle for civil rights with the travail of the Hebrews. The sermon ends with these words:

> Well, I don't know what will happen now. We've got some difficult days ahead. But it doesn't matter with me now. Because I've been to the mountain top. And I don't mind. Like anybody, I would like to live a long life. Longevity has its place. But I'm not concerned about that now. I just want to do God's will. And He's allowed me to go up to the mountain. And I've looked over. And I've seen the promised land. I may not get there with you. But I want you to know tonight, that we, as a people will get to the promised land. And I'm happy, tonight. I'm not worried about anything. I'm not fearing any man. Mine eyes have seen the glory of the coming of the Lord.[11]

This too is (retrojective) typology. With these words, King interpreted the present by way of the past. The link is not historical, it is metahistorical. By connecting the achievement of civil rights with entrance into the land of biblical promise, King interpreted the movement he led religiously, asserting that within the struggle was the guiding hand of God. For some King was Communist-inspired. For the movement, and in King's own mind, he was a type of Moses viewing from afar a future he would not live to see.

10. Ibid., 360.
11. From "I've Been to the Mountaintop," a sermon delivered at the Mason Temple in Memphis, on April 3, 1968. See A Call to Conscience: The Landmark Speeches of Martin Luther King, Jr., ed. Clayborne Carson and Kris Shephard (New York: Warner Books, 2001), 201–23.

Projective Typologies

Just as events of the past can be illuminated by a typological correlation with its prototype or antetype, so typologies can provide the language and imagery of a foreseen future redemption. An example of projective typologies can be found by turning to Second Isaiah. In 43:16–21 the prophet opens his oracle with the Lord identifying himself as the one who "makes a way in the sea, . . . who brings out [to defeat] chariot and horse" at the exodus. But immediately attention is turned to the future: "Do not remember the former things, or consider the things of old. I am about to do a new thing; now it springs forth, do you not perceive it? I will make a way in the wilderness and rivers in the desert" (vv. 18–20a). Here the original exodus provides not only a prototype for what is about to happen but a warrant for it as well.[12] It is however the *novum*, the new thing about to happen, that is of especial noteworthiness, for it is here that the linearity of history, even within the notion of reiteration so characteristic of typology, that is being confirmed. Time moves in a line, and yet there emerges within time that which is unforeseen in any normal sense. It is left to the prophet to discern the new acts of God about to take place.

Most striking in this regard, says Fishbane, is the theological reversal found in Isaiah 19:19–25.[13] In this eschatological oracle we are startled to find a complete reversal of the traditional schema of redemption. *The enslaving peoples become the peoples to be redeemed.* In what Fishbane calls a "sustained exegetical counterpoint," the language of the original account of redemption, the story of the exodus as recorded in Exodus 3:7–9 and 8:16–24, is recast to apply to the Egyptians themselves, not to the Israelites! This time it is the Egyptians who are oppressed, who cry to the Lord. It is they who build an altar as a sign and a witness to the Lord. Now the Lord will make himself known to the Egyptians. He will send them a savior and will defend and deliver them. As part of this redemptive process chastisement will occur. The Lord will "strike" (send plagues upon) Egypt, but when they turn to him in supplication, he will heal them. In such an oracle, Fishbane suggests, the phenomenon of historical typologies is brought to its conceivable limit. "For hereby the subject-matter has been inverted to such an extent that just that redemptive event which constituted Israel's particular destiny has become the prototype by which a more universal, messianic reconciliation is envisaged."[14]

---

12. Fishbane, *Biblical Interpretation*, 364.
13. Ibid., 367.
14. Ibid., 367–68.

Now we must note: So radical was this idea of universalism to later readers that the language was altered, reversing Isaiah's own reversal. That change occurs in the Septuagint translation of the Hebrew text, undertaken by hellenized Jews in Alexandria. The rendition of Isaiah 19:25 in the Septuagint is altered to identify the people in question as "[God's] people in Egypt and in Assyria," rather than the Egyptians and Assyrians themselves. The theological insight of Isaiah was lost in translation. The translator was a traitor!

Typologies of a Spatial Nature

Just as Israel's religious imagination perceived a sacred history unfolding in temporal events, so it tended also to identify places within a sacred geography. In this regard Israel drew upon the universal human inclination to externalize and give concrete locality to the inner experience of and longing for harmony and peace, a place where the Divine touches the earth and makes it sacred. Of the biblical images most enduring in this regard is that of Eden. It is the garden divinely established, watered by four rivers that go forth to nourish the earth; it is a garden whose trees possess the secret powers of life and knowledge. It is, however, also a garden that because of human sin no longer exists. Its location in the primordial past thus symbolizes an original "harmony and order" lost by human culpability and now replaced by the travail of historical existence. As a spatial symbol it represents paradise lost when employed in retrojective typologies; conversely, in projective typologies it looks forward in hope to paradise regained. Thus spatial typologies are never completely divorced from time.

As in real life Jerusalem constituted the center of Judean existence, so in biblical imagination its status is profoundly deepened, Fishbane suggests, by its identification with Eden and with the "mountain of the Lord," Zion.[15] It is at Zion that the "foundation stone" is laid, being "an ancient symbol of sacred geography," the place of order and harmony. With the destruction of the land and the temple, spatial imagery takes on an even more critical and vital aspect in the exilic and postexilic period. Both Deutero-Isaiah and Ezekiel turn to Edenic imagery to describe the land to which the exiles will return. "For the LORD will comfort Zion; . . . and will make her wilderness like Eden, her desert like the garden of the LORD" (Isa. 51:3). Fishbane proposes that, in

---

15. Fishbane (ibid., 369) discusses Pss. 48:2–4, 12–14; 46:5 (all MT).

Ezekiel, the imagery of the old Eden restored (36:35), juxtaposed to the parable of the dry bones, in which the prophet envisages the re-creation of the corporate body of Israel, evokes the idea of a new Adam. By this coupling, it is suggested, nostalgia for a lost national dignity and fantasies of a primordial paradise are fused together.

Typologies of a Biographical Nature

Typologies of a biographical nature are abundant and varied throughout the Scriptures. In Genesis 9:1–9, for example, Noah is depicted as a new Adam who is to preside over a renewed creation. Typological reiteration holds the key to certain scenarios that are repeated throughout the partriarchal narratives, such as the barrenness of the matriarchs, fraternal strife with the younger sibling triumphing over the elder, drought leading to migration to a foreign land, patriarchal duplicity regarding the status of his wife, and so on.

Fishbane notes that correlations between type and antetype (which for simplicity's sake are my terms, not his) are often not physical, as in the narratives of genealogical descent in Genesis, but based on spiritual parallels or relationships, as in the identification of Joshua with Moses, or the depiction of Elijah or Ezekiel as a new Moses.[16] The purpose of such correlations (as M. L. King's identification with Moses) is to legitimate the successor of an earlier leader, and to show that there exists a deep similarity of character that, in this case, underlies Israel's spiritual leadership. This can be seen in the motif of preparing the mouth of the prophet for his spiritual role, the antetype for which occurs when Moses is instructed to be the spokesman for the Lord (Exod. 4:10–12). The motif is repeated in the commissioning scenes of Jeremiah, Isaiah, and Ezekiel. That this virtue should be extended to all of Israel is a postexilic hope (Isa. 59:21; cf. Joel 3:1–2).

In the postexilic period, a time of displacement and return, the figure of Abraham also becomes an archetype of responsive obedience. Deutero-Isaiah calls upon the exiles to "look to Abraham your father . . . for he was but one when I called him, but I blessed him and made him many" (Isa. 51:2). The implication being that Abraham is a type for the proper response to the prophet's (and therefore the Lord's) command to return to the promised land. "And, just as Abraham was promised a great seed and blessing (Gen. 12:1–3)—a bounty realized

16. Ibid., 373.

in subsequent history—so are the exiles implicitly guaranteed national renewal if they follow his example."[17]

TYPOLOGY IN THE NEW TESTAMENT

The New Testament church took up the task of finding meaning in history. The conundrum at hand involved "the things about Jesus of Nazareth" (Luke 24:19), and above all, his crucifixion and resurrection. The church interpreted Jesus and the events of his life in much the same way as historical events had always been interpreted within Judaism: typologically.

Typologies of a Cosmological-Historical Nature

In the Hebrew Bible, cosmological-historical typology typically serves to signal *a redemption to come*. In the New Testament, by contrast, the redemption is portrayed both as *already inaugurated* and as *yet to be fulfilled*. Thus the New Testament may be said to use cosmological-historical typology in both a retrojective and projective manner.

Retrojective Cosmological-Historical Typology

The prologue to the Gospel of John is the most obvious, and certainly the most provocative, of those cosmological typologies that speak of redemption as an event having already occurred. The opening verses of the Gospel recall the opening verses of the first book of the Bible, in which the Word of God serves as the agent by which creation is initiated "in the beginning" (cf. Ps. 33:6). The Word (Greek *logos*) by which all things were created, says John, has now become flesh "and lived among us" (John 1:14). That Word is the "only Son"; that is, he is *the* type of the Father. The Word/Son is therefore full of the same divine glory (cf. Exod. 33:22; John 1:14), grace, and truth that characterizes the Creator/Father. Thus, whereas at creation the Lord speaks and things come to be, Jesus is himself the incarnate Word by which God orders life and truth out of the chaos of human existence. As such, Jesus is the Way, the Truth, and the Life: the themes of the Gospel. In

17. Ibid., 375.

John's Gospel, receiving sight is but a metaphor for the more profound gift of understanding the truth revealed in Jesus (John 9). The creation of light as the first act of creation, separating out darkness, becomes the antetype of spiritual illumination given in Christ, the Light of the world (John 1:4–9; 3:19–21; 8:12; *et passim*). To be thus enlightened is to be born from above (3:3–8); it is to be reborn into true life.

Projective Cosmological-Historical Typology

Projective cosmological-historical typology is found at several points in the New Testament, but above all in the Revelation to John. Revelation employs Exodus traditions to provide the typology by which the future may be foretold. The lurid detail by which John lays out the destruction of the sinful world relies on the Exodus account of the plagues in Egypt (chaps. 7–10).[18] But in the telling of the ultimate end of time, the end is as it was in the beginning, in primordial times. The Lord starts afresh. There is a new heaven and a new earth, for the first heaven and the first earth pass away. The sea of chaos is gone. As was paradise, so the new Jerusalem is graced by a river flowing through it, and on either side grow trees of life. Here, as in paradise before the fall, there is no death, or mourning, or crying, or pain, "for the former things have passed away" (Rev. 21–22). The end is as the beginning. In Pauline language, ultimately God becomes "all in all" (1 Cor. 15:28).

Typologies of a Historical Nature

The question central to the Gospels is Jesus' own: "Who do you say that I am?" The four Gospels set out to answer it, and the task was not easy. Luke tells us as much in the prologue to his Gospel (1:1–4): prior efforts have lacked order, which he will now provide. To the mind of faith the resurrection of Jesus had proved that Jesus was God's Anointed, the Messiah. The difficulty arose in the fact that neither crucifixion nor resurrection fit any Old Testament or contemporary expectation of a messianic figure. The Gospel writers could have said, as the Muslim's Qur'an does say (2:73; 3:55, 56; 5:111; 4:158; 5:11; 23:51), that Jesus did not suffer death on the cross but died of old age in a mountainous

---

18. See, e.g., Leonhard Goppelt, *Typos: The Typological Interpretation of the Old Testament in the New*, trans. D. H. Madvig (Grand Rapids: Eerdmans, 1982), 197, n. 81.

region (Kashmir). The evangelists did not say that, not only because the shocking cruelty of his death was too real to be denied, but because they sensed that in a deeply mysterious way Jesus' death was key to his whole history, a decisive clue to who he was before God and humankind. The resurrection, to be sure, negated Jesus' death, but it affirmed his life, including his suffering and dying. Now the question was: How does Scripture help us understand the suffering and death of the Lord's anointed?

One way the New Testament answers this question is by historical typology that draws on the portrait of an unidentified Servant of the LORD found in Deutero-Isaiah (Isa. 40–55). The early church read Isaiah's depiction of the Lord's Servant as a prophetic description or foreshadowing of Jesus. For them, and the church ever since, Isaiah 52–53 explained the suffering death of Jesus and provided the language for the Christian doctrine of atonement. The Servant provided the type, Jesus the antitype. I quote only the central section of the Song of the Servant.

> Surely he has borne our infirmities
>   and carried our diseases;
> yet we accounted him stricken,
>   struck down by God, and afflicted.
> But he was wounded for our transgressions,
>   crushed for our iniquities;
> upon him was the punishment that made us whole,
>   and by his bruises we are healed.
> All we like sheep have gone astray;
>   we have all turned to our own way,
> and the LORD has laid on him
>   the iniquity of us all.
>
> (Isa. 53:4–6)

The typological correspondence between the Servant of the Lord in Isaiah and Jesus, seen retrospectively, needs to be spelled out. The messenger of the Lord has come upon the mountains (Zion/Jerusalem) bearing the good news of Israel's salvation: that God reigns, that his kingdom has come (Isa. 52:7; cf. Luke 10:9, 11, *et passim*). The Lord's Servant, who grew up in obscurity with nothing in his appearance to commend him (Isa. 53:2), was one so reviled, despised, and rejected that people turned their faces from him (v. 3; cf. Mark 6:4ff. par.), "although he had done no violence and there was no deceit in his mouth" (Isa. 53:9; cf. Mark 15:14). Like a lamb led to slaughter, the Servant "opens not his mouth." He who commanded love, even of the enemy, does not waver, he does not revile in return. He dies and is buried (Mark 15:42ff. par.). To their (lit. "our") horror, this is brought about by those who come to recognize in the Servant's death their own complicity and guilt, and they come to understand what they had never even conceived of before (Matt. 27:3–10). They now know that instead of being smitten by God (Isa. 53:4), the Lord had "laid on him the iniquity of us all" (v. 6), and in this understanding a complete change is wrought in their lives. By his "stripes" they have been healed (v. 5 KJV). Their sins have been borne away (e.g., 1 Cor. 15:3). Even now, exalted by God, the Servant of the Lord makes intercession for transgressors (Rom. 8:34). So astonishing is this, so contrary to worldly expectation, that the nations are startled and even kings fall silent (Isa. 52:15).

By way of these verses, the crucifixion of Jesus came to be understood. To make this connection between the Servant of the Lord and Jesus was to come to faith; not to make the connection was to remain in unbelief. This is clearly portrayed in Luke's account of a minister in the court of Queen Candace of Ethiopia, who is reading Isaiah 52–53 without comprehension as he rides homeward from Jerusalem in his chariot (Acts 8:26–39). The apostle Philip, directed by the Spirit, appears on the same road and asks the court official if he understands what he is reading. No, the Ethiopian responds; "How can I, unless someone guides me [or: "will give me the clue," New English Bible]?" About whom is the prophet speaking, he asks. Is it about himself or someone else? The official, a eunuch, is looking for a historical referent. To whom does the prophecy refer? Philip, on the other hand, having personally accompanied Jesus, was faced with a different question: What theological sense could be made of Jesus' life, teachings, and death—and his resurrection from the dead? That had to be explained by searching the Scriptures, as Jesus had instructed them (John 5:35), and Isaiah 52–53 fit Jesus perfectly. Once the eunuch understands the good news that Jesus of Nazareth was this Suffering Servant, he too is astonished and, recognizing the transformation taking place in his own mind, asks to be baptized. Here we have a good example of the hermeneutical circle once again: Isaiah explains Jesus (for Philip); Jesus explains Isaiah (for the Ethiopian). Or: idea (Isaiah) becomes event in Jesus' suffering; event becomes idea in the gospel.

Typologies of a Spatial Nature

In the New Testament, the reality most comparable to Judaism's understanding of "the land" is the envisioned "new Jerusalem" (Rev. 21:2). Until that city has become manifest, the New Testament writings seem to know of no place, city, or land differing in inherent holiness or sacrality from any other. Indeed, it is the whole argument of the epistle to the Hebrews that the entire earthly system of sacrifice (temple, priests, offerings, etc.) is but a copy and shadow of the heavenly realm, where the true sanctuary is located, and that it is there in heaven that Christ has appeared to offer himself once and for all as a sacrifice for sin (9:24). In the meantime, Christians hold to the truth that where the Spirit of the Lord is, there is holiness. And since the Spirit blows where it wills (John 3:8), any time or any place is potentially holy. In this regard, the Johannine doctrine of the Holy Spirit is Christian theology's uncertainty principle. Given God's freedom, the Christian may speak with assurance, but not with certainty, about where the Holy Spirit is or what it is up to. That "not with certainty" produces the "I don't know" humility of the wise and tolerant.

Typologies of a Biographical Nature

Like Deutero-Isaiah's Suffering Servant, so other biblical figures provided biographical typologies for discovering and explaining who Jesus was. He came to be seen as the Second Adam (Rom. 5; 1 Cor. 15), as a priest in the order of Melchizedek (Heb. 5–7), as a kind of Jonah (Matt. 12:39–41; 16:4; Luke 11:29–32), and most of all, appealing to no particular biblical figure but to that single relationship upon which continuity of kingship depended, as Son of David (e.g., Matt. 1:20; 9:27; Luke 2:4) and Son of God (passim). In what may be a pre-Pauline formula, the two titles are uniquely combined in Paul's summary of the gospel in the opening salutation of his Letter to the Romans, the gospel "concerning [God's] Son, who was descended from David according to the flesh and was declared to be Son of God with power according to the spirit of holiness by resurrection from the dead" (Rom. 1:3). The deep significance of typological sonship is expressed most unambiguously in John's Gospel: "No one has ever seen God. It is God the only Son, who is close to the Father's heart, who has made him known" (1:14). To know the Son is to know the Father also (John 8:19). The language of typology is continued in the letter to the Hebrews, where the Son is described as having "the exact imprint [Greek *charaktēr*] of God's very being" (1:3). Sonship and fatherhood are made inextricable.

The New Testament also uses typology of a biographical nature to illumine the life of Christians, whose experience is in turn patterned on that of Christ. Through the waters of baptism, in sacramental death with Christ, the old self dies to sin, so that the new self in Christ might arise a new creation, to live in newness of life, the old having passed away (Rom. 6). Those who are "in Christ" walk "according to the Spirit," for their minds are set on "the things of the Spirit." And the hard lesson follows that "anyone who does not have the Spirit of Christ does not belong to him" (Rom. 8:1–10). The "things of the Spirit" are synonymous with "the fruit of the Spirit" and are enumerated by Paul for those who may be uncertain: "love, joy, peace, patience, kindness, generosity, faithfulness, gentleness, and self-control" (Gal. 5:22–23). The person who takes on this identity, who wants by imitation to be a type of Christ, is called a "Christian." Typology is thus the key to understanding and living a worthy life. "The meaning of Christ and the meaning of existence . . . mutually decipher each other."[19]

CONCLUSION

Although typology is not the only way in which the Bible interprets itself, it is a central, and perhaps even, *the* central way. Western secular historians have rigorously eschewed the idea of a providential hand in history, let alone a telos within history or of a metahistorical meaning above history. Similarly, secular historians balk at the idea of God acting in history, at any time or for any reason. For them God is not and cannot be a participant in the drama of humanity. Faith sees it, and must see it, otherwise. To speak of events within time as revelatory of the mind and will of God is to speak collectively of a history of "the acts of God," or of "redemptive history." Such language presupposes that finite existence, human existence, is not what it ought to be, but that what is can and will become what it ought to be, by the

19. Paul Ricoeur, *Essays on Biblical Interpretation*, ed. Lewis S. Mudge (Philadelphia: Fortress, 1980), 52.

providence and power of God. Of course everything has its immediate cause. It cannot be otherwise.[20] The religious task is to know which of these events (such as the founding of Israel in 1948 or the civil rights movement of the 1960s) has a future built into it and which do not, which are pleasing in God's sight and which are not. For this purpose, the typological interpretation of Scripture is—and will remain—an indispensable task.

20. See the discussion in Karl Barth, *The Epistle to the Romans*, trans. from the 6th ed. by Edwyn C. Hoskyns (London: Oxford University Press, 1933), 357.

Chapter 6
What Did the Early Church Leaders Say?

CHANGE AND CONTINUITY

The early church leaders (sometimes called "the church fathers") are so designated because they were pivotal figures in articulating, shaping, and defending what came to be recognized as the orthodox faith of the Christian church. A study of what these leaders said reveals that they did not always speak with one voice, and that what seemed right and orthodox at one time could prove not to be so at another time. Yet the greater irony, as Jaroslav Pelikan has illustrated so thoroughly, is that even as the church leaders consciously expressed the ancient faith in new and diverse ways, they confidently affirmed their continuity with "the faith that was once for all entrusted to the saints" (Jude 3).[1]

A striking illustration of this appears in the development of the Nicene Creed. When first adopted in 325, the creed carried the accompanying warning that "the catholic and apostolic church anathematizes" any who would deviate from the creed or would presume to alter it. In 380 Emperor Theodosius I went a step further by identifying the Nicene Creed with the "faith which we believe to have been communicated by the apostle Peter to the Romans and maintained in its

1. See Jaroslav Pelikan, *Credo: Historical and Theological Guide to Creeds and Confessions of Faith in the Christian Tradition* (New Haven: Yale University Press, 2003), 9; and *The Christian Tradition: A History of the Development of Doctrine,* 5 vols. (Chicago: University of Chicago Press, 1971–1989). These have served as an essential source for this chapter; and, in a like manner, John J. O'Keefe and R. R. Reno's monograph, *Sanctified Vision: An Introduction to Early Christian Interpretation of the Bible* (Baltimore: Johns Hopkins University Press, 2005).

traditional form to the present day." Yet in 381 the Second Ecumenical Council issued a revision of the Nicene Creed that amplified both the doctrine of God and the doctrine of the Holy Spirit. Nevertheless, it too declared that "the profession of faith of the holy fathers who gathered in Nicea" was "not to be abrogated" but was to "remain in force."[2] It is this revised creed, known by historians as the Niceno-Constantinopolitan Creed, that is recited by creedal churches the world over as the Nicene Creed.

The affirmation of steadfast continuity amid obvious change is a characteristic feature of patristic biblical interpretation. But it is also, in fairness, a characteristic feature of the biblical canon itself. In the New Testament we find both the confident affirmation that Jesus Christ is "the same yesterday, today, and forever," and the unembarrassed display of diverse portraits of Christ. Perhaps, then, we should say that the church fathers do after all continue in a path set forth by the Scriptures themselves, at least in this respect. And if in this respect, then perhaps in others as well.

Since a survey of the biblical interpretation of the church fathers is impossible here, I shall sample three seminal figures, Irenaeus, Origen, and Augustine. Among them, they illustrate patristic biblical interpretation as it took shape in the Greek-speaking East before the Council of Nicea, and in the Latin West in the post-Nicene age.

IRENAEUS, BISHOP OF LYON (CA. 135–200)

Irenaeus was born in Asia Minor (western Turkey), perhaps in Smyrna. He tells of sitting enthralled as a youth in the household of the "blessed" Polycarp, who had himself learned Christian faith from John, the author (as Polycarp related) of the Fourth Gospel.[3]

Like John, his theological grandfather, Irenaeus was a fierce opponent of Gnosticism, a teaching that affirmed salvation in Christ but severed that salvation from the material world, thereby denying the very essence of the incarnation. (Irenaeus compares gnostics to those who take mosaic pieces, intended to form the image of a king, and rearrange them to form a dog or fox; cf. *Against Heresies* 1.8.1.) According to Irenaeus, the gnostics fell into error because they failed to read

---

2. Quoted by Pelikan (*Credo*, 10) from the *Theodosian Code* 16.1.2.
3. See Johannes Quasten, *The Beginnings of Patristic Literature* (vol. 1 of *Patrology*; Westminster, Md.: Newman Press, 1962), 287–88.

the Scriptures according to "the rule of faith" (*regula fidei*). The rule of faith is a brief summary of the Christian confession that provides a guide to the interpretation of the Scriptures, Old and New. In the *Demonstration of the Apostolic Preaching*, a distillation of his thought, Irenaeus provides this description of the rule of faith:

> This then is the order of the rule of our faith, and the foundation of the [church] . . . : God, the Father, not made, not material, invisible; one God, the creator of all things: this is the first point of our faith. The second point is: The Word of God, Son of God, Christ Jesus our Lord, who was manifested to the prophets according to the form of their prophesying and according to the method of the dispensation of the Father: through whom all things were made; who also at the end of the times, to complete and gather up all things, was made man among men, visible and tangible, in order to abolish death and show forth life and produce a community of union between God and man. And the third point is: The Holy Spirit, through whom the prophets prophesied, and the fathers learned the things of God, and the righteous were led forth into the way of righteousness; and who in the end of the times was poured out in a new way upon mankind in all the earth, renewing man unto God.
>
> (Sec. 6.)[4]

Elsewhere, Irenaeus formulates the rule of faith in slightly different language but with the same basic content. The rule of faith thus provides a flexible summary of God's identity and of God's action, its beginning, its turning point, and its anticipated outcome. It did not settle questions of method or points of detail, but enabled interpretation by supplying the "overarching story" in which the quest for meaning could take place.[5]

A notable feature of Irenaeus's reading of Scripture is the strong linkage of creation and redemption. The God who creates humankind in the image of God is also the God who redeems humankind through Christ. Both Testaments, Old and New, are required to complete the story. Those without the Old Testament possessed no common narrative for speaking of creation or the fall. Those without the "memoirs of the apostles" (the Gospels) had no common narrative for speaking

4. Translation by J. Armitage Robinson as reproduced in Iain M. Mackenzie, *Irenaeus's* Demonstration of the Apostolic Preaching: *A Theological Commentary and Translation* (Burlington, VT: Ashgate, 2002), 3. See also *Against Heresies* 1.10.1.

5. See Rowan A. Greer, "The Christian Bible and Its Interpretation," in James L. Kugel and Greer, *Early Biblical Interpretation* (Philadelphia: Westminster, 1986), 109–99; Frances M. Young, *Biblical Exegesis and the Formation of Christian Culture* (Cambridge: Cambridge University Press, 1997).

of redemption in Christ or of the consummation of creation. Only the two Testaments conjoined could tell the story from creation to the consummation of creation, from beginning to end, with fall and redemption constituting the middle.

Another feature of Irenaeus's reading is the climactic place assigned to Christ, the incarnation of God's eternal Word. As the incarnate Word, Christ brings about a double movement of reversal and completion of all that has gone before. Christ undoes or reverses everything that has gone awry since Adam's fall, while completing every good purpose that God had begun in previous ages. "By his obedience unto death, Christ undoes the fatal consequences of Adam's disobedience to the God of life. . . . At the same time, Christ the Second Adam establishes for the first time the likeness between God and humankind that was the goal of creation from the time of Adam."[6] The task of the Christian today is to imitate that new man made visible in Christ, "making progress day by day, and ascending towards the perfect, that is, approximating to the uncreated One."[7] Led by the Holy Spirit, this is the function of the church into which all who obey God's call are admitted until they "come to maturity, to the measure of the full stature of Christ" (Eph. 4:13).

ORIGEN (CA. 185–254)

The life and work of Origen is rather startling for several reasons. A citizen of Alexandria in Egypt, he was but sixteen when he tried to join his father in martyrdom, failing only because his mother had hidden his clothes! At eighteen, because of his intellectual gifts, he was chosen to head the catechetical school in the great city, a position formerly held by his teacher, the famous Clement of Alexandria. He startles us because of his asceticism: he owned few clothes, ate little, accustomed himself to sleeping on the ground (Matt. 6:31), and was known to walk for miles without sandals (10:10).[8] He startles us because, "for the sake of the kingdom of heaven" and to attain spiritual perfection, he is reputed to have castrated himself (19:12) to ward against slander, since

6. R. Kendall Soulen, *The God of Israel and Christian Theology* (Philadelphia: Fortress, 1996), 44.
7. For this English translation, see *Against Heresies* in *The Ante-Nicene Fathers,* ed. A. Roberts and J. Donaldson (Grand Rapids: Eerdman, 1985), vol. 1, 315–567.
8. See Paul L. Maier, *Eusebius—The Church History: A New Translation with Commentary* (Grand Rapids: Kregel, 1999), 6.1–3.

young women would be among his students.[9] He startles us because of his sheer intellectual inventiveness, psychic energy, and devotion to the church—for which he was given the surname Adamantius. He is credited with writing the first complete dogmatics (*De principiis, Contra Celsum*), the first critical text (the Hexapla), and the first systematic biblical exegesis (commentaries and homilies). Origen startles us by the tenacity of his scholarship and the sheer volume of his literary output. The Hexapla was itself sixty-five hundred pages in length. To this are thousands of additional pages of commentaries, homilies (the earliest corpus of Christian sermons in existence), and scholia or detailed notes on Scripture, most of which have been lost. For these works Jerome called Origen an "immortal genius" and the greatest "teacher of wisdom and knowledge in the church after the apostles"[10]—before finding it politically expedient to repudiate Origen's allegorical extremes. He startles us because even at an elderly age he courageously endured torture, from which he died a "confessor's" death in Tyre in 254.

lost?

Finally, Origen startles us because, in spite of his inimitable devotion to Christ and his church, he was ultimately condemned by the church as a heretic. Epiphanius of Salamis (ca. 315–403) called Origen "the father of Arius" (condemned by the Council of Nicea in 325) and "the root of all other heresies."[11] He was condemned by Emperor Justinian in 543 and denounced as erroneous by the Second Council of Constantinople in 553, for ideas such as the preexistence of souls and the spherical form of resurrection bodies—ideas that the noted Catholic scholar, Hans Urs von Balthasar, discounts in the estimate of Origen's worth as "impoverished remains."[12] In von Balthasar's judgment, it is "all but impossible to overestimate Origen and his importance for the history of Christian thought."[13] In any case, Origen was prepared for condemnation: "If I give offence . . . to the Church," he said, "then I hope the whole Church will unite with one consent and cast me off" (*Homiliae in Josue* 7.6).[14] That offense arose from the conviction that Origen went too far in his spiritual interpretation of Scripture, that

9. Ibid., 6.8.

10. Quoted by Rufinus in the preface to his Latin translation of Origen's *De principiis* (Kessinger Reprints: www.kessinger.net).

11. Karl Baus, et al., eds., *The Imperial Church from Constantine to the Early Middle Ages*, trans. Anselm Biggs (vol. 2 of *History of the Church*, ed. Hubert Jedin and John Dolan, New York: Crossroad, 1980), 123.

12. *The von Balthasar Reader*, ed. Medard Kehl and Werner Löser, trans. Robert J. Daly and Fred Lawrence (New York: Crossroad, 1982), 384. The great nineteenth-century church historian Philip Schaff called them "grand and fascinating errors" (*History of the Christian Church*, Vol. 1 [New York: Scribner's, 1882], 505).

13. *Von Balthasar Reader*, 384.

14. Jean Daniélou, *Origen*, trans. Walter Mitchell (New York: Sheed & Ward, 1955), 8.

his ideas were discontinuous with the traditions of the church and had to be rejected. This is nowhere more evident than in his cosmology, derived and defended by flights of allegorical imagination.

Origen's Cosmology

The opening chapters of Origen's *On First Principles* (*De principiis*) are in many ways a poetic thought experiment. They are an effort to expound in detail the architecture of eternity, inspired by what Origen believed were mysteries hidden in Scripture and in the natural world. These themes appear scattered throughout his writings but particularly in his commentaries on Genesis and the Gospel of John and in the eighth book of *Against Celsus* (*Contra Celsum*). Combining ruminations on classical and contemporary philosophy with his own deep reflections on Genesis 1:1, John 1:1, and Romans 1:20 ("since the creation of the world God's invisible qualities—his eternal power and divine nature—have been clearly seen, being understood from what has been made"), Origen engages his imagination to divine Divinity and sketch the choreography of heaven. The deeper meaning of the natural world, like Scripture itself, lies not in what is obvious to the eye (its literal sense, what is "written without," as he calls it), but in that higher realm toward which it points (that is, what is "written within"). It is an intuition differently conceptualized but not alien to modern theoretical physics. In his commentary on the Song of Songs he writes, "I think that He who made all things in wisdom so created all the species of visible things upon the earth that He placed in some of them some teaching and knowledge of things invisible and heavenly, whereby the human mind might mount to spiritual understanding and seek the grounds of things in heaven."[15]

Of course, among those in whom was placed "some teaching and knowledge of things invisible and heavenly" Origen counted himself. His reflections on this invisible world before time are from the beginning inescapably Trinitarian: from the supreme, incorporeal, and invisible God as God the Father comes God the Son and God the Holy Spirit. Since this describes Divinity within eternity and before time, one is not to suppose there was a time when the Father was ever without the Son or without the Holy Spirit. They are coeternal. As the

---

15. *The Song of Songs, Commentary and Homilies*, trans. R. P. Lawson (London: Longmans, Green, 1957), 220.

"invisible image of the invisible God," the Son as divine Logos is the agent of creation,[16] and so creates a finite number of rational, immortal souls which, because of free will and a cooling of their ardor for contemplating the Godhead, fall away from their intended purpose.

With the goal of restoration, God through the Logos then creates the visible and invisible world as the place where these incorporeal souls might be rehabilitated. The form souls take (whether as stars, angels, demons, or human beings, etc.) is a function of the coolness of their ardor, which in turn determines the degree of their fallenness. That soul that fell first and farthest is the devil;[17] and that supremely exalted soul which did not fall, being sinless, became the soul of Jesus Christ, the God-Man.[18] Human beings, being weak souls inhabiting mortal bodies,[19] need assistance if they are to be restored to the fellowship and contemplation of the Divine. The incarnation, culminating in the cross, is the supreme act of that redemption; but the plethora of rational creatures, assuming stations within the visible and invisible realms according to merit (such as angels and archangels), also have pedagogical roles in salvation (for example, announcing the birth of Jesus). The telos of creation is thus the restoration of all immortal souls back into the heavenly kingdom that God might once again be all in all.

The Interpretation of Scripture

For Origen, Scripture, like the natural world itself, exists for the contemplation of heaven, not world history, or even Jesus and his church. For this reason, until one becomes familiar with the architecture of heaven as Origen describes it, it is difficult to understand what he is doing when he sets himself to the task of interpreting Scripture. Perhaps also for this reason he does not explain his method of scriptural interpretation until the fourth book of *First Principles,* that is, until after he has laid out the doctrines of his theology.[20] In Origen's mind,

---

16. Origen suggests that "perhaps" it is to Christ God is speaking when he says, in the imperative, "Let there be light" (Gen. 1:3; *Comm. Jo.* 1.110).

17. For Origen (as for Augustine later), evil is the absence of good, hence, ontologically speaking, it is nothing; it is nonbeing.

18. Origen is the first to speak of the two natures of Christ, human and divine, which led to the christological controversies of the fourth century. No less controversial was his extreme sexual asceticism.

19. The Greek text describes "men" as "souls that make use of bodies," whereas the Latin translation reads, "souls that are located in bodies" (cf. *First Principles,* 4.2.7). A similar softening of the Greek is found throughout the Latin text.

20. The translation cited in this section is that of G. W. Butterworth, *Origen on First Principles* (London: Society for Promoting Christian Knowledge, 1936).

the sacred books are the work of the Holy Spirit. They are the result of a kenosis (emptying) of the Logos into human words, just as Jesus is a kenosis of the Logos into human flesh.[21] The preeminent concern of the Holy Spirit is the "unspeakable mysteries connected with the affairs of men." Thus the Spirit's purpose in inspiring Scripture is to reveal to those "capable of being taught" the "deep things" hidden therein in order for them to become partakers "of all the doctrines of the Spirit's counsel" and thus be assisted in reaching perfection and hence salvation (*First Principles*, 4.2.7).

The sequence of spiritual truths hidden within the narratives and laws of Scripture is for Origen the real subject matter of Scripture (its unitive thrust or *skopos*).[22] The literal wording of the text was merely the vehicle of those truths. The story line of Scripture may occasionally contain "something which did not happen, occasionally something which could not happen, and occasionally something which might have happened but in fact did not" (4.2.9). This can be said of the New Testament as well as the Old because the same Spirit is at work in both Testaments. Clearly, he says, there are things in the New Testament, including laws and commandments, which are "not reasonable." Interpreting Scripture literally, therefore, is simply silly, for how can one suppose, as Genesis 1 suggests, that days can exist before the sun and moon have been created, or that God walked in the garden in the cool of the day, or that the devil could have taken Jesus to a mountain high enough for all the kingdoms of the world to be seen, and so on (4.3.1). There are, he writes, a "thousand other passages in the Gospels" of a similar nature that cannot, and were not intended to be, taken literally, including the radical moral commands of Christ. Thus all Scripture "has a spiritual meaning, but not all a bodily [literal] meaning" (4.3.5).

This pertains particularly to the Old Testament, but in ways different from the New. Before Christ's sojourn on earth, which was visible and bodily, he came spiritually to those in whom "the fullness of time" (Gal. 4:4) was already spiritually present: the patriarchs, Moses (cf. Heb. 3:5), and the prophets—enabling them to contemplate the coming glory of Christ (*Commentary on John* 1.37–38). So although the gospel is not present in the Old Testament, it is nevertheless "stored up in all the scriptures" (*Commentary on John* 1.36). Since the Jews do not accept Christ, they deny the key by which their own Scriptures are to

---

21. See R. Gögler, *Zur Theologie des biblischen Wortes bei Origenes* (Düsseldorf: Patmos, 1963), 390.
22. See Richard N. Soulen and R. Kendall Soulen, *Handbook of Biblical Criticism,* 3rd ed. (Louisville: Westminster John Knox, 2001), 168–69, "Scope." Also Young, *Biblical Exegesis,* 21–27.

be understood, causing God to end his covenant with them and hand them a "bill of divorce." Here, as with many other exegetical remarks, Origen added to the fateful anti-Judaism that was to plague the church, even though it is clear from his homilies and commentary on Romans that he believed Paul had it right in Romans 9–11, that in the end "all Israel will be saved" (11:26).

At the surface, therefore, the Scriptures are like the Suffering Servant of Isaiah 53, that is, "without form or comeliness" (KJV). Like human beings, Scripture is a composite entity possessing body, soul, and spirit, in which the body, or literal wording, is the vehicle of something more important—moral (soul) and spiritual (spirit) truth. In practice, however, Origen is less clear or consistent in assigning what is to be deemed the "soul" and what the "spirit" of a text. Nor is it possible always to prescind when a passage is to be taken literally and when figuratively, even though he states that whatever is absurd or impossible must be taken figuratively—and this in part because the real meaning of Scripture "must be worthy of the divine majesty" (*Homily on Leviticus* 7.5). Thus Origen can judge the story of the ark historical while concluding that the account of Jesus' cleansing of the temple cannot be, since it is unworthy of the dignity of Christ and does not conform to the deeper intent or *skopos* of the gospel.

For this reason, Origen's commentaries can be a source of infinite frustration to the modern mind. One finds there not close exegetical studies as one might expect of the author of the Hexapla; rather, the reader is confronted by flights of allegorical fantasy and freewheeling word associations. As Origen writes in *Against Celsus*: "Such, indeed, was the abounding love which He had for men, that He gave to the more learned a theology capable of raising the soul far above all earthly things; while with no less consideration He comes down to the weaker capacities of ignorant men, of simple women, of slaves, and, in short, of all those who from Jesus alone could have received that help for the better regulation of their lives" (7.41). Of course, Origen is here referring to his own theology, and to himself as one of the "more learned" to whom God's abounding love had given a theology "capable of raising the soul," while the incarnation was for men and women with "weaker capacities."[23]

It was not without reason that Origen was condemned. Nevertheless, it is to Origen, more than to any other of the early church leaders,

---

23. *The Ante-Nicene Fathers*, vol. 4: *Tertullian, Part Fourth; Minucius Felix; Commodian; Origen, Parts First and Second*, ed. Alexander Roberts and James Donaldson (Peabody, MA: Hendrickson, 1994 reprint).

that we owe the church's doctrine of the Bible as Word of God. Perhaps this is his most important legacy.

AUGUSTINE, BISHOP OF HIPPO (354–430)

Augustine was born in Thagaste, North Africa (modern Souk Ahras, Algeria), one hundred years after Origen's death; yet there is much to compare between the two men and, given the limited scope of this essay, doing so provides us with an easy entrée into his complex life.

Both men were profoundly influenced by a devout parent, Origen by his father, Augustine by his mother; both were recognized for their intellectual brilliance while still young; both ardently explored a wide range of disciplines in search of wisdom; both were prolific, their writings widely disseminated; both attained fame across the Roman Empire within their own lifetimes; both viewed themselves as loyal churchmen contributing to the treasury of Christian thought; both were recognized by the Catholic Church for the significance and power of their writings, one to condemnation, with the destruction of major portions of his literary legacy, the other to sainthood and the collection, indexing, and archiving of almost everything he wrote; both died in old age as their worlds collapsed, one of torture during imperial persecution in Palestine, the other of natural causes while Arian Vandals lay siege to his city in North Africa. But these are similarities writ large.

Their differences are more revealing. By his late teens Origen had castrated himself to suppress the temptations of the flesh; at a comparable age Augustine had fathered a son by a concubine, and even a decade later could still mockingly implore of the Lord, "Grant me chastity and continence, but not yet!" (*Confessions* 8.7.17).[24] Origen was from childhood innately ascetic, Augustine an accomplished aesthete—as one wit put it: "His name should rhyme with fine and wine and dine."[25] Origen studied Christian heresies the better to defend against them; Augustine was enamored of one, known as Manichaeism, for more than a decade. Origen came to Platonic and Neoplatonic thought early, as well as to the allurements of allegorical interpretation; Augustine was thirty years of age at the time of his philosophic conversion under Ambrose, bishop

---

24. *St. Augustine's Confessions: A New Translation by Henry Chadwick* (Oxford: Oxford University Press, 1991), 145.

25. Classroom lecture by Professor Edwin Prince Booth (1898–1969), Boston University School of Theology, spring semester, 1957. Alternative pronunciations, it was suggested, would rhyme with mean and spleen, or "disgust'n", neither of which was said to be appropriate.

of Milan, who also taught him the value of allegory in the interpretation of Scripture. Origen loved scholarly minutia and cosmological speculation; Augustine enjoyed speculation too, as on the nature of the Trinity, but considered such preoccupations irrelevant to the day-to-day moral and theological concerns of the parish. Origen was on a rigorous pilgrimage of perfection, as were the heresies of Augustine's time: Manichaeism, Donatism, and Pelagianism; Augustine was humbled both by the memory of sin and the experience of divine grace, and he thought the notion of salvation by works a heretical absurdity.[26] Origen saw mysteries hidden in Scripture and in the natural world as the key to the spiritual cosmos above; Augustine found Scripture a path to the will within. Origen never experienced a "before" and "after" in his spiritual life; for Augustine conversion to Christ and to the authority of the Catholic Church provided the key both to the world without and to the world within. Origen's preoccupation was with humankind's ascent to God attainable in reality only by an elite few, like himself, capping their lives with martyrdom; Augustine's preoccupation was with the "startling, active love of God for humankind," a gift freely given regardless of station or religious achievement.[27] Finally, Origen left us no autobiography; Augustine did.

The Confessions

Augustine's dramatic conversion to Christianity is superseded only by that of the apostle Paul in terms of its significance for the life and thought of the Christian church in the West. It is described in what is widely recognized as the greatest spiritual autobiography in the Western world, *The Confessions*,[28] written ten years after his conversion and after being consecrated a bishop in the Catholic Church in North Africa. No synopsis can do it justice. To comprehend the mind of Augustine one must think his thoughts with him page by page. He does not simply recall the past; he searchingly deconstructs the motivations and feelings surrounding the events of his life, placing them all before God as in prayer. Not until Augustine does one find in extant literature of the antique world the kind of introspection found here. The reader

---

26. See *On Christian Doctrine* 1.35.39.

27. Peter Brown, *Augustine of Hippo: A Biography* (Berkeley: University of California Press, 1967), 508.

28. See *The Confessions*, trans. Maria Boulding (New York: Vintage Books, 1998); and Henry J. Chadwick, *Confessions* (Oxford: Oxford University Press, 1991).

of the *Confessions*, it is said, witnesses the birth of the introspective conscience, the birth of the modern mind.[29] We must leave aside the validity of this judgment as an issue, just as we must eschew retelling the fascinating story of his conversion in which he experienced the transformation of his will, just as we must forgo a discussion of the role this experience played in his rejection of Pelagianism and the notion of free will. In order to understand his approach to Scripture, however, it is helpful to review what Augustine thought was a central insight into his life brought about by his conversion to Christian faith as related in his *Confessions* and elsewhere.

Having possessed a will totally captive to the sensate world of beauty and pleasure, his conversion experience of divine grace enabled Augustine to turn away from the world to God, the "very life of life." All his loves were affected by this revelation: the love of his mother Monica, of a friend whose unexpected death had cast him into unrelieved depression, of a woman he would not marry but whose embrace he adored. In each instance the love he experienced was reciprocal: his love for the other, the other's love for him. And in each case, seen in the new light of faith, he recognized in the nature of his love both his own sin and theirs. He had loved the other for his own enjoyment, just as they had loved him. Now, in the light of God's grace, he knew he had neither looked upon nor loved the other as they were "in God." To love the other as God's possession and gift and not one's own: this is the insight into which Augustine is converted. It becomes his foremost interpretive principle. In his work *On Christian Doctrine*, begun around 396, hence essentially contemporaneous with the *Confessions*, Augustine explains, "When you enjoy a man in God, it is God rather than the man whom you enjoy; for you take joy in Him who will make you blessed" (1.33.37).[30] Herein lies the essence of *agape* or love (which Jerome and Old Latin versions of the Bible translated "charity"): "I call 'charity' the motion of the soul toward the enjoyment of God for His own sake, and the enjoyment of one's self and one's neighbor for the sake of God; but 'cupidity' is the motion of the soul toward the enjoyment of one's self, one's neighbor, or any corporal thing for the sake of something other than God" (3.10.16). The purpose of all temporal delight, which in itself is transitory, is to lead the soul to the love of

---

29. The initial text usually cited here is that of Krister Stendahl, *Paul among Jews and Gentiles* (Philadelphia: Fortress, 1976). Chapter 2, "The Apostle Paul and the Interpretive Conscience of the West," 78–96.

30. Citations are from *Saint Augustine: On Christian Doctrine*, trans. D. W. Robertson Jr. (New York: Liberal Arts, 1958).

God, who alone is unchanging. This, too, is the function of the Word become flesh: to prepare the way for the love of God. The same can be said of the Law and of all sacred Scripture. Their purpose is "the love of a Being which is to be enjoyed and of a being that can share that enjoyment with us" (1.35.39).

The implication for any interpretation of Scripture, says Augustine, is clear: "Whoever thinks that he understands the divine Scriptures, or any part of them so that it does not build the double love of God and neighbor does not understand it at all" (1.36.40). And he who finds there a lesson useful to the building of charity, even though he misses the author's intent, has not been deceived, nor is he untruthful. In fact, Augustine concludes, "a man supported by faith, hope, and charity, with an unshaken hold upon them, does not need the Scriptures except for the instruction of others" (1.39.43)!

On the Interpretation of Scripture

Since Augustine's rules for the interpretation of Scripture shaped that subject for monks throughout the Middle Ages, they warrant our attention more closely. The principles are laid out in the little book *On Christian Doctrine*, more aptly named by some, *On Christian Teaching*. I have already noted above the foremost of all the principles of interpretation: charity, or love.

Augustine notes two things necessary in the treatment of Scripture: a way of discerning what is to be understood (his hermeneutical methodology), and a way of teaching what has been learned (his pedagogical theory, which, for Augustine, was rhetoric). The first is dealt with in the first three books; the latter is not addressed until 427, when it is added as book 4, shortly before his death. In order to discover what is to be understood, Augustine tells us (in what is the first discussion of semiotics[31] or theory of signs) it is necessary to distinguish between things and signs. Things are familiar to us: wood, rocks, trees, and so on; things have meaning in and of themselves and are not as such signs of anything else. However, words are always signs, and since Scripture is made up entirely of words, the hermeneutical task is to ascertain what those signs mean, whether they are to be taken literally (pointing to things) or figuratively (pointing beyond mere things to "other" realms of significance).

---

31. See Soulen and Soulen, *Handbook of Biblical Criticism,* 170–71, "Semiotics."

So far as Scripture at its literal level is concerned, pagan historians are of value. They are helpful in ascertaining the temporal accuracy of events, persons, and places described in Scripture. Augustine even suggests that it would be helpful to create an encyclopedia of information on such things as the geography of place names, the identification of foreign rulers, as well as types of animals, plants, stones, metals, and so on (2.39.59). He acknowledges that most people may simply wish to understand the thoughts and intentions of those who wrote Scripture, and in so doing haply discover the will of God (2.5.6). The difficulty arises, he suggests, when Scripture is obscure or ambiguous, or worse, when it is absurd or unworthy. Taken literally, Scripture can lead the unlearned astray. In such instances, Scripture must be taken figuratively (allegorically), not literally. To say that Scripture is divinely inspired does not mean that its literal wording is sacrosanct. Like Origen before him, Augustine is convinced that because all Scripture is inspired these hard places have been put there by God to humble the proud and to ward against contempt for the familiar (2.6.7). He illustrates his point with reference to the Song of Songs. Here the poet praises his beloved for her beauty: "Thy teeth as flocks of sheep, that are shorn, which come up from the washing, all with twins: and there is none barren among them" (4:2 Douay-Rheims translation). The verse can be understood as it is, but "in a strange way," Augustine admits, he finds it more pleasant "when I envisage them [figuratively] as the teeth of the Church cutting off men from their errors and transferring them to her body . . . having put aside the burdens of the world like so much fleece, and as ascending from the washing, which is baptism, all to create twins, which are the two precepts of love, and I see no one of them sterile of this holy fruit" (2.6.7). Just why he finds this type of allegorical interpretation more pleasant, Augustine admits, "is difficult to say" (2.6.7).

Whereas Origen uses allegorical interpretation to overcome Scripture's crudity and obscurity or to divine the cosmology of heaven as he imagines it, this is not so with Augustine, who is far more orthodox or "Catholic." Augustine simply declares, "Scripture teaches nothing but charity, nor condemns anything except cupidity. . . . Again, if the minds of men are subject to some erroneous opinion, they think that whatever Scripture says contrary to that opinion is figurative. But [Scripture] asserts nothing except the catholic faith" (3.10.15). Whereas the modern mind might see this as eisegesis, for Augustine the Catholic Church and its rule of faith provided the objectivity of a consistent interpretive principle independent of the interpreter's own judgment. Augustine's famous allegorical interpretation of the parable of the Good Samaritan shows the role of church doctrine as an interpretive principle:

> *A certain man went down from Jerusalem to Jericho:* Adam himself is meant; *Jerusalem* is the holy city of peace from whose blessedness Adam fell; *Jericho* means the moon, and signifies our mortality, because it is born, waxes, wanes, and dies. *Thieves* are the devil and his angels. *Who strip him,* namely, of his immortality; *and beat him,* by persuading him to sin; *and left him half-dead,* because in so far as man can understand and know God, he lives, but in so far as he is wasted and oppressed by sin, he is dead; he is therefore called *half-dead.* The *priest* and *Levite* who saw him and passed by, signify the priesthood and ministry of the Old Testament, which could profit nothing for salvation. *Samaritan* means Guardian, and therefore the Lord Himself is signified by this name. The *binding of the wounds* is the restraint of sin. *Oil* is the comfort of good hope; *wine* the exhortation to work with fervent spirit. The *beast* is the flesh in which He deigned to come to us. The being *set upon the beast* is belief in the incarnation of Christ. The *inn* is the Church, where travelers are refreshed on their return from pilgrimage to their heavenly country. The *morrow* is after the resurrection of the Lord. The *two pence* are either the two precepts of love, or the promise of this life and of that which is to come. The *innkeeper* is the Apostle (Paul). The supererogatory payment is either his counsel of celibacy, or the fact that he worked with his own hands lest he should be a burden to any of the weaker brethren when the Gospel was new, though it was lawful for him "to live by the Gospel."
>
> (*Quaestionum evangelicarum* 2.19)[32]

The interpretation is not subjective, or simply "according to the opinions of the interpreter," because the interpretation follows the rule of faith. It is not of his devising. It is the authoritative teaching of the church: Adam is assisted in his movement toward God by the healing love (charity) of Christ, in the figure of the Good Samaritan, while the cupidity of both priest and Levite leave them even less close to God than before. Nor has Augustine forgotten his own rule that any interpretation of a scriptural passage that does not result in advocating love of God and neighbor has not yet understood what is being said. His first choice in divining the right interpretation for the two pence is "the two precepts of love" (of God and neighbor).

---

32. Slightly abridged by C. H. Dodd, *The Parables of the Kingdom,* 3rd ed. (London: James Nisbet, 1936), 11–12.

We recall that Augustine defines charity as the motion of the soul toward the enjoyment of God for God's own sake, and toward one's self and one's neighbor for the sake of God; while cupidity is the motion of the soul toward the enjoyment of one's self, or the neighbor, or any corporal thing (e.g., nature itself) for any reason other than God (3.10.16). Thus if Scripture assigns to God words or acts or emotions of bitterness or anger toward the destruction of cupidity, it is to be taken literally; but in other instances, as in the words of Jeremiah, "Lo, I have set thee this day over the nations, and kingdoms, to root up and to pull down, and to waste and to destroy" (Jer. 1:10 Douay-Rheims), then the words are to be taken figuratively (3.11.17), since it is the kingdom of cupidity that is being addressed, not earthly kingdoms. This principle applies to other difficulties of interpretation. No reasonable person, Augustine avers, would think that shameful deeds are being commended by Scripture, and those that appear that way to the inexperienced must be understood figuratively. In other instances, such as the practice of polygamy by the patriarchs, Scripture must be understood historically and literally, as well as figuratively and prophetically, so that the purpose of Scripture—the increase of charity—be promoted (3.12.20). Hence, determining whether a text is the one or the other is obviously "of first importance" (3.24.34).

Another rule for interpreting difficult passages is simply to let Scripture interpret Scripture. When trying to elucidate problematic passages, he advises, the wise expositor will "draw examples from the plainer passages to throw light upon the more obscure, and use the evidence of passages about which there is no doubt to remove all hesitation in regard to the doubtful passages" (2.9.14).

For the serious student of Scripture Augustine does have specific advice: Read all of Scripture, even if you do not understand it, memorizing passages where possible. Read different translations of the same passage, not just one, realizing that no one translation is perfect. Become knowledgeable of languages (Hebrew and Greek) and of things mentioned in Scripture, such as the nature of animals, or stones, or plants. Lack of such knowledge, he asserts, makes the figurative meaning obscure; for example (and here again Augustine shows his love of allegory), knowledge of the ways of serpents clarifies the Lord's admonition that we should be wise as serpents: as the serpent protects its head, so the faithful Christian should offer his body to protect Christ, the head of the church; as the serpent sheds its skin, so we are to "put off the old man" and "put on the new," and so on (2.16.24).

Augustine does not doubt the events as they are narrated, and he is aware that each human author of Scripture was directed by a particular intention in writing; but neither the events as such nor the intention of the author are of ultimate importance, since the purposes of the Holy Spirit who inspires all of Scripture may be achieved just as effectively in the person who hears and interprets the text, even if the result is contrary to the intent of the author. (We shall meet these ideas again in later chapters.) We have seen in chapter 4 how this Augustinian principle applies also to translators. As Augustine sees it, there is no need to go back to the Hebrew text of the Old Testament, because the same Spirit who inspired it was equally at work in the translators who produced its Greek equivalent, the Septuagint.

For Augustine, following Pythagorean and Neoplatonic thought, numbers are the key to cosmic order and also the vehicles of figurative and mystical meanings, and he contends that ignorance of their allegorical freight causes misunderstanding. For instance, in a rather torturous way he alleges that the fact that Moses, Elijah, and Jesus all fasted forty days cannot be understood apart from consideration of this number. "For it contains four tens, to indicate the knowledge of all things involved in times. . . . the number ten signifies a knowledge of the Creator and the creatures; for the trinity is the Creator and the septenary [group of seven] indicates the creature by reason of his life and body. For with reference to life there are three, whence we should love God with all our hearts, with all our souls, and with all our minds; and with reference to our body there are very obviously four elements of which it is made [earth, water, air, and fire] . . . thus . . . we are admonished to live chastely and continently and without temporal delight, or, that is, to fast for forty days" (2.16.25). In an exercise of this sort, Augustine thought of himself, through the use of reason, as being able to penetrate beyond the realm of sense into the eternal realm of perfect number, and thus to God.[33] Scriptural legitimacy for numerology he found in the Wisdom of Solomon: "You [Lord] have disposed [ordered] all things by measure, and number, and weight" (11:20b New American Bible); empirical legitimacy for this truth he found in art (music) and architecture.[34]

Finally, interpreting Scripture, and training the exegete for that task, is the sacred work of the church. It would be unthinkable to Augustine

---

33. See Jeremy S. Begbie's discussion of Augustine's early essay, On Music, in Theology, Music, and Time (Cambridge: Cambridge University Press, 2000), 75–86.

34. See his treatises De ordine and De musica (On Music) written within months following his conversion, in 386–87.

that anyone not committed to the authority of the Catholic Church and to its rule of faith could faithfully understand or interpret the sacred text. Understanding presupposes conversion.[35] The classic statement concerning the relationship of faith to understanding is found in Augustine's commentary on the Gospel of John: "Understanding is the reward of faith. Therefore seek not to understand in order to believe but believe in order to understand."[36]

Faith, for Augustine, is the precondition of interpretation. But it is only the first requirement. Augustine recognizes seven steps toward wisdom. Fear of the Lord, the first step, is awareness of one's mortality, and the willingness to nail the desires of the flesh to the wood of the cross (2.7.9). Fear gives rise to humble piety, so that the exegete neither contradicts Scripture nor thinks himself or herself wiser than Scripture, even when Scripture is obscure.[37] The third virtue is the knowledge that Scripture teaches the exegete nothing other than "that God is to be loved for Himself and his neighbor for the sake of God" (2.7.10). When the exegete reflects on this twofold command, she or he will recognize how much the world has been loved instead; and this, when rightly acknowledged, will give rise to fear and to the awareness that one's own piety is insufficient and that there is no recourse other than to trust in the authority of the sacred Scriptures and in prayer. This leads then to the fourth step, to resolution in the hungering and thirsting for justice that leads to the love of eternal things, such as the Trinity. The fifth step is the counsel of compassion, which entails perfecting love of neighbor. When such love includes the enemy, the exegete has arrived at the sixth step, in which the soul is cleansed for a vision of God insofar as that is possible for those who have "died to the world" (2.7.11), for even they "see through a glass darkly" (1 Cor. 13:12) and therefore "walk by faith rather than by sight" (2 Cor. 5:7). In this way the exegete ascends to wisdom and the enjoyment of peace and tranquility, the seventh step.

CONCLUSION

Even this brief review of Irenaeus, Origen, and Augustine amply demonstrates how greatly they differ, not only from one another, but also from the Scriptures they seek to interpret. Yet, in the final analysis, one

---

35. Gerald L. Bruns, *Hermeneutics: Ancient and Modern* (New Haven: Yale University Press, 1992).
36. *On the Gospel according to St. John* 29.6.
37. See *Confessions* 3.5.9.

may argue that these church leaders differ less in the fundamental judgments that they make about God, Christ, the Spirit, and the world than in the conceptualities they use to express those judgments. However expressed, whether in the language of Hebrew narrative or in Greek speculative thought about that narrative, their viewpoints converge at the common point: the Galilean Jew named Jesus, and everything to do with him, from birth to death—from words to deeds to resurrection—is revelatory of God's nature and will.

Chapter 7
How Many Senses Does Scripture Have?

THE QUADRIGA

That a passage of Scripture can have more than one valid meaning or "sense" was, for most of Christian history, a self-evident teaching of Scripture itself (cf. Gal. 4; 2 Cor. 3). But how many senses can a single passage of Scripture have? More exactly, how many different *kinds* of sense can a passage of Scripture have or make? Today the question may strike us as odd, but it was not to Christians of an earlier time. Christians did not typically assume that there was only one valid kind of scriptural meaning, that is, *the literal sense*, as some do today. Rather, they tended to think that Scripture made sense in a limited variety of ways, each of which was suited to foster the Christian life in a specific way. There was the literal sense, of course. But there was also the spiritual sense, which could, in turn, be subdivided into even more senses. According to one common division, there were four senses of Scripture in all, four different ways a person could make good sense of a single passage of Scripture. In time, these four modes of interpretation came to be known as the Quadriga, after a chariot drawn by four horses. Just as four horses pull a heavy carriage better than one, so the four senses of Scripture build up the Christian life better than one alone.

John Cassian (ca. 360–435) is generally credited with being the first to distinguish the four senses of Scripture. The key passage comes from Cassian's treatise "On Spiritual Knowledge":

The practical side of knowledge is hived off among many professions and disciplines. The contemplative side is divided into two
parts, namely, historical interpretation and spiritual insight. . . .

Now there are three kinds of spiritual lore, namely, tropology,[1]
allegory, and anagoge. This is what Proverbs has to say about them:
"Write these three times over the spread of your heart" (Prv 22:20).

History embraces the knowledge of things which are past and
which are perceptible. The apostle gives an example: "It is written
that Abraham had two sons, one by a servant and one by a free
woman" (Gal 4:22–23).

What follows is *allegorical,* because the things which actually
happened are said to have prefigured another mystery. "These two
women stand for the two covenants . . ." (Gal 4:24–25).

Anagoge climbs up from spiritual mysteries to the higher and
more august secrets of heaven, such as what the apostle adds: "The
Jerusalem above is free and is our mother" (Gal 4:26–27).

Tropology is moral teaching designed for the amendment of life
and for instruction in asceticism. It is as if by these two covenants
we were to mean the practical discipline and the contemplative, or
else we could take Jerusalem or Sion to be the human soul, as the
following words express it: "Praise Jerusalem the Lord, praise Sion
your God" (Ps 147:12).

And if we wish it, these four modes of representation flow into a
unity so that the one Jerusalem can be understood in four different
ways, in the historical sense as the city of the Jews, in allegory as the
church of Christ, in anagoge as the heavenly city of God "which
is mother to us all" (Gal. 4:26), in the tropological sense as the
human soul.[2]

Note that Cassian's "four modes of representation" are really about different ways the interpreter can usefully understand the scriptural text.
Each "sense" of the text corresponds to a certain activity or perspective
on the part of the exegete, as well as to a dimension of meaning in the
text itself.[3]

Not everyone followed Cassian's lead in finding four senses of Scripture. Pope Gregory the Great (590–604), for example, the "Father of
Western medieval spirituality,"[4] identified only three senses when

---

1. The term comes from the Greek word *tropos,* referring to one's way of life, conduct, or character; cf. Heb. 13:5.
2. John Cassian, *Conferences,* trans. Colm Luibheid (*Classics of Western Spirituality;* New York: Paulist Press, 1985), 160. Italics added.
3. Cf. Frances M. Young, *Biblical Exegesis and the Formation of Christian Culture* (Cambridge: Cambridge University Press, 1997), 175.
4. See John Anthony McGuckin, "Gregory the Great," *The Westminster Handbook to Patristic Theology* (Louisville: Westminster John Knox, 2004), 153–55. Also *The Letters of Gregory the Great, Books 1–4* (trans. with an introduction and notes by John R. Martyn; Toronto: Pontifical Institute of Medieval Studies, 2004).

offering guidance for the "spiritual reading" (*lectio divina*): "First we lay the foundations in history; then, by pursuing a symbolical sense, we erect an intellectual edifice to be a stronghold of faith; and lastly, by the grace of moral instruction, we as it were paint the fabric in fair colours."[5] Gregory's division is substantially similar to Cassian's, but he employs other terms for what Cassian called the allegorical and tropological sense, and he omits anagogy altogether.

Still, by the later Middle Ages, the Quadriga had acquired a certain canonical status of its own. Sometime around 1260, a Scandinavian by the name of Augustine of Dacia enshrined the fourfold schema of interpretation in an easily memorized poem (others have attributed the quatrain to Nicholas of Lyra, who quoted it in 1330):

> Litera gesta docent, quid credas allegoria,
> Moralis quid agas, quo tendas anagogia.
> The letter teaches events, allegory what you should believe,
> Morality teaches what you should do, anagogy what mark you
>   should be aiming for.[6]

In the twentieth century, opinion about the value of the Quadriga was varied. A leading Catholic theologian and medieval historian, Henri de Lubac, could defend it as bearing "a certain fundamentally Catholic attitude in the face of the Word of God." Others, also Catholic, have impatiently thrust it aside as "entirely artificial," an "inevitable distraction," and as having "nothing to recommend" it.[7]

On the contrary, the idea of a fourfold sense of Scripture is not artificial at all and has much to recommend it. With a little reflection, it is not hard to see that the three "spiritual senses" correspond to the three theological virtues of Paul (1 Cor. 13): faith (allegorical interpretation), love (tropological interpretation), and hope (anagogic interpretation). They correspond as well to the three temporal orientations of life: the past (as "the faith we believe"), the present (as "love of God, self, and neighbor"), and the future (as "the hope that is in us"). However much this or that medieval exegete may have missed the mark in any given exegetical endeavor, it is these three virtues—founded upon and growing out of the historical sense—that the Quadriga is designed to serve and cultivate.

5. Gregory the Great, *Epistle* 5.53a, trans. in F. Homes Dudden, *Gregory the Great: His Place in History and Thought* (2 vols.; New York: Longmans, Green, 1905), 1:193.

6. See Henri de Lubac, *Medieval Exegesis*, vol. 1: *The Four Senses of Scripture*, trans. Mark Sebanc (Grand Rapids: Eerdmans, 1998), 1.

7. Ibid., 9–10.

In what follows, we shall explore the various senses of Scripture by focusing on three men who lived at the beginning of what is called the Twelfth-Century Renaissance. Our three pivotal figures are the abbot Suger of St.-Denis, the saint Bernard of Clairvaux, and the "heretic" Peter Abelard. In turn they represent the origin of the Gothic style in church architecture, the last of the church fathers, and the beginning of the science of theology. I have chosen them not only because they were instrumental in shaping the era in which they lived, but because each highlights a distinct way of making sense of Scripture, loosely captured in the terms *anagogia* (Suger), *tropologia* (Bernard), and *historia* (Abelard). Allegory is present throughout.

ABBOT SUGER AND THE ANAGOGICAL SENSE

A worldly and multifaceted man, Abbot Suger of St.-Denis (ca. 1081–1151) is best known today as the genius who supervised the reconstruction of the abbey of St.-Denis in Paris and in so doing introduced elements of style that provided inspiration for the great Gothic cathedrals of Europe. Remarkably, Suger left to posterity a retrospective account of his intention in reconstructing the church. This account gives us unparalleled insight into Suger's architectural vision and makes explicit the abbot's interest in the anagogic dimension of Christian faith. Suger knew that most of the pilgrims who entered his church were illiterate. The only "Scripture" they could read would be its walls of stone and glass. Suger wished to devise an architectural style that would inspire those who visited the abbey with the hope of the new Jerusalem, as mentioned by Paul in Galatians 4 and gloriously portrayed in the final visions of Scripture (Rev. 22–24).

The decaying chapel he inherited, Suger informs his reader, was Romanesque, dark and inadequate for the pilgrimages of high holy days, and "unworthy of the dignity of the Royal House of France," with which St.-Denis had become identified. The old building was also out of keeping with the theological vision of its namesake, Dionysius the Areopagite, the Neoplatonic mystic from whose writings Suger drew much of his inspiration.[8] In *The Celestial Hierarchy*, Dionysius wrote of ascending

---

8. The church's namesake actually represented three saintly figures who had melded over time into one: Dionysius the Areopagite, the companion of Paul (Acts 17:34); Saint Denis, the actual apostle to the Gauls of the third century; and Pseudo-Dionysius, the anonymous metaphysical mystic of the sixth century whose writings were the immediate source of inspiration for Abbot Suger.

steps of spiritual progress that lead from the human to the Divine, from the mundane to the celestial realm of the "Father of Lights."

> A hierarchy is a sacred order, a state of understanding and an activity approximating as closely as possible to the divine. And it is uplifted [*anagogia*] to the imitation of God in proportion to the enlightenments divinely given to it. The beauty of God—so simple, so good, so much the source of perfection—is completely uncontaminated by dissimilarity. It reaches out to grant every being, according to merit, a share of light and then through a divine sacrament, in harmony and in peace, it bestows on each of those being perfected its own form.[9]

Inspired by Dionysius, Suger was intent on a design that would fill the interior with light, symbolic of the Light of lights and the light of the new covenant. Suger devised pointed windows and high-vaulted arches that were intended to lift the pilgrim's eyes upward to ever greater luminosity, as "from the material to the immaterial," from the mundane to the celestial, just as the scenes of heavenly peace depicted above were to enlighten the minds of the humblest pilgrim.

In his account of "what was done under [my] administration," Suger recalls his own anagogic experience of being "called away" from the material world of "external cares" to the "immaterial": "Then it seems to me that I see myself dwelling, as it were, in some strange region of the universe which neither exists in the slime of the earth nor entirely in the purity of heaven."[10] Such was the experience Suger wanted everyone who entered through the church's portals to share: an experience of the Celestial City. Every detail of the structure was conceived to this end. In a poem of his own composition, written in honor of the bronze reliefs of the passion and resurrection of Christ on the west portal doors, Suger wrote:

> Whoever thou art, if thou seekest to extol the glory of these doors,
> Marvel not at the gold and the expense but at the craftsmanship of
> the work.
> Bright is the noble work; but, being nobly bright, the work
> Should brighten the minds so that they may travel, through the
> true lights,
> To the True Light where Christ is the true door.
> In what manner it be inherent in the world the golden door
> defines:

9. *The Celestial Hierarchy* 3.1 in *Pseudo-Dionysius: The Complete Works* (trans. Colm Luibheid; Classics of Western Spirituality; New York: Paulist Press, 1987), 153–54.

10. Erwin Panofsky, *Abbot Suger: On the Abbey Church of St.-Denis and Its Art Treasures*, 2nd ed. by Gerda Panofsky-Soergel; Princeton: Princeton University Press, 1976), 64–65.

> The dull mind rises to truth through that which is material
> And, in seeing this light, is resurrected from its former
> submersion.[11]

Elsewhere Suger refers to the movement of spiritual ascent as ana-gogy. The verbal sense of the term _anagogia_ is "to lead up," and that is what Suger intended both the geometry of the architecture and the art of the chapel to do.

The elements of Gothic style introduced by Suger at St.-Denis were quickly taken up and developed by succeeding generations, and remain visible today in the cathedrals of Sens (1130ff.), Canterbury (1174), Notre-Dame (Paris, 1179), Chartres (Gothic, 1194), to name only a few. These structures, cruciform in shape and oriented toward the east, can be understood as translations of Scripture into stone. Like any good translation, the Gothic cathedrals accord great weight to the _literal_ sense of Scripture. In myriad ways, in stone, bronze, and colored glass, they relate the story of salvation, depicting Adam and Eve in paradise, the fall, and exile; the Old Testament saints and prophets; and above all, of course, the Christ, whose mother was the Virgin Mary, the betrothed of Joseph; whose baptizer was John; whose disciples were the Twelve, led by the fishermen Peter, Andrew, James, and John; whose intimate friends were John the Beloved, Mary and Martha, Mary of Magdala, Salome, and others; whose betrayer was Judas; whose evangelists were Matthew, Mark, Luke, and John; whose apostle was Paul; whose martyrs were Stephen, Dionysius, Polycarp, Justin; and on and on. All of these are faithfully recorded in the cathedrals' windows, murals, and sculptures with a profusion of detail comparable only to the Bible itself.

But the inimitable genius of the Gothic cathedral is not to be found in its graphic depiction of the Scripture's literal sense alone. It is to be found in the way they fulfill Suger's vision of an architecture that will entice spirits to see through the letter of faith to the Spirit, to see through the houses of worship of this passing age the glory of the Heavenly City to come.

BERNARD OF CLAIRVAUX AND THE TROPOLOGICAL SENSE

Bernard of Clairvaux (1090–1153) was a man of fiery love. Bernard's contemporaries recognized this, not least Abbot Suger himself. When both men were young, Bernard wrote to Suger upbraiding him for trav-

---

11. Ibid., 23.

eling about Europe on behalf of the king with "pomp and splendour." But when they were old, and Suger lay dying, Bernard wrote to him tenderly as his "dearest and most intimate friend." Subsequent generations have also remembered Bernard as a "guide for those who follow the path of love in Christian spirituality." This is seen in Dante's *Divine Comedy*. After Dante's love of Beatrice had drawn him as far as it could, it is Bernard who leads Dante onward into a vision of God and to "the Love that moves the sun and the other stars."[12]

Love, human but especially divine, is a cardinal theme of Bernard's biblical interpretation. Indeed, Bernard's aim in commenting on Scripture was to lead his readers into an experience of God's love. Apart from the *experience* of God's love, Bernard believed, it was impossible to have true knowledge or understanding in spiritual affairs. As he wrote to Pope Eugene III (ca. 1150) in his *Book on Consideration*: "If you are a saint, you have comprehended and you know; if you are not, be one and you will know through your own experience" (5.30).

Bernard's sermons on the Song of Songs offer an instructive illustration of his approach to biblical interpretation. The book is a collection of love poems between two lovers, and allegorical interpretation of the poetry was already an ancient tradition by Bernard's time. Bernard follows suit. He interprets the identity of the beloved in a variety of ways as fits the occasion: the soul, the church, the Word of God. Indeed, the identity of the beloved may change within a single sermon as he walks around viewing as flowers the metaphors of the Song. Again, Bernard may emphasize, *allegorically*, a doctrine of faith, concerning the resurrection or the church; he may emphasize, *tropologically*, the qualities of a spiritual director; he may emphasize, *anagogically*, the eschatological goal, the heavenly Jerusalem for which the soul aspires.

Yet, for all their variety, Bernard's sermons on the Song of Songs are principally designed to entice his hearers into longing for union with God. In this sense, the dominant mode of Bernard's exegesis is *tropological*. His sermons are performative utterances designed to effect the inward transformation of the hearer though love. They seek so to relate to the hearer as to effect longing within him or her. As Evelyn Underhill notes in her classic study on mysticism, "awakening" is the first step

---

12. Ewert H. Cousins in his preface to *Bernard of Clairvaux: Selected Works*, trans. G. R. Evans (Classics of Western Spirituality; New York: Paulist Press, 1987), 5. Not all in his own day regarded Bernard the epitome of love, particularly concerning his treatment of Abelard. Peter the Venerable abbot of Cluny chided Bernard: "You perform all the difficult religious duties; you fast, you watch, you suffer; but you will not endure the easy ones—you do not love." Quoted by Ralph Adams Cram in Peter Abelard, *Historia Calamitatum: The Story of My Misfortunes* (St. Paul, Minn.: Thomas A. Boyd, 1922), xvi.

toward the experience of mystical union, and this is what Bernard is about in his instruction to his monks of Clairvaux.[13] For this reason he willingly dwells on natural desire as the mode proper to devotion. Ultimately his intent was to lead his hearers into an experience of God's love. That was after all the purpose of the contemplative life and the goal of the spiritual exercises.

The homilies on the Song of Songs are rife with the rhetoric of desire. In the second of a long series of sermons,[14] the abbot opens with an exposition of the very first line of the book: "Let him kiss me with the kiss of his mouth." Bernard interprets the speaker as a patriarch of the Old Testament longing for the incarnation of Christ. As in Underhill's first step in the mystic's progression, Bernard "awakens" the hearer's interest by using the erotic language of the Song and then deftly lifts the hearer's mind up from the physical to the spiritual plane. The movement is anagogical, but the purpose is to entice the soul into the mystical union of love; that is, it is tropological.

> Very soon now there will be great rejoicing as we celebrate the feast of Christ's birth. But how I wish it were inspired by his birth! All the more therefore do I pray that the intense longing of those men of old, their heartfelt expectation, may be enkindled in me by these words: "Let him kiss me with the kiss of his mouth" [Song 1:1]. Many an upright man in those far-off times sensed within himself how profuse the graciousness that would be poured upon those lips. An intense desire springing from that perception impelled him to utter: "Let him kiss me with the kiss of his mouth," hoping with every fiber of his being that he might not be deprived of a share in a pleasure so great.
>
> The conscientious man of those days might repeat to himself: "Of what use to me the wordy effusions of the prophets? Rather let him who is the most handsome of the sons of men, let him kiss me with the kiss of his mouth. No longer am I satisfied to listen to Moses . . . Isaiah . . . Jeremiah. . . . For his living, active word is to me a kiss, not indeed an adhering of the lips that can sometimes belie a union of hearts, but an unreserved infusion of joys, a revealing of mysteries, a marvellous and indistinguishable mingling of the divine light with the enlightened mind, which, joined in truth to God, is one spirit with him.[15]

13. Evelyn Underhill, *Mysticism: A Study in the Nature and Development of Man's Spiritual Consciousness*, 12th ed. (New York: Noonday Press, 1955), 176–97.

14. *On the Song of Songs I* (vol. 2 of *Bernard of Clairvaux: Selected Works*; trans. Kilian Walsh; Cistercian Fathers Series 4. Spenser, Mass.: Cistercian Publications, 1971), 8.

15. *On the Song of Songs I*, 8–9.

For Bernard, the dance is in the dancing. In the words of Gerald Brun, "the point is not just to interpret the text but to experience it and be transformed by it."[16] The rhetor's pride lies in such a performance. It is not to *inform* his hearers but to *arouse* with the rhetoric of passion their sleeping souls. So in the sermon at hand, Bernard begins with the language of carnal love, as of course the poem itself does, but as the sermon proceeds affective language is left behind, and he lifts the hearer into a contemplation of the Word made flesh in Jesus. The sermon ends with the words: "this kiss is no other than the Mediator between God and man, himself a man, Christ Jesus, who with the Father and Holy Spirit lives and reigns as God for ever and ever. Amen."[17]

Elsewhere Bernard clarifies his intent: "since we are carnal and born of carnal desire (Rom 7:14), it is unavoidable that our desire and love should begin with the body and if it is rightly directed, it will then proceed by grace through certain stages, until the spirit is fulfilled (Gal 3:3)."[18] The concept of "stages of ascent" is fundamental to mysticism, as Bernard illustrates.

As noted earlier, Bernard and Abbot Suger were intimate friends who did not always see eye to eye. "What has gold to do with the sanctuary of Christ?" Bernard would ask the jewel-entranced abbot of St.-Denis. Suger believed that things perceptible, like sapphires on crosses and chalices of gold (prized for their luminosity), could lead to truths conceptual, like Light Eternal. Bernard entertained no such idea. He thought the height, length, and breadth of the new chapels being built by monasteries to be an obscene denial of the vow of poverty and humility. Yet we have seen how the abbot of Clairvaux did not blush to appeal to carnal desire to awaken in his hearers a longing for God who transcended materiality. The two abbots were not on the same track, but their common commitment to the Scriptures, interpreted by the Quadriga, meant that they were, for all that, still headed in the same direction.

PETER ABELARD AND THE ALLEGORICAL SENSE

Allegorical interpretation searches the literal or historical sense of Scripture with the aim of finding in it parables of the enduring mysteries of faith. For allegorical interpretation, the details of Scripture are never

---

16. Gerald Bruns, *Hermeneutics Ancient and Modern* (New Haven: Yale University Press, 1992), 140.
17. *On the Song of Songs I*, 15.
18. *Bernard of Clairvaux: Selected Works*, 204.

incidental or happenstance, but always signs of larger-than-life truths, about God, the world, and the economy of salvation. Allegorical interpretation requires the leaven of imagination, but it is often a highly rational and didactic enterprise. Its aim is not principally to entertain, but to instruct and to edify.

To illustrate allegorical interpretation, I have chosen to focus on Peter Abelard (1079–1143), not least because his own story is larger than life, and was already viewed by many of his own contemporaries as a text rich with moral and spiritual lessons, albeit not always of a positive kind.

If anyone seemed to be fortune's child from birth, it was Abelard. Firstborn in a family of minor French nobility, raised to be a soldier, Peter declined all rights of primogeniture and chose to pursue "Minerva rather than Mars" and live the life of "a peripatetic philosopher" in the cultured environs of Paris.[19] Handsome and talented in the composition of love songs, he is said to have had a voice that enflamed the admiration of married women and girls alike. Brilliant and supremely self-confident in philosophy, he bested the most famous teachers of his day in disputation. Fearlessly rational, he authored works that marked watersheds in intellectual history, and founded an institution of learning that eventually became the University of Paris. Finally, and most famously, he was one-half of the most celebrated love affair of the Middle Ages, together with Heloise, the most intellectually accomplished woman of her era.[20]

Yet, when Abelard finally authored his memoirs, he titled them *A History of Calamities*.[21]

He was, it seems, one of those people "whose infallible instinct leads straight to dangerous questions and provoking replies."[22] Hired by the canon of Notre-Dame to serve as tutor to his teenage niece Heloise, Abelard seduced her and was castrated in revenge. Investigating Dionysius the Aeropagite, Abelard characteristically but ill-advisedly proved the famous theologian could not have been the same man as the patron saint of the Abbey of St.-Denis, thereby invalidating the abbey's sacred relics, threatening its prestige as a site of pilgrimage, and jeopardizing

---

19. See Peter Abelard, *Historia Calamitatum: The Story of My Misfortune* (St. Paul, Minn.: Thomas A. Boyd, 1922), chap. 1. The *Historia* is the primary source for Abelard's life. For the intellectual setting of Abelard's life, see the brief but provocative introduction in this volume by Ralph Adams Cram.

20. See Elizabeth M. McNamer, *The Education of Heloise: Methods, Contents, and Purpose of Learning in the Twelfth Century* (Medieval Studies 8; Lewiston: Edwin Mellen, 1991).

21. A recent reprint of the Thomas A. Boyd publication is *Peter Abelard: The History of My Misfortune* (Mineola, N.Y.: Dover, 2005).

22. M. T. Clanchy, *Abelard: A Medieval Life* (Oxford: Blackwell, 1997), 331. The judgment is that of Etienne Gilson, *Heloise and Abelard* (Ann Arbor: University of Michigan Press, 1960), 105.

its major source of income. (Abelard escaped to Provins in Champaign, and his discovery was suppressed.) In his work *Sic et Non* (*Yes and No*), Abelard demonstrated that the authority of the church fathers could be summoned on both sides of a host of controversial issues, and thereby incurred the wrath of more tradition-minded theologians such as Bernard of Clairvaux. Abelard was forced to burn another of his own books, *Theologia Summi Boni*, with his own hands. And, if that were not enough, Abelard was formally condemned at the Council of Sens in 1141, two years before his death.

Already in his lifetime, estimates of Abelard varied widely.[23] To Heloise, Abelard was "the most famous man in the whole world"; he was her Socrates, her lord, and the father of her son Astralabe. To the students who came to him from all over Europe, he was the greatest dialectician since Aristotle. To Anselm of Laon (d. ca. 1117), his former teacher and adversary, Abelard was a "troublemaker," well deserving ecclesial condemnation. To Adam, then abbot of St.-Denis (where Abelard had found refuge from the enraged canon of Notre-Dame), Abelard was a traitor for discrediting the abbey's sacred myth. To the nuns of Heloise's convent called the Paraclete, Abelard was the exquisite composer of liturgical songs. To Bernard of Clairvaux, who orchestrated his condemnation at the Council of Sens (1140), he was "a monk without a rule, a prelate without responsibility, an abbot without discipline." To Abbot Peter the Venerable of Cluny, Abelard was a man "without equal, without superior," he was France's Socrates, the West's Plato, and Christ's own philosopher.

To himself, Abelard was "absolutely outstanding in logic" and, because of logic, "hateful to the world." By his own estimate, his writings were not attacks on faith, but efforts to illuminate the true character of faith by reason. To his writings we now turn, with special emphasis on the relation of *historia* and *allegoria* in his biblical interpretation.

The Quadriga

Like everyone schooled in Scripture in the Middle Ages, Abelard was well acquainted with the multiple senses of Scripture.[24] Exegetes often

---

23. For contemporary and modern estimates of Abelard, see M. T. Clanchy, *Abelard: A Medieval Life.*

24. For this analysis I am indebted to Rolf Peppermüller's work, *Abaelards Auslegung des Römerbriefes* (Beiträge zur Geschichte der Philosophie und Theologie des Mittelalters, new series, vol. 10; Münster: Aschendorff, 1972), 23–27. Also A. Victor Murray, *Abelard and St. Bernard: A Study in Twelfth Century 'Modernism'* (Manchester: Manchester University Press, 1967).

made pro forma reference to the Quadriga at the beginning of commentaries and then abandoned the terminology in its application. In his treatise on Romans Abelard follows this pattern. However, in his commentary on the six days of creation (the Hexameron),[25] which at Heloise's persistent urging he prepared for the nuns of the Paraclete, Abelard employs as sectional rubrics the terms *allegoria* and *moralitas*, with the stated acknowledgment that *historia* is the basis of all exegesis. What one discovers, however, is that Abelard's distinction among the various hermeneutical perspectives is highly fluid. What Abelard regards as Scripture's "literal sense" is profoundly shaped by allegorical and typological interpretation from the outset.

For example, commenting on the literal sense of the phrase, "And God said . . . and there was . . . ," Abelard sees God first reasoning ("And God said") and then acting ("and there was") according to a pattern of archetype-type. Using Platonic categories as his hermeneutic, Abelard employs typology to distinguish "between the intelligible and the sensible, the eternal and the temporal, between word and deed." All of this hinges, says the rationalist Abelard, "upon the recognition that the Word of God, first silent and in the mind, then spoken and completed in deed, is rational, providential and perfect," thereby proving that the created order is the product of God's love.[26]

In the opening verses of Genesis Abelard also discovers the Trinity hidden mystically in the words. He identifies the "spirit/wind" of God in 1:2 with the Holy Spirit, and he finds the Son within the scriptural "*God said*" (*dixit Deus*—implying the presence of "the Word," the second person of the Trinity). He also finds here a foreshadowing of the restoration of the image of God (the *imago Dei*), lost in the fall: the spirit of God, disturbing the waters like wind on the sea, is a sign of the Lord's regenerative act through the waters of baptism. Such waters, he says, are pervasive throughout the universe in their function as the re-creative power of God's love.

Other examples of allegorical interpretation could easily be cited. In a long excursus on circumcision in his commentary on Romans, Abelard notes that just as the Israelites had to pass through the waters of the Red Sea to reach the land of promise, so no one reaches the heavenly Jerusalem through the waters of baptism without the outpouring

---

25. *Expositio in Hexaemeron.* See Eileen Kearney, "Peter Abelard as Biblical Commentator: A Study of the *Expositio in Hexaemeron*" in *Petrus Abaelardus (1079–1142): Person, Werk und Wirkung,* ed. Rudolf Thomas, et al. (Trierer theologische Studien 38; Trier: Paulinus-Verlag, 1980), 199–210.

26. Ibid., 201.

of the (red) blood of Christ. But these examples suffice to show that in Abelard's exegetical practice, *historia* and *allegoria* pass easily and quickly into each other. *Historia* is the nominal foundation of allegory, but *historia* is itself already charged with allegorical significance from the outset. In this respect, Abelard simply exemplifies a trait common to many theologians of his day.[27]

Reason and Tradition

What marked Abelard out as a dangerous man in the eyes of many contemporaries was his confidence that reason—rather than tradition—must be primary in drawing out the deeper meaning of faith. Abelard's *Sic et Non* juxtaposed quotations from the Bible and the church fathers in such a way as to highlight their mutual contradiction, their yes *and* no. By showing that patristic witnesses could be summoned on both sides of a theological or scriptural issue, Abelard effectively discredited the church fathers as an authoritative source in disputation and underscored the role of reason in deciding between conflicting interpretations.

Abelard's opponents feared and despised his dialectics. To Bernard of Clairvaux, Abelard's method was little more than "arguing with boys" too immature to handle sacred things. To William of St. Thierry, confidant of Bernard of Clairvaux, Abelard was "the maddest and most dangerous" monk alive, because he elevated personal opinion over sacred tradition. But for Abelard, the internal dissonances within the patristic tradition served perfectly to fulfill the heuristic motto he had chosen for himself and his students: "By doubting we come to inquiry, and by inquiry we perceive the truth." It is this emphasis on the independence of reason that the school founded by Abelard on Mont-Sainte-Geneviève was to live on in the form of the University of Paris, that is, *outside* the monastery in the secular world.

The Historia of Jesus and the Revelation of Eternal Love

Abelard's bold reading of Scripture, and even bolder confidence in the power of reason to guide such reading, led him to propose his own

27. Ibid., 208.

account of the nature of the atonement.[28] If God is love, Abelard reasons, then it would be improper to speak of an act of divine love, such
as the redemption of humankind, as being compelled or necessitated
by something extrinsic to God's nature. In Abelard's view, this was the
weakness of two traditional theories of the atonement still current in his
day. According to one, Jesus' death was a result of a transaction between
God and the devil, from whom God ransomed humankind after Adam's
fall. According to the second, Christ's death was occasioned by the need
to satisfy the affront to God's dignity occasioned by sin. Neither theory,
Abelard reasons, measures up to the logic of divine love. Both theories
imply that God became something he had not been before the transaction of Christ's death. Abelard reasoned that if God is love, that love
must be constant, ubiquitous, and unchanging. God is love *before* and
after the fall of Adam, *before* and *after* the crucifixion. In a sense, for
Abelard the assertion that "God is love" is an axiom that precedes the
historia of Christ, and therefore sets the context for its interpretation.

But how does Abelard know that God is love? The answer, of
course, is the gospel story of Jesus, and the literal or historical sense of
Scripture. In the Gospel of John Jesus says, "Greater love has no man
than this, that a man lay down his life for his friends" (15:13 RSV).
When Heloise writes Abelard (Letter Four) imploring him to reassure
her that his love for her had been pure and not simply lust, he quotes
this verse in an effort to console her (Letter Five).[29] Whatever her love
for him, Christ is worthy of a still greater love. Her mind should be
set on Christ, not on Abelard! Similarly, whatever Christ's love, God's
love is greater still. For Jesus himself said, "The Father is greater than
I" (John 14:28). If Christ dies in demonstration of his love, then how
much more must God's love be! This is the conclusion the apostle Paul
reaches: "Why, one will hardly die for a righteous man—though perhaps for a good man one will dare even to die. But God shows his
love for us in that while we were yet sinners Christ died for us" (Rom.
5:7–8 RSV). Through the interpretive principle of "from the lesser to
the greater," based on Scripture itself, Abelard reasons that God's love
cannot be less than what is revealed in Jesus Christ.

The term Abelard uses to describe the work of Christ, rather than
redemption or *atonement*, is reconciliation (2 Cor. 5:18–19). God's love

---

28. The book to read is Richard E. Weingart, *The Logic of Divine Love: A Critical Analysis of the Soteriology of Peter Abelard* (Cambridge: Cambridge University Press, 1970).

29. See *The Letters of Abelard and Heloise,* translated with an introduction by Betty Radice (New York: Penguin, 1974).

is *from the beginning* reconciling love, and it is from the beginning *pro nobis* ("for us"). We alone as human beings are the object of God's act in Christ—not the devil, not some aspect of God needing appeasement. Sin is an act against God's love. Sin estranges the sinner from God. The sinner is reconciled, is brought back into relationship with God, by the prevenient love (grace) of God manifested everywhere in creation and nowhere more than in the life and death of Jesus Christ, who is the divine Word (Logos) and Son of God. Jesus is God's representative in the world; he is humankind's representative before God. When Jesus graciously heals the sick, gives sight to the blind, enables the lame to walk, and forgives the sinner, he incarnates and bestows the gift of God's reconciling love by arousing compassionate love in return. These thoughts appear in the second stanza in a Good Friday hymn composed for the nuns of the Paraclete:

> For they are ours, O Lord, our deeds, our deeds,
>   Why must thou suffer torture for our sin,
> Let our hearts suffer for thy passion, O Lord,
> That shear compassion may thy mercy win.[30]

It is this logic of divine love that causes Abelard to see evidence of God's love in all creation. God's love is prevenient and is experienced as grace. It is extended to us objectively before we recognize its presence subjectively.

For Abelard, the central mystery of Christian faith is that the grace-filled acts of Jesus should be extended even to the point of accepting the terrible suffering of crucifixion and death. Sacrifice is truly involved. But it is a sacrifice whose why and wherefore is to be found solely and exclusively in Christ's love for others. Self-sacrifice is simply what love does. It seeks reconciliation at all costs: "Father, forgive them, for they know not what they do." At the same time, Jesus is the revelation of the eternal being of God. God cannot *be* less than what Jesus *does*. This makes what takes place on the cross cosmic in scope and significance. Jesus is none other than the Word of God, the Logos become flesh, the revelation of the burning heart of God.

At this point, in the biblical portrait of Christ, the literal sense of Scripture is revelatory and redemptive in itself. It needs no allegorical interpretation. Instead, it has the power to make everything else into

---

30. Titled, "For Good Friday: The Third Nocturne," in *The Letters of Abelard and Heloise*, trans. with an introduction by Betty Radice (New York: Penguin, 1974), 295.

an allegory, or type, of itself—even perhaps the calamitous life of Peter Abelard, who died condemned by the church, but who lives on in its memory as one who truly was in his time, in the words of Peter the Venerable, "Christ's own philosopher."

CONCLUSION

Different as they were in so many ways, Suger, Bernard, and Abelard shared with one another and with other theologians of their age the conviction that a single passage of Scripture could be validly interpreted in a variety of different ways. For them, the Quadriga was not an artificial and useless distraction from the real meaning of Scripture, but a helpful guide to plumbing its depths of spiritual meaning, now in the mode of what we can hope for (*anagogia*), now in the mode of how we are to live (*tropologia*), now in the mode of what we are to believe (*allegoria*).

Chapter 8
What Is the Center of Scripture?

Does the Bible have a center? Physically, it does. Open the Bible at the middle and you find yourself in the book of Psalms. From there one can work backward to the Pentateuch and historical books or forward to the Wisdom literature and the Prophets. This is a handy trick to know, because otherwise the sheer size of the Bible makes it hard to find one's way around.

Does the Bible likewise have a *thematic* center, a focal point for interpretation? If it did, that too would be good to know, since it could aid the exegete in the work of interpretation. Indeed, the Christian tradition has generally affirmed that the Scriptures *do* have a center, as we have already seen. Irenaeus's rule of faith represented one effort to articulate the central thrust of Scripture. For Athanasius in his dispute with Arius in the early fourth century, the canon's center or *scope* (Greek *skopos*, "target" or "aim") was Christ in his humanity and deity. Nevertheless, from time to time, the church's interpretation of Scripture has been so overwhelmed by the proliferation of detail, ornament, and tangents that the center has been hard to identify. When this has happened, Christians have found it necessary to renew the question: What is the center of Scripture?

One era when the church renewed its search for the thematic center of Scripture was the Reformation. One key figure in this renewed search was Martin Luther (1486–1546), who found the center of Scripture in the good news of justification by faith alone. Luther's understanding of

113

the center of Scripture influenced many subsequent generations. But, as we shall see, Luther's theological heirs have also at time modified Luther's understanding in subtle but important ways.

THE CENTER OF SCRIPTURE
AND LUTHER'S REFORMATION

"I am seeking and thirsting for nothing else than a gracious God," Luther wrote to his young friend and colleague Philipp Melanchthon (1497–1560).[1] For many years, despite hours of intense Bible study and prayer, Luther could not find what he was looking for. He was in anguish. In a retrospective written in 1545, a year before his death, Luther set down an account of what the problem had been. Luther kept stumbling over a troublesome verse in Romans: "For [in the gospel] the righteousness of God is revealed through faith for faith" (1:17). Luther hated the expression "the righteousness of God" because, he tells us, he understood it to mean "the righteousness through which God is just and punishes sinners and the unjust." Such a God, the God who punishes, he could not love. "I hated him," he writes.

> At last . . . meditating day and night, I gave heed to the context of the words, namely, "For [in the gospel] is the righteousness of God revealed, as it is written, 'He who through faith is righteous shall live.'" There I began to understand that the righteousness of God is that by which the righteous lives by a gift of God, namely, by faith. And this is the meaning: the righteousness of God is revealed by the gospel, namely, the passive righteousness with which merciful God justifies us by faith, as it is written, "He who through faith is righteous shall live." Here I felt that I was altogether born again and had entered paradise itself through open gates.[2]

Running through Scripture with his memory, Luther recalled analogous genitival formulations that denoted an action on God's part: "the work of God, that is, what God does in us, the power of God, with which he makes us strong, the wisdom of God, with which he makes us wise, the strength of God, the salvation of God, the glory of God." In each instance, the reference is not something the believer performs

---

1. See *What Luther Says: An Anthology*, vol. 2, compiled by Ewald M. Plass (St. Louis: Concordia, 1959), 603, #1836.

2. From "Preface to the Complete Edition of Luther's Latin Writings, Wittenberg, 1545," quoted in *Martin Luther's Basic Theological Writings*, ed. Timothy F. Lull; rev. ed. (Minneapolis: Fortress, 2005), 8–9.

but something one receives, just as the earth does not produce rain but rather receives it (passively) from above. So too, Luther concluded, in the case of God's righteousness: "We are righteous only by the imputation of a merciful God through faith in His word."[3]

With this discovery, Luther came to a new understanding of the center of Scripture. The center of Scripture is the gospel, the good news that God forgives sins for Christ's sake, good news to be received by faith, and by faith alone. Christ alone (*sola Christus*) is God's Word incarnate and, since all have sinned and fall short of the glory of God, it is faith alone (*sola fides*) in Christ (Rom. 3:28) that puts human beings in a right relationship with God (Gal. 2:16),[4] not love as in Augustine (Gal. 5:22), or any "work" of the Law or act of penance or act of reason. God justifies the sinner as an act of pure grace alone (*sola gratia*; Rom. 3:21–26). As love alone binds two human beings in effable union, so faith alone binds the believer to God.

As these remarks suggest, Luther's conception of the center of Scripture has two poles, a more objective pole and a more subjective one. On the objective side, Luther understands the center of faith to be what God has done in Christ. According to this understanding, the center of Scripture is "what inculcates Christ" ("was Christum treibet"). "All the genuine sacred books agree in this, that all of them preach and inculcate Christ. For all the Scriptures show us Christ. . . . Whatever does not teach Christ is not yet apostolic, even though St. Peter or St. Paul does the teaching. Again, whatever preaches Christ would be apostolic, even if Judas, Annas, Pilate, and Herod were doing it."[5]

Luther also makes the point elsewhere with beautiful simplicity: the Scriptures are "the swaddling cloths and the manger in which Christ lies. . . . Simple and lowly are these swaddling cloths, but dear is the treasure, Christ, who lies in them."[6] On the subjective side, the center of Scripture is the teaching that God's forgiveness in Christ is to be received *by faith alone*. This is the doctrine of justification. For Luther, the gospel of justification was "the ruler and judge over all other Christian doctrines": "For if the doctrine of justification is lost, the whole of Christian doctrine is lost."[7]

---

3. *Lectures on Romans* (vol. 25 of *Luther's Works*; St. Louis: Concordia, 1957–1972), 274–75.
4. Luther translated Rom. 3:29 adding the word "alone," which is not in the Greek text; he defends his translation in "On Translating: An Open Letter," *Luther's Works*, 35:175–208.
5. *Luther's Works*, 35:396.
6. *Luther's Works*, 35:236.
7. First quotation from Weimarer Ausgabe 39, 1:205; the second from *Luther's Works*, 26: "Lectures on Galatians 1535, Chapters 1–4.9."

Luther did not come to his understanding of the center of Scripture all at once. Despite his recollections quoted above, Luther made gradual progress toward his new insight over the course of many years, as his early writings amply demonstrate. Nor did he draw the full consequences of his discovery all at once. Nevertheless, much of Luther's theology, both before and after his "Reformation discovery," can be understood in light of his Reformation understanding of the center of Scripture.

The Psalms (1513–1515) and the Quadriga

Luther's early approach to biblical interpretation offers a striking study in novelty and continuity with previous tradition. This is evident from Luther's early lectures on the Psalms, his first lectures as a young professor of Old Testament at the University of Wittenberg.

One of Luther's first acts as a teacher in Wittenberg was to instruct the university printer to produce an edition of the Psalms free of all the glosses and marginalia accumulated over the centuries.[8] Students were to receive the Psalms with wide blank margins and white spaces between the lines, unencumbered by the interpretation of the church fathers. The reverend doctor would himself engage the text, making philological observations, and quoting the church fathers as suited him, his favorites being Augustine, Ambrose, and Bernard. This act, Gerald Bruns suggests, symbolically marks the transition from ancient to modern hermeneutics: "In a stroke Luther wiped the Sacred Page clean as if to begin the history of interpretation over again, this time to get it right."[9]

Despite this, Luther's interpretation of the Psalms was quite traditional in important ways. Luther interpreted the Psalms as literal prophecies of Christ, whose spiritual meaning was to be unpacked by appeal to the various spiritual senses of the Quadriga. "Whatever is said literally concerning the Lord Jesus Christ as to His person must be understood allegorically of a help that is like Him and of the church conformed to Him in all things. And at the same time this must be understood tropologically of any spiritual and inner man against his flesh and the outer man."[10] At this point, Luther still thought of Christ as an example which we are to imitate, by modeling ourselves on his life of suffering humility.

---

8. The *Glossa Ordinaria* was compiled by Walafried Strabo (d. 849) and in the *Glossa Interlinearis* by Anselm of Laon (d. 1117).

9. *Hermeneutics Ancient and Modern* (New Haven: Yale University Press, 1992), 139–40.

10. *Luther's Works*, 10:7.

Over time, though, Luther's understanding of the Psalter and its application to the life of the Christian changed in a subtle way.[11] Increasingly, Luther understood the Psalms as setting forth Christ not as a model to be imitated, but as a promise to be grasped by faith. By the time he arrived at the later psalms in the lecture series, that is, in the second term (1514–1515), a hermeneutical shift had slowly begun to appear in Luther's exegesis in which he saw an analogous relationship between the life setting of the psalmist in the old covenant and that of the Christian in the new: he viewed both as living in faith in the good news of divine promise. The psalmist lived in expectation of God's promise concerning the future advent of the Messiah, the Christian in anticipation of Christ's spiritual advent in times of temptation and trial. Luther extended this interpretation anagogically to the second coming in which Christ will rise up against the antichrist enthroned in Rome. In all instances, the word of promise, the gospel of Christ, is heard in the inmost heart by faith alone.

According to James Preus, *the* seed of what was to become the Reformation principle of justification by faith alone (*sola fidei*) is already visible in Luther's later Psalm lectures.[12] Faith is life lived under the promises of God. Faith is not obedience or submission[13] to an external law that requires nothing of the heart. Faith is trust in God's word of promise. It is the confidence that God does not lie, that God's promises are trustworthy. Word and faith are thus inextricably linked, for God is known only in and through his Word. For Luther, therefore, tropology now has less to do with what *the believer* should do in ethical response to God's act in Christ than with what *God* does in conforming the believer to a life of faith in Christ as God's Word. This stood in contrast to the traditional view that the merits of Christ's faith and sacrifice were mystically conveyed to the individual through sacramental reenactment in the Eucharist. And Luther was still two years away from writing his 95 theses against Indulgences!

The Authority of Scripture

On April 17, 1521, Luther stood in the midst of the imperial assembly at the Diet of Worms before a table laden with his writings. Luther was

---

11. For this discussion, I am indebted to James Samuel Preus, *From Shadow to Promise: Old Testament Interpretation from Augustine to the Young Luther* (Cambridge: Harvard University Press, 1969).

12. Ibid., esp. chap. 13.

13. Luther faults "Mohammedans" (the lions at the eastern gates of Europe) in equal measure with Catholics in their misunderstanding of God's act in Christ.

asked two questions by Johann Eck: "Are these your books, and do you recant what is in them?"

The proceedings allowed for no debate. Luther's position was by now well known. In his view, the doctrines and practices of the church were, at significant points, no longer in continuity with the center of the Scriptures. In *The Babylonian Captivity of the Churches*, published in the previous year, Luther had reduced the number of sacraments from seven to two, accepting only those which contained both visible sign and—significantly—the *promise* of Christ: baptism and the Eucharist. He rejected the doctrine of transubstantiation as too philosophically speculative.[14] And he rejected the view of the Eucharist as a priestly work of sacrifice on the grounds that it voided the role of faith.

As for the position of the church, that too was well known. It had been enunciated at Rome in May 1518, by the papal court theologian, and in Luther's presence at Augsburg in October 1518, by Cardinal Cajetan, and at the Leipzig Debate in July 1519, by the Dominican friar Johannes Eck: The hierarchy of the church is the outer manifestation of an inner spiritual order, with the pope acting simply as the visible representative of Christ, the invisible head of the church.[15] The authority of the pope and the councils is greater than that of the Scriptures, for the church and its councils are prior to the Scriptures, as the Scriptures themselves bear witness (Acts 15; Gal. 2). The Scriptures are therefore not authentic without the authority of the church, which decides between conflicting opinions. While it is true that the councils, like the papacy, are made up of fallible men, through the guidance of the Holy Spirit their pronouncements are infallible.

As the reader knows full well, Luther did not recant. His reply on the next morning before the assembly was direct: "Unless I am convinced by scripture and plain reason—I do not accept the authority of popes and councils, for they have contradicted each other—my conscience is captive to the word of God. I cannot and will not recant anything, for to go against conscience is neither right nor safe. Here I stand; I can not do otherwise. God help me. Amen."[16]

---

14. Luther argued that Aquinas, the author of the doctrine, had misunderstood Aristotle, upon whom the doctrine was based. See *The Babylonian Captivity of the Church*. "The Babylonian Captivity of the Church, 1520," trans. A. T. W. Steinhaeuser et al. in *Selected Writings of Martin Luther*, vol. 1: *1517–1520*, ed. Theodore G. Tappert (Minneapolis: Fortress, 2007), 355–478. The doctrine was first introduced by Peter Comestor (ca. 1100–1179) in a treatise on the sacraments; it was adopted by the Fourth Lateran Council in 1215.

15. See Anton Bodem, *Das Wesen der Kirche nach Kardinal Cajetan: Ein Beitrag zur Ekklesiologie im Zeitalter der Reformation* (Trierer theologische Studien 25; Trier: Paulinus-Verlag, 1971), 211.

16. See Roland Bainton, *Here I Stand: A Life of Martin Luther* (New York: Abingdon-Cokesbury, 1950), 185.

For Luther, the Scriptures' news of a gracious God was the most precious thing in heaven—or on earth. It could not be sacrificed or subordinated to any human power, no matter how exalted. It was this conviction that brought Luther into conflict with the authorities of his day. As Luther was to argue over his lifetime, the Scriptures have supreme authority in matters of faith because the Scriptures alone (*sola scriptura*) proclaim the good news of God's saving grace in Jesus Christ. Having found at last a gracious God in the Scriptures, Luther was not going to let any human authority muffle its liberating voice.

The Center of Scripture and the Nature of the Canon

Luther's understanding of the center of the Scriptures had important implications for his understanding of the canon as a whole. One way this expressed itself was in terms of the distinction between law and gospel. According to Luther, God's law sets before us what God expects *of* us, while the gospel sets forth what God does *for* us in Christ. The Scriptures contain both law and gospel, but in the final analysis it is only the gospel that is *unique* to Scripture. God's law is known to all humankind through conscience and by reason. But the gospel is known only where it is actively proclaimed, for faith comes "from hearing" (*ex auditu*; cf. Rom. 10:17).

One consequence of this view is that Luther placed special value on those portions of Scripture that in his view set forth the gospel most clearly. For Luther, this meant the Gospel of John and the letters of Paul, especially Romans and Galatians. In the language of contemporary scholarship, these books served as Luther's canon within the canon. They set forth the key themes in light of which the rest of the Bible was to be interpreted.

Another consequence of Luther's view was his readiness to question the apostolic authority of any book in the Bible that did not in his view "inculcate Christ." A case in point is the Epistle of James, which Luther famously referred to as an "epistle of straw." Although the letter speaks of faith in God, it does not once mention Christ's passion, resurrection, office, or set forth the promise of the forgiveness of sins by faith. Luther held a similar view of Hebrews, Jude, and Revelation. Accordingly, Luther placed these books at the back of his translation of the New Testament (1522), where he lists them *unnumbered*. The boldness of Luther's verdict may continue to shock us today. Still, it flows logically from Luther's conviction that "whatever does not teach Christ is not yet apostolic, even though St. Peter or St. Paul does the teaching."

THE CENTER OF SCRIPTURE
AND PROTESTANT SCHOLASTICISM

In the generation immediately after the Reformation, Luther's understanding of the center of Scripture remained highly influential among Protestants. But Luther's heirs also changed Luther's vision in subtle but important ways, often without being aware that they were doing so. Some Protestants lay greater emphasis on what they took to be the *objective* side of Luther's insight. Chief among these were a group of theologians who belonged to a movement that has come to be known as Protestant scholasticism.

Protestant scholasticism was a university-based movement that flourished chiefly in German-speaking lands from 1550 to 1750. These Protestant scholastics wanted to be loyal guardians of the Reformation, but gradually they developed an approach to the Bible that differed markedly from that of Luther and the other Reformers. In place of Luther's emphasis on Christ himself as the center of Scripture (the "treasure" wrapped up in Scripture), the scholastics began to conceive of the heart of Scripture as doctrine *about* Christ. The Bible now was less a book of *news* to be heard and trusted, as it was a book of *teaching* to be understood and believed. To describe that doctrine as accurately as possible, they reintroduced the vocabulary of medieval scholasticism that the Reformers had generally avoided (hence the movement's name). In fairness, the scholastics never lost touch with the importance of repentance, faith, and obedience. However, they increasingly interpreted all this in terms of giving intellectual assent to the doctrines contained in Scripture.

The Protestant scholastics were also preoccupied with establishing the supreme authority of Scripture over against Roman Catholic claims on behalf of the pope. In the process, they gave the doctrine of biblical inspiration a prominence far beyond anything it had in Luther's thought. The scholastics argued that since God directly dictated every word of Scripture (verbal inspiration), the Bible mirrored God's own perfect truthfulness, and was free from error in every respect (plenary inspiration). In the words of Johannes Quenstedt (1617–1688), professor of theology at the University of Wittenberg, "each and every-thing presented to us in Scripture is absolutely true, whether it pertains to doctrine, ethics, history, chronology, topography, or onomastics."[17] This is a long way from Luther's verdict that James is an epistle of straw. The New Testament historian William Baird summarizes the difference: "For [Luther] the Bible was the word of God, for [Lutheran orthodoxy] the words of the Bible were the words of God."[18]

While Protestant scholasticism had largely died out in Europe by the early 1800s, it lived on in America well into the nineteenth century at schools such as Princeton Theological Seminary. Charles Hodge (1797–1878), a professor at the seminary, declared, "Faith . . . in Christ involves faith in the Scriptures as the Word of God, and faith in the Scriptures as the Word of God is faith in their plenary inspiration. That is, it is the persuasion that they are not the product of the fallible intellect of man but of the infallible intellect of God."[19] In the early twentieth century, the newly born fundamentalist movement identified biblical inerrancy as one of the fundamentals of Christian faith, helping to ensure that this understanding of the "center" of Scripture would remain influential up to the present day.

THE CENTER OF SCRIPTURE AND PIETISM

Given the religious and social turmoil in Europe following the death of Luther in 1546, culminating in the devastating Thirty Years' War of Religion (1618–1648), it is little wonder that many Christians sought refuge in an unyielding creedal and sacramental orthodoxy. In time, however, there arose within German Protestantism, weary of war and the aridity of doctrinal controversy, a new spiritual awakening that moved in a different direction. This movement, which has come to be known as Pietism, sought the center of Scripture on the *subjective* side of Luther's correlation of Christ and faith.[20]

17. Johannes Quenstedt, *Systema*, P. 1 C. 4, S. 2, q. 5. Quoted in Robert D. Preus, *The Theology of Post-Reformation Lutheranism*, vol. 1: *A Study of Theological Prolegomena* (St. Louis: Concordia Publishing House, 1970), 346.

18. William Baird, *From Deism to Tübingen* (vol. 1 of *History of New Testament Research*; Minneapolis: Fortress, 1992), 58.

19. Charles Hodge, "The Inspiration of Holy Scripture, Its Nature and Proof," in *The Princeton Theology, 1812–1921*, ed. Mark A. Noll (Phillipsburg, N.J.: Presbyterian & Reformed Publishing, 1983), 137.

20. The definitions of Pietism, particularly its development after 1750, are wide-ranging, with one scholar equating it with German Protestantism as such (see, e.g., Michel Godfroid, "Gab es den deutschen Pietismus? Geschichte eines zur Polemik geschaffenen Begriffs," in *Zur neueren Pietismusforschung*, ed. Martin Greschat (Darmstadt: Wissenschaftliche Buchgesellschaft, 1977), 91–110.

Pietism has proven to be an enormously influential movement since its birth in the later 1600s. In view of its importance, we shall examine it in some detail, focusing especially on two key figures, Philipp Jakob Spener, and August Hermann Francke.

Philipp Jakob Spener (1635–1705)

The origins of Pietism in Germany are often associated with the publication in 1675 of Philipp Jakob Spener's *Pia Desideria* ("Pious Wishes"), a short work that bore the subtitle: "Heartfelt Desire for a God-pleasing Reform of the True Evangelical Church."[21] But Spener's work appeared first as the preface to a reprint of a series of sermons by Johann Arndt (1555–1621), and it is worth taking a short look at Arndt's sermons before turning to *Pia Desideria*.

Arndt's sermons were first published in 1605 under the title *True Christianity*. For Arndt, interpreting the Bible literally meant internalizing its injunctions: "God did not reveal the Holy Scriptures so that they might externally on paper remain a dead letter, but that they might become living in us in spirit and faith and that a completely new inner man might arise. [If this does not occur], the Scriptures are of no use to us."[22] This theme suffuses the whole of *True Christianity*:

> As we have inherited, through the physical birth, the sins from Adam, so we must inherit righteousness through faith from Christ. And as we inherited pride, covetousness, lust, and all impurity through the flesh of Adam, so we must be made holy, purified, and renewed in our nature by the Holy Spirit and all pride, covetousness, lust, and envy must die in us and we must receive, from Christ, a new spirit, a new heart, thoughts, and mind, just as we received sinful flesh out of Adam.
>
> . . . All works that are to be pleasing to God must come from this new birth, out of Christ, out of the Holy Spirit, and out of faith.
>
> Thus, we live in the new birth and the new birth in us. Thus, we live in Christ and Christ in us (Gal. 2:20). Thus, we live in the spirit and the spirit of Christ in us. This new birth and the fruits of this birth Saint Paul describes in Ephesians 4:23 . . . 2 Corinthians 3:17 . . . Colossians 3:10 . . . Titus 3:5 . . . Ezekiel 11:18 [*sic*]. . . .

21. *Pia Desideria*, trans. and ed. with an introduction by Theodore G. Tappert (Eugene, Or: Wipf & Stock, 2002).
22. *Johann Arndt: True Christianity*, trans. with an introduction by Peter Erb (Classics of Western Spirituality; New York: Paulist Press, 1979), 49.

The new birth thus arises from the incarnation of Christ. . . . Since Christ walked his humble path on earth among men, so he must live in you, and renew the image of God in you.[23]

Already in Arndt's work, we see a refocusing of the center of Scripture in terms of *Christ's presence* in the life of the believer. Arndt's *True Christianity* was reissued numerous times after its first publication in 1605. Decades later it was the first book to be printed in the German language in America by Benjamin Franklin in Philadelphia. A century and a half after that, it shaped the childhood piety of Albert Schweitzer, the most famous of all Protestant missionaries in the first half of the twentieth century and one of that century's greatest New Testament scholars.[24] No wonder *True Christianity* has been called "the classic devotional book of Protestantism."[25]

Spener's *Pia Desideria,* originally published as a preface to Arndt's sermons, soon appeared as a stand-alone volume. The work provided needed direction to a little movement in Frankfurt known as the *Collegium Pietatis* (whence "Pietism"), which Spener had initiated in his own home in 1670. This marked the beginnings of Pietism as both a religious and a social movement.[26]

Spener's first proposal called for making Scripture the focus of every Christian's life through the daily, verse-by-verse reading of the Bible, both privately and within the household. This approach was undoubtedly influenced by his student years in Strasbourg and Geneva among Calvinists where he had become acquainted with the Reformed church's emphasis on biblical exegesis, church discipline, and catechetical instruction. This injunction to study Scripture must also be noted in stark contrast, as Spener himself does, to the contemporary papal encyclical prohibiting the reading of the Bible by Catholic laity.[27]

More controversial to Lutheran orthodoxy was Spener's second proposal calling for the reintroduction of the "ancient and apostolic kind of church meeting," based on 1 Corinthians 14:26–40, to form as it were an *ecclesiola in ecclesia* (a "little church within the church"). In

---

23. Ibid., 39.
24. Ibid., 1.
25. Johannes Wallmann, "Johann Arndt (1555–1621)," in *The Pietist Theologians,* ed. Carter Lindberg (Oxford: Blackwell, 2005), 21.
26. On pietism as a social and political movement, see "Der hallische Pietismus als politisch-soziale Reformbewegung des 18. Jahrhunderts (1953)," by Carl Hinrichs in *Zur neueren Pietismusforschung,* ed. Greschat, 243–58. On Spener see K. James Stein, "Philipp Jakob Spener (1635–1705)," in *Pietist Theologians,* ed. Lindberg, 84–99; also Stein's biography, *Philipp Jakob Spener: Pietist Patriarch* (Chicago: Covenant Press, 1986).
27. *Pia Desideria,* 95.

these conventicles lies the origin of the Protestant Bible study group; its purpose was rooted more in the pedagogy of spiritual formation than in the mastery of theology. These groups were to be led by pastors or trained laymen—not simply for the sake of disseminating biblical knowledge, but to transform the lives of the participants into a "spiritual priesthood"—thereby fulfilling more intentionally Luther's doctrine of the priesthood of all believers.[28]

Spener's third through sixth proposals are as follows. The third sets forth the admonition that the hallmark of the practicing Christian is not knowledge but love (so John 13:34–35; 15:12; 1 John 3:10, 18; 4:7–8, 11–13, 21),[29] or as Luther put it quoting Paul, faith active in love (Gal. 5:6), something Pietists believed was lacking in all kinds of theological orthodoxy. Spener's fourth proposal is a response to the intolerant and divisive sectarian controversies that had characterized the church of the post-Reformation period, namely, to practice heartfelt love toward the heretic and the unbeliever, following the Samaritan's example in Christ's parable (Luke 10:29–37). At the same time (the fifth proposal), the believer was to give a forceful, but modest defense, based on Scripture, of the truth of what he believed.[30] The sixth proposal pertained to the reform of education, especially the training of theological students. Spener set the ground rules for what was to become, in Germany at least, the mind-set of rational, academic discussion, including such mundane artifacts of thoughtful interchange as the scholarly journal, the alphabetical index, and the footnote.[31]

Taken together, Spener's proposals represent a powerful way of conceiving the center of Scripture. If Christ was the center of Scripture, as Luther insisted, then Christ had to become the center of the Christian's life. Nothing demonstrated this Jesus-centered faith more than the hymnody of Pietism, which lives on today in countless hymnbooks.[32] According to Martin Gerl, Pietism's emphasis upon being Christian in word and deed created a real alternative to the harder, intolerant face of orthodoxy. But more than this, Pietism (again through its public disputes with doctrinaire Lutheranism) promoted the concept of free

---

28. In 1739 in England, John Wesley formed "United Societies," dividing them into "classes" of twelve persons of Bible study and mutual betterment, to be guided by "General Rules" that Wesley devised. These rules may be found in *The Book of Discipline of the United Methodist Church*. The earliest recorded Christian "societies" in England date to 1678 in London. See C. T. Winchester, *The Life of John Wesley* (London: Macmillan, 1924), 65.

29. *Pia Desideria*, 95.

30. Ibid., 98.

31. See Martin Gierl, *Pietismus und Aufklärung* (Göttingen: Vandenhoeck & Ruprecht, 1997), 576.

32. For English-speaking Pietist hymn writers none excelled Isaac Watts (1674–1748), Charles Wesley (1707–1788), and Fanny J. Crosby (1820–1915).

association (Spener's *ecclesiola in ecclesia*), the unfettered and public dissemination of opinion, the spiritual autonomy and therefore elevation of the individual, and the spirit of critical self-examination and tolerance.

For Spener, imitating Christ also meant moderation in dress, food, and drink as well as the prohibition of such "indifferent things" (adiaphora) as card playing, dancing, and attendance at the theater. Not surprisingly, perhaps, the Pietist movement aroused charges of "Pharisaic hypocrisy" and heresy. Eventually, Pietists were even expelled from clerical and public office, and occasionally imprisoned. The most accomplished of those so persecuted during the latter part of the seventeenth century in Germany was August Hermann Francke, whose work remains the high watermark of Pietism in that country. More than any other person, it is Franke, Spener's student and protégé, who applied the Arndt/Spener emphasis on spiritual rebirth to biblical hermeneutics, the art and task of interpretation.

August Hermann Francke (1663–1727)

Francke was a trained philologian, preacher, pedagogue, entrepreneur, social activist, and organizational genius. Starting with "four Taler and 16 Groschen" (ca. five dollars),[33] he founded multilevel schools for poor children, including an orphanage, along with commercial enterprises and farms to provide his numerous institutions with sustained material support. His work became a model for Christian activists across the Christian world. The almost fifty buildings of the Franckesche Stiftungen, now restored with a cultural and pedagogical focus, still stand in Halle an die Salle (Germany), the center of Francke's activities.

Francke's own spiritual rebirth had occurred in 1687 after years of theological training in Leipzig and Lüneberg and, as often observed, is reminiscent of Augustine's garden experience.[34] Like Paul's and Luther's experiences as well, with their definitive before and after, Francke's own experience of spiritual rebirth became for him the sine qua non of every true Christian believer and the indispensable hermeneutical principle for all true biblical interpretation. It was, however,

33. Erich Beyreuther, *August Hermann Francke (1663–1727): Zeuge des lebendigen Gottes* (Marburg an der Lahn: Francke-Buchhandlung, 1956), 243.
34. Francke's account is quoted by Markus Matthias in "August Herman Franke (1663–1727)," in *Pietist Theologians*, ed. Lindberg, 103–4. For the story of Augustine's conversion, see book 8 of his *Confessions*.

an experience neither Arndt nor Spener recorded as his own, and it put Francke at odds with the emerging spirit of the Enlightenment. Of this experience Francke was to write, "True faith is a divine work in us, which transforms us and bestows upon us the new birth from God, which kills the old Adam, and fashions us into a new man who is entirely different in heart, soul, mind, and in all his powers."[35] Like Luther, Francke believed that the wrath of God preceded the mercy of God, mortification ("killing the old Adam") preceding vivification (rebirth). As elsewhere in the Bible, Francke finds the concept of rebirth in Psalm 17:15: "I will behold your face in righteousness; I will be satisfied if I awake according to your image." Writing on "The Foretaste of Eternal Life" (a foretaste he found in the conversion experience itself), Francke explains:

> Literally translated from the Hebrew, these last words are: "If your image awakes." What does David mean by this? He wishes to say: Because the image of God in man has faded through the fall, indeed is lost, one cannot have rest in anything. . . . However, if the image of God toward which a person was initially created is awakened in him once again (which occurs if he is once again enlightened by the Holy Spirit so that his eyes are opened to see what kind of wretched state the whole of his life stands in, and how he is lacking the true way and can have this only in Christ Jesus), then he refreshes himself and experiences how joyous and gracious the Lord is.[36]

Rebirth as the personal experience of God's grace is for Francke evidence of God's providence and proof of the truth and efficacy of Scripture. It is the requisite sign of true Christian faith—a notion too subjective and emotionally oriented to be happily received by many of his contemporaries.[37]

In addition to his broad pedagogical vision and his advocacy for the poor, Francke's effect on biblical studies, both in his own country and worldwide, was immense. It was his schools that provided the first Protestant missionaries and it was his influence that brought about the first Bible institute explicitly dedicated to the publication and dissemination of the Bible in whole and in part. Still in existence, the publishing house preceded by one hundred years its counterpart in other

35. Quoted by Baird, *From Deism to Tübingen*, 63.

36. See *The Pietists: Selected Writings*, ed. Emilie Griffin and Peter C. Erb (San Francisco: HarperSanFrancisco, 2006), 55. Translation slightly revised.

37. See Erhard Peschke, *Studien zur Theologie August Hermann Franckes*, 2 vols. (Berlin: Evangelische Verlagsanstalt, 1964–1966).

Western countries. His work very quickly became the model for schools founded in such diverse centers as Moscow, Sweden, Italy, South India, the Near East, Denmark, and England. According to the historian Kurt Aland, the leading textual critic of the twentieth century, a convincing line can be drawn, at least in Germany, from the appearance of German Pietism not only to the rise of Bible societies, institutes, and publishing houses, but ultimately to the rise of biblical criticism, most immediately in the form of textual criticism—the necessary first step in Bible translation.[38]

Hermeneutics

Arising out of his own personal experience of rebirth, Francke was convinced that there was an understanding of Scripture, a kind of "living" understanding that was distinguishable from and transcended all purely theoretical understanding.[39] To focus exegesis toward this goal, Francke employed the concept of the *scopus* (Latin for "scope," i.e., aim) of the biblical text, asserting that a text could not be understood apart from its intention, aim, or purpose. The concept of a text's *scopus* corresponds closely to what I have called "the center of Scripture." According to Francke, one could speak of the objective *scopus* of Scripture—to bring to conversion—and the subjective *scopus* of the reader—the reader's sincere intention to search for edification.

Francke believed the *scopus* of Scripture to be summed up in the famous passage of 2 Timothy 3:16: "All scripture is inspired by God and is useful for teaching, for reproof, for correction, and for training in righteousness." In this verse Francke found a listing of both the stages within the course of conversion and the various genre for addressing them:

> So all Scripture is given for the purpose that it be useful (1) for teaching (in order to liberate from ignorance as well as from error in teaching and life, and from tribulation and affliction of the heart); (2) for reproof (for the conviction by teaching); (3) for correction (that one be brought by important instruction and conviction to the right way); (4) for training in righteousness (that one who is set on the right path is continually directed as a child in its way).[40]

38. See "Der Deutsche Pietismus als Wegbreiter für die Arbeit der Bibelgesellschaften," in *On Language, Culture, and Religion: In Honor of Eugene A. Nida*, ed. Matthew Black and William A. Smalley (The Hague: Mouton, 1974), 3–21.

39. I am following here Markus Matthias's essay, "August Hermann Francke (1663–1727)," in *Pietist Theologians*, ed. Lindberg, 100–114.

40. Quoted by Matthias, ibid., 111, n. 9.

Elsewhere Francke equates the objective *scopus* of the biblical text with the hidden meaning, the *sensus mysticus,* which the Holy Spirit has conferred upon the text. As Markus Matthias explains, the *sensus mysticus* for Francke is not a second meaning, as in allegorical interpretation. Nor is it a meaning that the nonreborn are unable to recognize. Rather, the distinction lies in the nature of understanding itself: to the nonreborn understanding rises only to the level of theoretical knowledge (*cognitio literalis*), whereas for the reborn understanding rises to a "living" knowledge (*cognitio spiritualis*). Living knowledge entails that kind of understanding which only the reborn are able to discern through the affectation of the will. It is the level of understanding implied in Jesus' exhortation, "He who has ears to hear, let him hear" (Luke 14:35b). For Francke, only the reborn have such ears. Only the reborn know what the text is saying—literally (*sensus literalis*). And the reborn is the one in whom Jesus' rebirth has taken place in one's heart.

The previous considerations help us understand Francke's distinction between the *sensus literae* (the sense of the word) and the *sensus literalis* (literal sense). In Francke's mind the distinction (which I must greatly simplify here) was between what the author intended (the *sensus literalis*) and what the words in their simple and common sense (the *sensus literae*) conveyed, the latter being accessible on the grammatical level, the former only to proper exegesis: "The exegetical reading of Holy Scripture is that which concerns finding and explaining the literal sense intended by the Holy Spirit himself. We call it (1) the *sensum literalem*. For we distinguish it from the *sensus literae* which is the meaning of the words in their proper and innate signification according to that which is the principal object of grammatical reading."[41]

The grammatical reading included not only the logical examination of the text, but also a discovery of its historical determinants (its *lectio historica*). Such knowledge equated with merely the husk of the text, the kernel of which lay in its suprahistorical message. This is the distinction that was later to be made, for example, between the Jesus of history and the Christ of faith—the first could be known by anyone; the latter could only be known ("understood") by faith. One sees, as Francke himself did, that the distinction he is talking about is not to be found in the sense of the text itself but in its reading. He was thus driven to the

41. Quoted by Matthias, ibid., 105.

unpopular position of saying that "only rebirth or true piety . . . leads to a true, namely practically effective, understanding."[42]

Since the purpose of the text under the authorship of the Holy Spirit was just such a rebirth of the will, Francke, following Spener and others, believed that the task of exegesis was to raise the historical author of the Bible "from the dead" and to re-present him as "living," in terms of his emotion, life condition, and destiny. In that way, the affective power of the author (i.e., the Holy Spirit) that produced the text would be efficacious once again in the life of the interpreter.

The future of the Pietist movement after Francke was to be a rich and influential one. Its broad stream of direct influence encompasses such figures and movements as Nicholas Count von Zinzendorf (1700–1760; the founder of the Moravian church), Friedrich Schleiermacher (1768–1834), John Wesley (1703–1791, the founder of Methodism), the holiness movement, the Salvation Army, and countless twelve-step programs. What these share, different as they are in so many other ways, is a conviction that Christ, the center of Scripture, must come alive in the life of the reader in heartfelt, joyous assurance and active love.

CONCLUSION

The search for the center of Scripture is a perennial theme of Christian biblical interpretation. During the Reformation era, the search was taken up with renewed urgency for the purpose of reforming the church. The result, as we have seen, was not one uniform conception of the Scripture's center, but a family of closely related conceptions that remain influential into the present day.

---

42. The words are Matthias's, ibid., 105.

Chapter 9
What Is the Literal Sense of Scripture?

INTRODUCTION

What is the literal sense of Scripture? The question would appear to be simple, but the history of the Quadriga shows that it is not. One wants readily to agree with Brevard Childs's observation: "There are few more perplexing and yet important problems in the history of biblical interpretation than the issue of defining what is meant by the *sensus literalis* [literal sense] of the Bible."[1]

The task before us in this chapter is to illustrate how the question of the literal sense of Scripture was construed in the post-Reformation period, by those who despised the church, those who loved the church, and those who were largely indifferent toward it. For assistance we turn to one of the most significant writings of the twentieth century in the field of the history of biblical interpretation, Hans Frei's *Eclipse of Biblical Narrative*.[2] In this work Frei surveys the hermeneutical principles operative in the interpretation of Scripture in the eighteenth and nineteenth centuries. As the title suggests, central to Frei's thesis is that interpreters of Scripture, even into recent times, have tended to focus on what they perceive to be "the real subject matter" of biblical texts, rather

---

1. Childs, "The Sensus Literalis of Scripture: An Ancient and Modern Problem," in Beiträge *zur Alttestamentlichen Theologie: Festschrift* für Walther Zimmerli, ed. Herbert Donner, et al. (Göttingen: Vandenhoeck & Ruprecht, 1977), 80.
2. Hans Frei, *The Eclipse of Biblical Narrative* (New Haven: Yale University Press, 1974).

than on the words themselves in their narrative sense. Frei identifies three foci of biblical interpretation dominating this period, foci we have already seen operative in nuce in earlier times. The "real subject matter" of texts, that to which the texts are said literally to refer, during the period to which we now turn, has been variously identified with: (1) the historical event behind the text; (2) the authorial mind or intent as distinct from the words themselves; and (3) ideas or concepts independent of either history or authorial intent, even of the words themselves.[3]

We shall discuss a representative of each focus in turn. All were figures of the Enlightenment.

THE HISTORICAL EVENT BEHIND THE TEXT: REIMARUS

The Goal of Jesus and His Disciples (1778)[4] by Hermann Samuel Reimarus is "one of the greatest events in the history of criticism," wrote the famed historian of nineteenth-century life-of-Jesus research, Albert Schweitzer, because it is the first attempt to get behind the text to form a historical conception of the life of Jesus independent of the apostolic teachings about him, the first to seek a solution to the problem of the Jesus of history versus the Christ of faith by combining historical and literary criticism, and the first to recognize the role of eschatology and apocalyptic thought in late Judaism, the milieu in which Jesus lived.[5] Schweitzer continued in this judgment by adding, "seldom has there been a hate so eloquent, so lofty a scorn," as one finds in its pages.[6] Nothing escapes Reimarus's critique of the origin of the Christian church: not Jesus, not the disciples, not the evangelists or the apostle Paul, not the church's traditional interpretation of the gospel or the gospel story. It is therefore not a little revelatory of the man that "in the spirit of devotion and piety," Reimarus had for forty years been professor of Oriental languages in the secondary schools of Hamburg (Germany) and had regularly attended Christian services and participated in the Lord's Supper, while harboring opinions in the privacy of his study that were caustically at variance with his own social and religious practices. His scorn was lofty, but his fear of the state church and the professional and economic consequences of denouncing its sacred

3. Ibid., 268.
4. Trans. and an introduction by George Wesley Buchanan (Leiden: Brill, 1970).
5. Albert Schweitzer, *The Quest of the Historical Jesus*, trans. W. Montgomery (New York: Macmillan, 1956), 15, 22–23.
6. Ibid., 15.

Scripture soared higher still. It is little wonder, given the religious climate of the times, that the famed dramatist and philosopher G. E. Lessing (1729–1781) waited until ten years *after* Reimarus's death before presenting *The Goal of Jesus*, a brief essay of one hundred pages, to the public; even then Lessing published the manuscript under the guise of "another anonymous fragment from the Wolfenbüttel library," where Lessing served as librarian. Ironically, as we shall see, Reimarus attributed just such a fear of loss of status to the disciples of Jesus, transferring to them a deception that was his own.

Reimarus believed that behind the words of Scripture lay not the world of Christian piety and doctrine, nor the world the Gospel writers would have us believe, but the world as it had actually been, free of the distortions and fabrications of the disciples and evangelists. That real world behind the text was waiting to be disclosed to anyone willing to apply the analytical skills of simple logic. One had but to separate out the possible from the impossible (e.g., the miracles), the consistent from the contradictory (e.g., whether the Messiah's coming is present or future) and, most critically, the sayings of Jesus from the disingenuous statements of the early church about Jesus. When the New Testament is viewed in the light of natural reason and not in "holy, blindfolded naiveté," the rational person, Reimarus argued at the height of the Age of Reason, can only be appalled by the artful deceit revealed therein. The Old Testament is particularly lamentable when taken literally. Concerning the Hebrew Bible the professor of Oriental languages wrote:

> There is certainly . . . no book that is so full of contradictions as this, and in which God's name is so often and so shamefully misused, whereby all persons who are here cited as men of God, fraudulently occasion pure scandal, offense, and atrocity. In the whole record of this history, there is neither patriarch, judge, nor king whose genuine and earnest purpose it was to propagate a true understanding of God, virtue, and piety among men. They come from a fabric of pure foolish deeds, crimes, deception, and cruelty, for which the guiding force was principally the love of power and selfishness. Through such abominable dealings, every pretext of supernatural appearance of God and angels . . . is logically pure delusion, deceit, and misuse of the divine name.[7]

With such an attitude toward sacred Scripture, why, one may wonder, should Christian scholars take Reimarus seriously? Unlike Origen

---

7. Quoted by Buchanan, *Reimarus*, 4–5.

or Augustine, he offers no allegorical escape from the bleak picture he so pointedly draws. The reason for taking Reimarus seriously was recognized by Lessing himself. "Lessing's greatness," writes Albert Schweitzer, "[is] that he grasped the significance of [Reimarus's] criticism, and felt that it must lead either to the destruction or to the recasting of the idea of [biblical] revelation."[8] Reimarus is either right in his assessment of Scripture or he is not; if not, then the Christian must know why he is wrong and offer a corrective assessment. Lessing himself made lasting contributions toward this end.[9] By publishing the writings of Reimarus, Lessing became the midwife to the quest of the historical Jesus, the effort to find the truth about Jesus, which was to dominate the nineteenth century and the second half of the twentieth. That history is richly told elsewhere by Schweitzer and others and need not detain us here.[10]

We want instead to look at the world behind the text as Reimarus envisioned it. In fairness to Reimarus, however, we do need first to note that he wrote before the major historical and literary criticisms had come into being (see chap. 10 below), which is to say that his critique of the Gospels is precritical in every regard except one: he rightfully supposes that the world behind the text and the world he lived in were one and the same, that the laws of nature had not changed. We should also note in fairness that many of his exegetical judgments have remained unaltered.

According to Reimarus the four Gospels, when read according to their literal sense, contain two radically different *systema* (or points of view) that must be distinguished from each other literarily and historically. One accurately expresses the mind of Jesus, the other that of his disciples following Jesus' death. The first is this-worldly and secular; the second otherworldly and spiritual. Both can be gleaned from a close reading of the four evangelists. The first *systema* is simply the normative Jewish expectation of a Messiah who would liberate the Jews from the degradation of Roman occupation and lead the nation to unparalleled heights of material prosperity and dominion over its enemies. Amid that heightened expectation Jesus appears beside the river Jordan with John the Baptist and, as the result of a vision, announces that he is the Messiah promised of old.[11] For Reimarus, the "whole

8. Schweitzer, *Quest of the Historical Jesus*, 15.
9. See, e.g., G. E. Michalson Jr., *Lessing's 'Ugly Ditch': A Study of Theology and History* (University Park: Pennsylvania State University Press, 1985).
10. For bibliography see Richard N. Soulen and R. Kendall Soulen, *Handbook of Biblical Criticism*, 3rd ed. (Louisville: Westminster John Knox, 2001), 153–56.
11. *Reimarus*, 55.

content and the entire purpose of Jesus' teaching" is disclosed in the words: "'Repent and believe the gospel' [Mark 1:15], or as it is put elsewhere, 'Repent, for the kingdom of heaven has come near' [Matt. 4:17]." Since the terms "kingdom of heaven" and "kingdom of God" are nowhere defined, nor the title "Messiah," says Reimarus, one can only infer that Jesus naturally assumed every Jew would know that he was talking about a material kingdom, and that no further explanation was needed. His proclamation brought nothing new to Jewish thought or practice. What Jesus did spell out in contradistinction to normative Jewish expectation was the higher standard of righteousness required for entry into the messianic kingdom. It was a standard scribes and Pharisees failed to grasp because of their hypocritical habit of "straining gnats and swallowing camels" (Matt. 23:24).[12] Jesus' teachings imply no break with traditional Judaism with respect to the law (Matt. 5:17–20); he had no intention of establishing a new religion or of creating new rites such as baptism (John 4:2) or the Lord's Supper. He did not accede to himself divine status. Reference to himself as Son of God carries no other connotation than its Old Testament designation as one "beloved of God," as is said of Israel, David, Solomon, and so on.[13] It is just that in a preeminent sense the Messiah is "Son of God" and therefore "within the limits of humanity." Statements in John's Gospel of his relationship to the Father are in no wise metaphysical but simply Jesus' way of stating his love for God and God's love for him. The book of Acts shows that originally converts were baptized, not in the name of the Trinity as the early church would later have it (Matt. 28:19), but simply "in the name of Jesus" (10:48; 19:5; et passim), that is, in baptism the repentant acknowledges Jesus as the Messiah and commits himself to the true love of God and neighbor. The good news Jesus proclaims and calls others to believe in and trust is simply that he is the Messiah foretold.

Disciples are sent out to spread this good news, to gather adherents for a popular uprising, and thus to usher in the new age of the messianic kingdom (Matt. 10:23). With little response, Jesus boldly enters Jerusalem, dramatically and violently cleanses the temple, harangues the Pharisees and warns the Sanhedrin (Matt. 23). Animosity rises among religious and political leaders, and Jesus sadly discovers that his support among the people is meager and ephemeral. He is betrayed by

12. Ibid., 39.
13. Ibid., 45.

Judas, forsaken by all his disciples, and abandoned by God. His life ends ignominiously on a cross with a cry of despair. Hope that Jesus would be Israel's secular savior evaporates with the dawn.[14]

With the horrifying crucifixion of the would-be Messiah, the second *systema* of a "spiritual suffering savior for the whole human race" now begins to germinate in the minds of the disciples.[15] It had wafted about in Jewish consciousness since the time of Daniel and can be found in rabbinic sayings and elsewhere, as in Justin's *Dialogue with Trypho*. The Messiah would come a second time, not in human lowliness but supernaturally on the clouds of heaven to redeem the world. Like the first *systema*, the second *systema* too can be traced, woven into the Gospel narratives and the sayings of Jesus like the repair of a tattered tapestry. After fleeing Gethsemane and Peter's threefold denial, and being "overcome by anxiety and fear," the disciples find safety behind the closed doors of an upper room in Jerusalem, leaving Joseph of Arimathea, Nicodemus, and the women to take care of Jesus' burial.[16]

> Soon, however, one or another of them ventures to slip out. They hear that no further judicial investigation had been made for them. . . .They soon pluck up their courage and think . . . of their future fortune. . . . [They] were no longer accustomed to work. . . . Both [hardship and insult] were necessarily highly repugnant and painful to them, since this was the exact opposite of their continuously cherished purposes and hope. Whereas they had already had a small foretaste with their Master that teaching gives esteem and does not remain unrewarded. [Jesus received charitable gifts. Virtuous women provided material support. . . .] [Later e]vents show that the apostles really everywhere received high respect and that they usurped as much power over the common people as was possible. They dictate . . . not only what [the people] should believe, but also what they should do and not do, eat and drink. They scold; they threaten. . . ; they execute the ban and give people over to satan. They set over them bishops, administrators, elders. They compel the people to sell all they have and lay the proceeds at their (the apostles') feet, and then they distribute these as pleases them. . . .
>
> It is no wonder, then, that they did not immediately lose courage . . . but opened up for themselves a new way through a bold invention.[17]

14. Ibid., 80.
15. Ibid.
16. Ibid., 127.
17. Ibid., 127–29.

To lay the foundation for a new spiritual *systema* to replace the secular one of earthly expectation that had preoccupied Jesus, the disciples had to wait until the third day after Jesus' death, then steal the body from the tomb, leaving the stone rolled away to suggest bodily resurrection. "They wait with [the corpse] for a whole fifty days [until it has decomposed], so that after that, when it was too late to search for the body or to demand them to show the resurrected Jesus publicly, they could say all the more boldly that they had seen him here and there, that he had been with them, spoken with them, and eaten with them; and finally that he had left them and gone to heaven so that he might soon return again more gloriously."[18] "If . . . Jesus had spoken so clearly of his death and of his resurrection after three days, why, after he had really died and was buried, did this recent promise come to the mind of no single disciple, apostle, evangelist, or woman? . . . They apparently also knew nothing of such a promise."[19]

His suffering and death are to be interpreted in terms of the Suffering Servant of Isaiah 53 as an atonement for the sins of humankind. To appeal to the Gentiles, the Jewish law, its circumcision, Sabbath, new moons, sacrifices, and feasts will be abandoned. Baptism and the Lord's Supper will become the new sacraments for the remission of sins and entrance into the body of Christ, the church. By proclaiming this new gospel, the disciples' life of prestige and privilege will be preserved even if a few must die a martyr's death. To assure the continuation of material comfort, the device will be instituted whereby the wealthy share their possessions in common with the new community, held together by the fabricated promise that the Lord will soon return. Its (fictitious) delay will serve the splendid purpose of never having to be abandoned; it will keep the expectation alive among its adherents. This "enabled the apostles not only themselves to transform their meagerness to abundance, but also to lure thereby thousands of poor to the present enjoyment of these meager but soon to be abundantly rich possessions."[20] This fraud is then cleverly perpetuated throughout the region by being set down in written form in the Gospels and letters of the New Testament.

Reimarus concludes his essay:

So the new system [found in the Gospels] is not in agreement with history, but history must be made to conform to their new system. . . .

18. Ibid., 130.
19. Ibid., 81.
20. Ibid., 133.

then both history and system are to that degree unfounded. The history, because it was not taken from fact, experience and recollection. . . . The system, however, because it refers to the *facta* which first began after the system had been composed in the thoughts of the author, and are therefore simply fabricated and false.[21]

To what degree did Reimarus, discounting the narrative sense of the Gospels, find the world "as it actually happened" behind the text? That too is a question we cannot pursue here. It was Albert Schweitzer's judgment that Reimarus's great discovery was that Jesus' thought world was "essentially eschatological," his "sole mistake" being the "assumption that Jesus' eschatology was earthly and political in character."[22] Needless to say, eschatology became the cornerstone of Schweitzer's own reconstruction of the historical Jesus.

AUTHORIAL MIND OR INTENT: SCHLEIERMACHER

A second way of construing what a text literally means contends that it is to be found in the mind or intent of the author. For our illustration, we turn to Friedrich D. E. Schleiermacher (1768–1834). We do so because he is recognized as "the father of modern theology" and "the founder of modern hermeneutics"—a man one can fault, as the theologian Karl Barth once opined, but none has equaled.[23] In Schleiermacher's own lifetime he was renowned as a preacher and pastor, most notably at Trinity Cathedral in Berlin from 1809 until his death; as a philologian, whose translations of the works of Plato "have not been surpassed"; as a philosopher and pedagogue, being a central figure in founding the University of Berlin and the Berlin Academy of Sciences; and as a man of letters with a genius for social discourse. In his writings one can find the seeds of form and redaction criticism, of speech-act and reception theory, of the phenomenology of language and the quest of the historical Jesus, among other things. As is often observed, Schleiermacher marks the beginning of an era, not just a school.

Although Schleiermacher was a Reformed (Calvinist) clergyman who worked for unification with the Evangelical (Lutheran) Church

---

21. Ibid., 83–84.
22. Schweitzer, *Quest of the Historical Jesus*, 23.
23. Karl Barth, *From Rousseau to Ritschl* (London: SCM, 1959), 308.

in Germany, he referred to himself as a "Moravian of a higher order." Like Paul, Augustine, and Luther before him—even Francke to a lesser degree—Schleiermacher falls into that group of individuals for whom a profound religious experience brought together, over time and in the manner of an organizing principle, both thought and feeling into a conceptual whole. That religious experience occurred in his youth among the Moravian Brethren. Our task is to explain how it shaped his understanding, not only of himself and of human existence as such, but also of Scripture, and most specifically the Christ of the Gospel of John. In short, before we can understand Schleiermacher's concept of "authorial intent," we must do what Schleiermacher himself insisted upon: in order to understand a text in its literal sense we must place the text in its context—and ultimately that means within the life of the author and more specifically still within the intent of the author. A text can "literally" mean only what the author "intends" it to mean—as in the parable of the Sower, Jesus intended the "seed" to mean the gospel. We shall accordingly look first at the content of Schleiermacher's religious experience as he describes it and then at the hermeneutical method by which he applied insights derived from that experience to his interpretation of biblical texts. Concern for the centrality of experience is Schleiermacher's own. To Anselm's familiar saying, "Nor do I seek to understand in order that I may believe, but I believe in order that I may understand," Schleiermacher adds, "For he who does not believe does not experience, and he who does not experience, does not understand."[24]

The birthday of Schleiermacher's spiritual life occurred in 1783 in his fourteenth year during an extended family visit with the Moravians (*Herrnhuter*) of Gnadenfrei in eastern Saxony. His father, a Reformed chaplain to the Prussian army attracted to Pietism, had taken young Friedrich and his siblings to Gnadenfrei to enter them into the nearby Moravian school of Niesky. The religious experience occurring at that time, Schleiermacher wrote in 1802, was the beginning of "my awareness of our relation to a higher world."[25] We know little of the circumstances surrounding the event, but the role it was to play in his thought pervades his two most famous writings: *On Religion: Speeches*

24. These words were prefixed to the German edition of Schleiermacher's work, *The Christian Faith*, but do not appear in its English translation. They are quoted by Richard R. Niebuhr, *Schleiermacher on Christ and Religion: A New Introduction* (New York: Charles Scribner's Sons, 1964), 139.

25. In a letter to Georg Reimer, quoted by Martin Redeker, *Schleiermacher: Life and Thought*, trans. John Wallhausser (Philadelphia: Fortress, 1973), 9.

to Its Cultured Despisers, and his principal dogmatic work, *The Christian Faith*.[26] We do know that unlike Luther and Francke, Schleiermacher's experience did not juxtapose wrath and grace, or mortification and vivification, enabling one to posit a radical before and after; rather, it may be described simply as the universally accessible experience of dawning self-awareness. It is "that moment in which in any man a definite consciousness of his relation to the highest Being has, as it were, original birth, an individual religious life originates."[27]

Schleiermacher's preferred phrase for this experience is "the feeling [or immediate awareness] of absolute dependence." That feeling, he says, is the very heart and nature of religion: "The sum total of religion is to feel that, in its highest unity . . . our being and living is a being and living in and through God."[28] This awareness, being ontological in nature not psychological (as often misconstrued), is constitutive of true self-consciousness and forms the basis of genuine individuality and freedom. Absent this awareness, which is identical with a moral perception of being in the world (hence Schleiermacher's preoccupation with ethics), the self remains enmeshed within the transient values of earthly existence and "incomprehensive of the direction of God's creative activity in the world."

The feeling of absolute dependence may be viewed in two ways, let us say from below and from above. As the part (a human being) becomes aware of its dependence upon the whole (universe), so the whole is dependent on the part for its becoming. Richard R. Niebuhr summarizes this aspect of Schleiermacher's thought as follows: "Man-in-himself, archetypal man, is the apogee of the created order, the 'Earth-spirit,' the act though which the earth knows itself in 'its eternal being and in its ever changing becoming.'"[29] The religious experience must therefore be understood hermeneutically: as the individual discovering oneself within the totality of created order, and as the whole created order coming to self-awareness in the individual self. Here is the hermeneutical circle: the part within the whole, the whole within the part. As we shall see, according to Schleiermacher God and man meet in perfect unity in Christ. Christ is the second Adam, becoming the epitome of what Adam intended to be in perfect God-consciousness.

26. Friedrich Schleiermacher, *On Religion: Speeches to Its Cultured Despisers* (trans. John Oman; repr. Louisville: Westminster John Knox, 1994); *The Christian Faith* (1928; repr. Philadelphia: Fortress, 1976).
27. Schleiermacher, *On Religion*, 228.
28. Ibid., 49–50.
29. Niebuhr, *Schleiermacher on Christ and Religion*, 65.

Let us say here a little more about the circular movement of thought in the act of interpretation.

The Hermeneutical Circle and the "Art" of Interpretation

Interpretation is what all sentient beings do throughout every waking moment; it is constitutive of being in the world. We must assume that how that interpretation proceeds is identical in every case. Interpretation, whether of a noise in the night or a text, moves in a circle, at first cursorily, from the parts to the whole and then back again to the parts, until the thing itself is contextualized and "understood." Translators of foreign texts, moving from one language to another, are most conscious of the circle of interpretation. As a youth of twenty and already a confirmed autodidact, Schleiermacher began the translation of the works of Plato; it is here, one may assume, that this movement of interpretation became for him, as he later wrote, "the main thing," the "method according to which the whole and its unity is to be understood via the particulars."[30] The application of the circle is thus infinite in scope. It involves not only words in sentences, or sentences in paragraphs, or paragraphs in complete texts. The circle of incorporation may be extended to all the texts of a single author, to the author's historical setting, even to the place of the text within language itself. The circle goes further. One may ask, What effect did the text have on future texts, on the development of the language in which the text was written, and so on?[31] (Cf. chap. 3 above.) The technical term here is *intertextuality.* In his translation of the works of Plato, the young Schleiermacher had to decide which works attributed to the philosopher were authentic, which spurious. The question becomes: Does this allegedly authentic text fit into the whole body of texts known to be authentic? To make that determination, Schleiermacher recognized that he had to become acquainted with both the external (historical) circumstances of Plato's life as well as the internal (psychological) aspects of his mind, that is, his character, style, intention, manner of thought, and so on. The former involves objective historical criticism, the latter the subjective aspects or

---

30. Friedrich Schleiermacher, *Hermeneutics and Criticism: And Other Writings,* trans. and ed. Andrew Bowie (Cambridge: Cambridge University Press, 1998), 109.

31. Ibid., 15, para. 13. Schleiermacher speaks of Christianity's enormous "concept-forming power," a phenomenon referred to in the twentieth century as "language-gain." He uses the example of "righteousness" (*dikaiosynē*) in Paul's Letter to the Romans (p. 86), but examples are limitless.

"art" of interpretation, that is, hermeneutics. Hermeneutics is an "art" because although critical rules of interpretation can be spelled out, as Schleiermacher did, there are no rules for applying the rules themselves; in other words, the rules of interpretation must be *intuitively* applied.[32] Schleiermacher called this the "feminine" side of interpretation.[33]

Intuition concerning a past (or present) life is possible because all human beings share in a "common band of consciousness." Apart from that participation in (human) being no understanding between persons could take place. Because a past life, and all the texts pertaining to it, can be viewed as a whole and placed within its cultural era (which no living person can ever do), it is possible for a skilled interpreter to come to know a deceased author better than the author knew himself.[34] The interpreter would be able, as a matter of art, to put himself intuitively in the author's place. Psychological understanding of this kind is possible, however, only in those instances where one has access to texts of extended speech whose historical circumstances are known. Schleiermacher applied these principles to his analysis of 1 Timothy and was the first rightly to conclude that Paul could not have been the author of the epistle. The language and historical setting of the epistle did not conform to Paul's style, vocabulary, thought forms, or historical circumstances as found in his undisputed letters.

This emphasis upon the author of a text, rather than upon the text itself, arises from the hermeneutical circle. A text is but a moment in the total life-expression of its author. The literal meaning of a text therefore cannot be known until the text is placed back into its setting in the author's life, which means that *the intention of the author* in writing the text must be the ultimate focus of interpretation: What did the author intend to convey by this particular text? What does the text say about the conscious and unconscious motivations of the author? Schleiermacher coyly suggests that sacred Scripture could have arisen in a totally miraculous manner without using people (as is said, e.g., of the *Book of Mormon*), but since that is not the case, the Holy Spirit must have chosen to have everything traced back to individual authors—thereby negating any necessity for or possibility of the doctrine of verbal inspiration.[35]

---

32. Schleiermacher, *Hermeneutics and Criticism*, 14, para. 12. He called this aspect of interpretation "divinatorisch" (divinatory), perhaps inspired by his wife's otherwise disturbing interest in spiritualism. See Redeker, *Schleiermacher*, 211.
33. Schleiermacher, *Hermeneutics and Criticism*, 92–93.
34. Ibid., 23, para. 18.3.
35. Ibid., 17, para. 13.5.

Christ and the Gospels

The two aspects of Friedrich Schleiermacher's thought that we have discussed, one dealing with <u>content</u>, the other with <u>methodology</u>, come together in his treatment of Christ and the Gospels.

By the early nineteenth century the distinction in content and style between the Synoptic Gospels (Matthew, Mark, and Luke) and the Gospel of John was widely recognized. The question was: Which provided the more accurate picture of Christ, John's Gospel or the source(s) behind, and therefore earlier and more authentic than, the first three Gospels? In opposition to emerging opinion,[36] Schleiermacher <u>argued for the priority of John</u>, contending that the author of the Gospel was, as ancient tradition said, the <u>Beloved Disciple</u> and eyewitness who recorded from memory "what Christ actually said." In what is acclaimed to be the first critical effort to lecture (in Berlin) on the "life of Jesus," Schleiermacher wrote: "Nothing betrays less sense of the nature of Christianity and of the person of Christ Himself than the view that John has mixed much of his own with the speeches of Jesus. It even betrays small historical sense and understanding of what brings great events in general to pass, and of the nature the men must have on whom they are founded."[37]

The Synoptic Gospels, being little more than aggregations of short sayings and narratives, he argued, contained little or no direct discourse and often provide no setting whatever to the sayings they record. The <u>hermeneutical "art" of intuitively</u> getting into an author's mind in order to understand his intention in writing a particular text <u>could not be applied to these three Gospels</u>. The <u>context</u> of the sayings was <u>missing</u>. What was also required and still <u>lacking</u> (and here Schleiermacher anticipated redaction criticism of the mid-twentieth century) was <u>critical analysis</u> of <u>how</u> the individual <u>authors</u> (Matthew, Mark, and Luke) <u>organized and shaped the traditional material</u> in their Gospels. Absent that analysis, he said, we are left to ponder how the Synoptic Christ, with his "philanthropic disposition, somewhat Socratic morals, a few miracles . . . [and] talent for striking apothegms and parables . . . could have such an effect as to produce a new religion and a new church."[38]

36. Friedrich Schleiermacher, *The Life of Jesus*, ed. Jack C. Verheyden (Life of Jesus Series; Philadelphia: Fortress, 1975), 223.

37. Ibid., 262.

38. Ibid.

John's Gospel, on the other hand, was quite different. Here one finds extended direct discourses whose historical context is given as well: with Nicodemus in Jerusalem (3:1–21), with the Samaritan woman at Jacob's well (4:4–42), with critics of his work on the Sabbath (5:16–47), with a crowd beside the Sea of Galilee (6:25–50), and so on. This historical specificity, plus the internal coherence of the extended speeches themselves, provide the parameters needed for proper interpretation. By equating the Gospel writer with the Beloved Disciple, Schleiermacher justifies treating the discourses not as texts conveying the intent and perspective of the Gospel writer, as required in the case of the Synoptic Gospels, but of Christ himself! Thus the indispensable value of the speeches is that they reveal *the inner life of Christ*, that is, his self-consciousness. The external factors of Christ's life are largely absent from John, and the Synoptic Gospels are scarcely of more value in this regard; but knowledge of these things, including Christ's death and resurrection (!), Schleiermacher contends, is not essential for understanding the inner life of Christ, the place of divine indwelling.

Schleiermacher accepts the outline of the Gospel story about Jesus as derived from the four Gospels combined, but the Gospel of John provides the essential key to Christ's self-understanding. Knowing Christ's inner life (his God- and self-consciousness), Schleiermacher asserts, enables the interpreter to make historical judgments about the Gospel accounts of Christ's external life. This has crucial effects on Schleiermacher's interpretation of the literal sense of Scripture. For example, having learned from his mother the miracle of his messianic calling (the manner of his conception being irrelevant), Christ waits in sinless self-consciousness until he is of socially acknowledged maturity, that is, thirty years of age, to make public his identity. His baptism by John the Baptist is accomplished for John's benefit, not his own.[39] It enables John to fulfill his prophetic role of announcing the advent of the Messiah. Jesus' baptism is not a moment of personal insight or of divine adoption. Christ's self-consciousness also precludes the historicity of the forty days of temptation. The narrative is merely a parable. Otherwise Christ would be inconsistent with himself.[40] Similarly, Christ does not call Judas by mistake, nor does he call Judas to fulfill some predestined role in a divine drama of vicarious suffering for the sins of the world.[41] Judas's presence with Jesus is an

39. Ibid., 140–41.
40. Ibid., 150–51.
41. Ibid., 346.

act of Judas's own volition; he *joins* the disciples. Jesus does not weep in despair in the Garden of Gethsemane as though he were "under the power of dark ideas and confused feelings";[42] nor is it conceivable that he uttered a cry of dereliction from the cross. Such a cry would conflict with "Christ's whole state of mind as it is described in the discourses in the Gospel of John."[43]

None of these acts, Schleiermacher reasons, comports with the one who did "everything only under the form of the divine will" and saw "everything only in relation to God."[44] Here Schleiermacher is thinking of such Johannine sayings as: "I can do nothing on my own authority; . . . because I seek not my own will but the will of him who sent me" (5:30 RSV). "If you knew me, you would know my Father also" (8:19b). "I do nothing on my own authority but speak thus as the Father taught me. And he who sent me is with me; he has not left me alone, for I always do what is pleasing to him" (8:28b–29 RSV). "Whoever believes in me believes not in me but in him who sent me. And whoever sees me sees him who sent me" (12:44b–45). Consciousness of this double in-dwelling, of God in him and he in God, says Schleiermacher, explains the metaphorical character of Christ's self-reference as the Father's Son, which is not to be taken literally. "He calls himself Son, not in reference to something divine which is called Son in him, but rather because the Father is in him."[45] The same is to be said of Christ's use of spatial metaphors. To speak of being sent into the world (3:17, 31ff.; 7:16, 28–29; 8:42, *et passim*), or of having come down from above and returning (6:38, 62), has nothing to do with two worlds, one divine and eternal, the other temporal and human. Such statements "can be nothing else than a reference to his personal self-consciousness."[46] Similarly, in the Synoptic Gospels when Christ refers to himself as the fulfillment of Old Testament prophecy, he is not asserting something about the power of prophetic foresight; rather, Christ makes this identification because he knows himself to be the actualization, the coming into being, of the substance of what the prophets hoped for.[47] With this fulfillment of the prophetic hope, the Old Testament loses all relevance to the Christian church. The New has come.

42. Ibid., 395–96, also 417–18.
43. Ibid., 423.
44. Ibid., 103–4.
45. Ibid., 100.
46. Ibid., 271.
47. On Schleiermacher's interpretation of Christ and the Old Testament, see *Life of Jesus*, 244–69.

Christ is the Redeemer because he is "the maximum of the vitality of consciousness," "the veritable existence of God in him."[48] For this reason, Jesus is the historical archetype of God-consciousness, and redemption comes to the individual when that same immediate awareness of God becomes spirit and reality in the life of the believer. Jesus' death on the cross and his resurrection are at best irresolvable facts of the narrative, about which Schleiermacher is both ambiguous and ambivalent. The cry from the cross was probably just an involuntary response to pain. Such things relate to the external aspects of Christ's life, not to Christ's inner life, and are therefore nonessential details of the narrative. All that matters to Schleiermacher is the perfection of Jesus' God-consciousness, which may be mirrored but is not constituted by what he does and undergoes.[49]

This abbreviated sketch of Schleiermacher's *Life of Jesus* is sufficient for our purposes; yet the legitimacy of Albert Schweitzer's judgment should already be clear, that "its value lies in the sphere of dogmatics, not of history." "Schleiermacher is not in search of the historical Jesus, but of the Jesus Christ of his own system of theology; that is to say, of the historic figure which seems to him appropriate to the self-consciousness of the Redeemer as he represents it."[50] And, we might add, appropriate to his experience of redemption as a fourteen-year-old youth in a Moravian worship service centered on Christ, and for whom, as a nineteen-year-old, the Moravian doctrine of Christ's death as an expiatory sacrifice had become morally repugnant.[51] This is because, as Hans Frei has pointed out, Schleiermacher was not interested in the *Christus extra nos* but in *Christus pro nobis* or *in nobis*.[52] Few at least have been willing to concede that Schleiermacher discovered the literal sense of the Johannine texts in the intention of Jesus or that "authorial intent" can be intuited by any "art" of interpretation. Nevertheless, for Schleiermacher, the literal sense of Scripture, the "true" subject matter of the Gospel accounts of the life of Jesus, is to be found in Jesus' *intention* to convey to others his own God-consciousness and to arouse in others the same God-consciousness and the self-consciousness that arises from it. For Schleiermacher, that consciousness is present in the Christian church in continuity with its earliest beginnings, by virtue of its continued and literal reference to the life of Jesus of Nazareth, the

48. Schleiermacher, *Life of Jesus*, 88; *Christian Faith*, par. 94.
49. Hans Frei, *Types of Christian Theology* (New Haven: Yale University Press, 1992), 75.
50. Schweitzer, *Quest of the Historical Jesus*, 62.
51. Redeker, *Schleiermacher*, 13.
52. See Frei, *Types of Christian Theology*, 74.

unsurpassable originator of that experience. The Christ event, that "the Word was made flesh and dwelt among us," is not a symbol, but a life. For this reason, it is said, Schleiermacher gave rise to the *sensus literalis* as a natural mode of New Testament reading.[53]

It is reported that upon Schleiermacher's death at the age of sixty-five, tens of thousands of citizens of every class and station lined the streets of Berlin to watch his cortège pass by; it was an outpouring of respect unequaled in the city's history, perhaps in the grand intuition that they had witnessed piety (may one say God-consciousness?) of an order they had not seen before.[54]

IDEAS OR CONCEPTS INDEPENDENT OF EITHER HISTORY OR INTENT: JEFFERSON

Thomas Jefferson (1743–1826) is of interest to us, not because he has figured prominently in the history of biblical interpretation, but because as a son of the Enlightenment his treatment of Scripture illustrates the only theological tradition that was acceptable to the intellectuals of his day: Deism, a theology without a Trinity, without an incarnation, and without a cross. Like others of his remarkable era, Jefferson was a man enamored with ideas. He wanted to be remembered for three, which he had inscribed on his tomb at Monticello: author of *The Declaration of American Independence* and of the *Statute of Virginia on Religious Freedom*, and father of the University of Virginia. (Not, one quickly notes, his roles as president and as vice-president of the United States.) These ideas came into being—or became incarnate, if you will: an American nation independent of England, a land in which church and state were to be forever separate, and a university whose center was to be a library, not a chapel—to place reason before faith. Reason, not revelation, he declared, is "the only oracle which god [sic] has given us to determine between what really comes from him, and the phantasms of a disordered or deluded imagination."[55] So it is in the realm of ideas that Jefferson valued Jesus—not as the Word incarnate.[56] In a letter to John Adams, dated April 11, 1823, he proffers his own translation of the

53. See ibid., 65–69.
54. Redeker, *Schleiermacher*, 212–13.
55. Letter to Miles King, from Monticello, Sept. 26, 1814; see Dickenson W. Adams, ed., *Jefferson's Extracts from the Gospels* (Princeton: Princeton University Press, 1983), 360.
56. *Jefferson's Extracts*, 412.

opening verses of John's Gospel, which he calls Jesus' "doctrine of the Cosmogony of the world."

> [John 1:1–3] truly translated means "in the beginning God existed, and reason [or mind] was with God, and that mind was God. This was in the beginning with God. All things were created by it, and without it was made not one thing which was made." Yet this text, so plainly declaring the doctrine of Jesus that the world was created by the supreme, intelligent being, has been perverted by modern Christians to build up a second person of their tritheism by a mistranslation of the word *logos*. One of it's [*sic*] legitimate meanings indeed is "a word." But, in that sense, it makes an unmeaning jargon: while the other meaning "reason," equally legitimate, explains rationally the eternal preexistence of God, and his creation of the world.[57]

As a Deist, Jefferson did not think of God as *in* creation, or as one whose will could be manifested in a human being. He could only think of God as *before* creation, endowing it with attributes according to his will. The Christian concept of spirit was also meaningless to him: "Jesus tells us that 'God is a spirit.' 4. John 24. but without defining what a spirit is '*pnemma ho Theos*.'"[58]

A devotée of Isaac Newton, Francis Bacon, and John Locke, whose portraits still hang in the parlor of his Monticello estate, Jefferson thought only in terms of laws of nature, including the moral law inscribed on the human heart. The world of philosophical speculation, especially that of Plato and Plotinus, the very world that had enabled the incipient church to find a foothold in the Gentile world, was to Jefferson nothing other than "foggy dreams" and "puerilities"; they were "mysticisms incomprehensible to the human mind" upon which the priesthood of the Christian church in its doctrine of the Trinity had built up fabrications of "impenetrable darkness" as delirious as Plato's own "unintelligible jargon"—"that three are one, and one is three; and yet the one is not three, and the three are not one."[59] Moreover, he argued, again in Deist fashion, the priests of the church had created these fabrications because, having found the teachings of Jesus "too plain to need explanation," they "saw, in the mysticisms of Plato, materials with which they might build up an artificial system which

57. Ibid.
58. Ibid., 411.
59. Quotations respectively from letter to John Adams, July 5, 1814; letter to William Short, from Monticello, Oct. 31, 1819; letter to John Adams, from Monticello, Aug. 22, 1813; see *Jefferson's Extracts*, 359, 388, 347.

might, from it's [*sic*] indistinctness, admit everlasting controversy, give employment for their order, and introduce it to profit, power and pre-eminence."[60] Persons such as Athanasius, Loyola, and Calvin, he said, are "false shepherds" of Jesus' simple doctrines, whose "metaphisical insanities . . . are to my understanding, mere relapses into polytheism, differing from paganism only by being more unintelligible."[61]

In happy contrast to these metaphysicians and theologians stood the moral philosophers of antiquity in whom Jefferson was trained as a youth and at the College of William and Mary in Williamsburg: Pythagoras, Socrates, Epicurus, Epictetus, Seneca, and Cicero. The thought of these men, when "distilled from their superstitions and idolatries," met Jefferson's approbation. Among them Epicurus struck the most sympathetic chord. It was Epicurus whose "genuine (not the imputed) doctrines" he considered "as containing every thing rational in moral philosophy which Greece and Rome have left us"; and it is here in Epicurus that in 1776 Jefferson found that unalienable right with which the Creator had endowed every human being: "the pursuit of happiness." "I am an Epicurean," Jefferson wrote in 1819, and the tranquility he said he valued in those late years as "the highest good" is an Epicurean good.[62]

It is against the ideas of these moral philosophers and pressed by his friends Benjamin Rush, a Philadelphia physician, and Joseph Priestley, the famed chemist and Unitarian theologian, that Jefferson, then in his first term as president, set about to formulate his opinion of the moral teachings of Jesus. To do this, Jefferson said, he first had to distinguish the pure precepts of Jesus from the encrustations of the Gospel writers. Like Reimarus before him, he saw the Gospels as the work "of the most unlettered, and ignorant of men" who had mutilated and misstated the pure sayings of Jesus.[63] The task, which he thought quite straightforward, was to separate the "splendid conceptions" of Jesus from the evangelists' "superstitions, fanaticisms, and fabrications."[64] In an idiom reminiscent of Gnosticism, Jefferson compared the undertaking to extracting "diamonds from the dung hill."[65] For these reasons Jefferson readily illustrates the type of scriptural interpreter who has no interest in the historical setting of Jesus or of the Gospel writers, and who has

---

60. Letter to John Adams, July 5, 1814; *Jefferson's Extracts*, 359.
61. Letter to Jared Sparks, Nov. 4, 1820; *Jefferson's Extracts*, 401.
62. Letter to William Short, Oct. 31, 1819, *Jefferson's Extracts*, 388.
63. Letter to Benjamin Rush, Apr. 21, 1803; *Jefferson's Extracts*, 333.
64. Letter to William Short, Aug. 4, 1820; *Jefferson's Extracts*, 396.
65. Letter to William Short, Oct. 31, 1819; cf. Letter to John Adams, Oct. 12, 1813. See *Jefferson's Extracts*, 388 and 352.

little interest in Jesus' intention or the intention of those who wrote about him, or even of the words themselves. Nor for that matter was Jefferson really interested in a close reading of Jesus' moral teachings in the manner of a Johannes Arndt or a Jakob Spener, for whom Scripture was both revealed and sacred, or in the spirit of Paul's *imitatio Christi* (1 Cor. 11:1)—whom he called the grand Coryphaeus (choir master) of "the band of dupes and imposters" who first corrupted the doctrines of Jesus. In spite of these handicaps, Jefferson firmly believed that by way of his extracts he could lay bare the only true meaning Scripture could possibly have—just as Marcion had thought sixteen centuries before.

Lacking time for a complete treatise on the subject, Jefferson drew up a brief outline of what a full treatment might contain, adding that it would probably be all he would ever say on the subject. He entitled it, *Syllabus of an Estimate of the merit of the doctrines of Jesus, compared with those of others.*[66] Concerning Jesus he wrote:

2. His moral doctrines relating to kindred and friends were more pure and perfect, than those of the most correct of the philosophers, and greatly more so than those of the Jews.
   And they went far beyond both in inculcating universal philanthropy, not only to kindred and friends, to neighbors and countrymen, but to all mankind, gathering all into one family, under the bonds of love, charity, peace, common wants and common aids.
3. The precepts of Philosophy, and of the Hebrew code, laid hold of actions only.
   He pushed his scrutinies into the heart of man; erected his tribunal in the region of his thoughts, and purified the waters at the fountain head.
4. He taught, emphatically, the doctrine of a future state.

In his cover letter Jefferson answered Rush's underlying question concerning Jefferson's religious beliefs. It was a question much in the public domain due to newspaper articles alleging an illicit relationship with a slave girl named Sally Hemings and raising doubts about his fitness for public office: "I am a Christian, in the only sense in which he wished any one to be"; he answered Rush, "sincerely attached to his doctrines, in preference to all others; ascribing to himself every human excellence, and believing he never claimed any other."[67]

---

66. *Jefferson's Extracts*, 332–34.
67. See Jaroslav Pelikan, "Jefferson and His Contemporaries," in *Thomas Jefferson, The Jefferson Bible: The Life and Morals of Jesus of Nazareth* (Boston: Beacon, 1989), 149.

A few months later, in 1804, for "2. or 3. nights only," Jefferson sat down with two copies of the New Testament and, with a sangfroid that is "still a bit overwhelming to contemplate" (Pelikan), began cutting out "the diamonds from the dunghill," pasting the verses "of pure unsophisticated doctrine" he had thus salvaged in a blank book of forty-six folio pages without adding commentary of any kind. He called it *The Philosophy of Jesus.* With the original now lost, the work exists only in a facsimile based on the two copies of the New Testament from which it was taken. Also extant are copies of Jefferson's list of the Gospel verses included in the text.[68] The compilation opens with Luke 2:1 and ends with Jesus' cry of dereliction and death on the cross. There are few verses of chronological detail, although oddly the lengthy genealogy of Jesus is included, perhaps due to Jefferson's aristocratic predilections. Verses are predominantly from the Synoptic Gospels, with only John 8:1–11, 10:1–16, 12:24–25, and 13:2–16, 34–35, apart from Jesus' arrest and crucifixion—the very opposite of Schleiermacher's preference for the Fourth Gospel. Verses are arranged "in a certain order of time or subject." Nothing suggesting the miraculous or messianic awareness is included. In his "Table of the texts extracted from the gospels" Jefferson provides a summary phrase to identify the content of each grouping of verses, such as "Precepts for the Priesthood," "Preachers to be humble," "false teachers," "disciples should love one another," "man not to judge for God," "The duty of mutual forgiveness and forbearance," "general moral precepts," "deeds & not ceremonies avail," "words the fruit of the heart," "humility, pride, hypocrisy," "God no respecter of persons," "Prudence and firmness to duty," "mere justice no praise," "the merit of disinterested good," "acts better than professions," "submission to magistrates," and "the duty of improving our talents." Interspersed are selected parables. The eschatological parables do not make the cut.

By Jefferson's own admission he had done the work hastily and he was not particularly satisfied with it, as a second endeavor would prove, but it did fulfill a temporary need. "A more beautiful or precious morsel of ethics I have never seen," he wrote in 1816. "It is a document in proof that *I* am a *real Christian*, that is to say, a disciple of the doctrines of Jesus, very different from the Platonists, who call *me* infidel, and *themselves* Christians and preachers of the gospel, while they draw all their characteristic dogmas from what it's [*sic*] Author never said nor saw."[69]

Ego.

---

68. *Jefferson's Extracts* 46, text: 55–105.
69. Letter to Charles Thomson, from Monticello, Jan. 9, 1816; *Jefferson's Extracts*, 365. Jefferson's italics.

Sometime in 1819/1820 Jefferson started over, this time with copies of the New Testament that he had purchased fifteen years before,
two each in Greek, Latin, French, and English. He pasted the extracted
verses in parallel columns, with the King James Version on the right.
Once completed, he seems rarely to have mentioned its existence. It
remained unknown until the latter decades of the nineteenth century.
It too has no commentary whatever, and his thoughts are discerned
only by the inclusion and exclusion of the Gospel record. It differs
from *The Philosophy of Jesus* in that something of the course of Jesus'
life is included, resulting in a text approximately the length of Luke's
Gospel. He called it, *The Life and Morals of Jesus of Nazareth extracted
textually from the Gospels in Greek, Latin, French, & English*.[70]

Again, every hint of the miraculous is excluded. As a boy Jesus is
found in the temple, but that he is there about his Father's business
is omitted. Jesus is baptized, but that John's baptism was a "baptism
of repentance" is also omitted. Noticeable, too, is that Jefferson finds
space for almost every saying and parable related to money, labor, and
stewardship, occasionally including parallel passages (such as the parable of the Pounds [Matt. 25] and the parable of the Talents [Luke 19].
The beheading of John the Baptist (Mark 6:17–28) has its place both
as a narrative in his "Bible" and as a capacious painting in his parlor
at Monticello—but one would not know explicitly from Jefferson's
text that John the Baptist was a prophet. Kept also is the Johannine
story of the woman caught in adultery (7:53–8:11). The parables of
the Prodigal Son, the Good Samaritan, the Laborers in the Vineyard,
the Unjust Steward, and others are present. There is no temptation or
Satan; there are no demons or angels. Both Schleiermacher's concept
of Jesus' "God-consciousness" and corresponding "self-consciousness,"
ubiquitous examples of which are found in the Gospel of John and
elsewhere, are absent from the composite figure of Jesus.

The last days of Jesus, as in the Gospels themselves, are told at length,
largely from the Gospel of John. At the Last Supper predictions of
betrayal by one of the disciples, and Peter's threefold denial, are made,
but there is no reference to an eschatological kingdom where they will
again sup with one another. There is a footwashing, but there are no
words instituting the bread and wine as a memorial of Jesus' life and
sacrifice. The arrest, Peter's denial, the trials with Caiaphas, Pilate, and
Herod, and the details of the crucifixion are told, pieced together from

---

70. In its printed edition it is titled *The Jefferson Bible* (Boston: Beacon, 1989).

the four sources. Jesus' last words are limited to three. Absent are the assuring words to the malefactor ("Truly I tell you, today you will be with me in Paradise," Luke 23:43b), "Father, into your hands I commend my spirit" (Luke 23:46), "I am thirsty" (John 19:28b), and "It is finished" (John 19:30b). Jesus' life ends with a cry of dereliction from the cross; there is no tearing of the veil of the temple, no earthquake releasing the dead from their graves, no confession by a centurion that Jesus was the Son of God. The women watch from afar as Jesus' body is removed from the cross and taken by Joseph of Arimathea and Nicodemus with the permission of Pilate. They roll a great stone before the sepulcher and depart. *The Life and Morals of Jesus of Nazareth* thus ends without an empty tomb and without resurrection appearances.

There is one curious omission. In neither *The Philosophy* nor in *The Life and Morals of Jesus* does Jefferson include the account of Jesus' reading Isaiah 61 in the synagogue at Nazareth, or of its application to his own ministry: "to preach deliverance to the captives . . . to set at liberty them that are bruised" (KJV).

In a letter to his former secretary, William Short, written in 1820, Jefferson compared himself as a materialist with Jesus, who took "the side of spiritualism": "He preaches the efficacy of repentance towards forgiveness of sin, I require a counterpoise of good works to redeem it."[71] Jefferson's good works are world renowned and justifiably praised. Posterity, however, knowing that Jefferson's will ordered the selling of 150 men, women, and children to reduce the enormous debt incurred in his pursuit of happiness, that his will manumitted only five persons, and that it neither acknowledged Sally Hemings, who had borne him five children, nor set her free, will have to decide whether sin is likely to be overcome by good works without repentance. Or, to put the matter differently, can one know the Christ without knowing him as Redeemer?[72]

SUMMARY

It comes as no surprise to the reader, having taken the rubrics of this chapter from Hans Frei's *Eclipse of Biblical Narrative*, that not one of our three interpreters identified "the literal sense of Scripture" with the

71. Letter to William Short, Apr. 13, 1820; *Jefferson's Extracts*, 391–92.
72. On the relationship of faith, sin, and redemption, see Hans Frei's discussion in *Types of Christian Theology*, ed. George Hunsinger and William C. Placher (New Haven: Yale University Press, 1992), esp. chap. 6.

biblical narrative itself. Each was quite certain that the true meaning and real reference of the Gospel texts lay elsewhere: in the historical events behind the text (Reimarus), in authorial intent (Schleiermacher), or in the abstract realm of moral precepts (Jefferson). That the literal meaning of Scripture lay in the biblical narrative itself continued to be overlooked for the next 150 years. But the reader will also note the curious correlation that existed between the lives of the three men and their interpretation of Scripture.

Chapter 10
What Is Modern Biblical Interpretation?

MODERN AND POSTMODERN

What is modern biblical criticism? Some might be tempted to say it means interpreting the Bible on the basis of reason rather than faith. But this is simplistic, and it is false. Biblical interpretation before the modern period (that is, before 1700) employed reason, and modern biblical interpretation relies on faith. There is, however, a significant shift in the way in which reason and faith are used in each instance.

In premodern interpretation, the story told by the Bible provided the comprehensive frame of reference in terms of which the stories of nations and individuals were placed and from which they derived their ultimate meaning. The Gothic cathedral of the Middle Ages provides a graphic expression of this biblically oriented view of cosmic reality. Reason and understanding are essential for interpretation, but they are guided by faith in the reality and truth of the world portrayed by the Bible.

With the rise of modern biblical criticism, the direction of interpretation is basically reversed. What the interpreter already and independently believes to be true about the world provides the comprehensive context for interpreting the Bible. The Bible is simply another artifact within the larger world, to be investigated and understood like any other ancient text. The meaning of the narrative events in the Bible, such as the flood, the exodus, or the resurrection, was judged to depend upon their proven historicity and conformity with secular knowledge, not on their location in sacred Scripture or in the story of God's dealing with the world. This viewpoint may seem to be independent of all faith, but in reality it is not. Modern biblical criticism assumes a secular (or this-worldly) understanding of the cosmos, and assumes that human beings can achieve a neutral and objective view of reality, resulting in knowledge of things as they actually are and have been.

Modern biblical criticism has brought many genuine gains to our understanding of the Bible. Most importantly perhaps, they have given many modern readers of the Bible an unprecedented appreciation for what one might call the Bible's *humanity*. The Bible did not fall from the sky but was born from a deeply human and enormously intricate history. Just as modern medicine consists of many different subdisciplines, each of which focuses on the human body (cardiology, podiatry, etc.), so modern biblical criticism consists of many different approaches and methods, each of which brings a certain aspect of the biblical text into sharper focus. Philology and comparative linguistics study languages in their ancient settings; biblical archaeology seeks extrabiblical evidence relevant for biblical interpretation; textual criticism searches for the best text based on the oldest and best manuscripts of the Old and New Testaments; historical criticism attempts to verify the historical data of Scripture by reference to secular knowledge of antiquity; comparative religions draws parallels or lines of development between biblical narratives, laws, psalms, and so on, and their counterpart in other cultures; psychological criticism applies current psychological theory to the interpretation of biblical figures; sociological criticism endeavors to describe the social and cultural setting of biblical events, cultic practices, mores, and institutions; rhetorical criticism analyzes the writings of the Bible according to the rules of ancient Greek rhetoric. These are only some of the newer methods at work in biblical scholarship today.[1]

Out of this vast field, we shall look at only three of the major methodologies most contributory to the modern understanding of biblical texts: source, form, and redaction criticism.

(1)   Source criticism inaugurated the modern period in biblical interpretation in the seventeenth and eighteenth centuries with the recognition that the literary idiosyncrasies of Scripture, such as changes in

---

1. These and other terms are defined more fully in Richard N. Soulen and R. Kendall Soulen, *Handbook of Biblical Criticism*, 3rd ed. (Louisville: Westminster John Knox, 2001).

vocabulary, contradictions, repetitions, doublets, anachronisms, and so forth, particularly in the Pentateuch, could be explained by a theory of composition involving multiple sources. By the beginning of the nineteenth century the Gospels were similarly examined, with a resulting four-source hypothesis to explain the similarities and differences between the first three (or Synoptic) Gospels.[2]

In the first decades of the twentieth century, analysis of the composition of the Old Testament, which was now known to have occurred over extended periods of time and from divergent points of view, led to even closer interest in the smaller linguistic genres of which the source materials were composed: historical narratives, sagas, legends, folktales, laws, hymns, prophetic oracles, curses, laments, benedictions, proverbs, and so on. Genre criticism, or form criticism as it is commonly known, enabled scholars to imaginatively locate, even more precisely than source criticism, the social setting of individual texts according to the nature and function of the various genres, such as folktales told around a nomad's campfire (e.g., Gen. 12), personal laments in times of sorrow (Pss. 22; 130), laws pertaining to the annual celebration of covenant renewal (e.g., the Decalogue of Exod. 20), or songs of praise for the coronation of a king (Pss. 2; 110), or, in the period of the early church, the gospel message or kerygma (Acts 2:14–39; 3:13–26; etc.), liturgical formulas (e.g., for the Lord's Supper; 1 Cor. 11:23–26), miracle stories for the propagation of faith (Matt. 8), or parables of eschatological warning (e.g., parable of the Weeds; Matt. 13:24–30). Both source and form criticism, however, fragmented the canonical text, extracted individual texts from their narrative world of sacred time, and placed them in the privileged world of the exegete, dissipating Scripture's efficacy as sacred text. Moreover, both source and form critics tended to be disinterested in the canonical shape of the individual writings in their effort to re-create the social world behind the text.

Dissatisfaction with the dislocation of texts from their narrative context led in the mid-twentieth century, particularly in Gospel studies, to the third critical method discussed here, known as redaction criticism—foreseen by Friedrich Schleiermacher. Redaction criticism wants to know how the compositional elements of Scripture were edited by the redactor ("editor" or "author") of the completed work, such as

---

2. The four sources are known as *Quelle* (siglum: Q), Mark, M (or special Matthean material), and L (or special Lukan material).

Matthew and Luke in the New Testament or the Chronicler in the Hebrew Bible, in order to make his source materials fit his own historical and theological point of view. Whereas some critics (like Jefferson or Reimarus) looked upon the Gospel writers as unlettered and deceitfully self-serving, redaction critics began to see them as theologians in their own right rethinking the gospel under new historical circumstances. Neither Reimarus, Schleiermacher, nor Jefferson interpreted Scripture with the benefit of insights from these methodologies.

SOURCE CRITICISM

Source criticism asks, Is the text at hand the work of a single author or is it composite, a compilation of different sources?[3] If the text is composite, then can the different sources be characterized in terms of specific historical circumstances, religious practices, theological points of view, ethical and moral concerns, and so on? Further, can the sources be located within a known historical setting?[4]

In source-critical theory it is now generally believed that sometime in the sixth century BCE priests of Israel added historical commentary and a more pronounced literary framework to an "embryonic" Pentateuch, then consisting of an amalgam of three ancient traditions identified with Judah in the south, Ephraim in the north, and Jerusalem. The compilers of these three traditions are commonly referred to as the Yahwist (tenth–ninth century BCE; siglum J), the Elohist (ninth–eighth century BCE; siglum E), and the Deuteronomist (seventh-sixth century BCE; siglum D). The fourth tradition, though never existing independently, wove these preexisting texts or traditions together over time to give the Pentateuch its present shape sometime in the sixth or fifth century BCE. An example of the organizing handiwork of the priests, known by the siglum P (Priestly tradition), is seen in its repeated demarcation of time from the origin of the world to the election of Israel and the creation of its sacred institutions, down to settlement in Canaan. The binding thread of P is easily traced; for example, in Genesis alone one finds the following:

---

3. Source criticism, as distinct from general literary and historical questions (such as the Mosaic authorship of the Pentateuch or the time of the deluge), first appeared in Old Testament study in the persons of Richard Simon (1638–1712) and Jean Astruc (1684–1766).

4. See Robert H. Pfeiffer, *Introduction to the Old Testament*, rev. ed. (New York: Harper & Brothers, 1948), 129ff., for a characterization of the four primary sources.

2:4a: "These are the generations of the heavens and of the earth when they were created" (thought originally to belong to Gen. 1:1 and now glossed by 2:4b).

5:1a: "This is the list of the descendants of Adam"

6:9a: "These are the descendants of Noah"

10:1a: "These are the descendants of Noah's sons, Shem, Ham, and Japheth" (the same phrase recurs in 11:10a; 11:27a; 25:12, 19a; 36:1; 37:2a).

The next example of source criticism is from Exodus 24, the sealing of the divine covenant with Moses. It illustrates how source-critical investigations of a text can clarify a text's apparent doublets, intrusions, and contradictions while at the same time inevitably fragmenting its narrative sense. Source criticism does this by attributing verses, or partial verses, to different oral or written sources, dividing what was once whole into its several parts. The division of Exodus 24 below is itself a simplified resolution of the inherent ambiguity of the narrative.[5]

J or E

1. Then he said to Moses, "Come up to the LORD, you and Aaron, Nadab, and Abihu, and seventy of the elders of Israel, and worship at a distance. 2. Moses alone shall come near the LORD; but the others shall not come near, and the people shall not come up with him."

E

3–8. The sacramental sealing of the covenant.

9. Then Moses and Aaron, Nadab, and Abihu, and seventy of the elders of Israel went up, 10. and they saw the God of Israel. Under his feet there was something like a pavement of sapphire stone, like the very heaven for clearness. 11. God did not lay his hand on the chief men of the people of Israel; also they beheld God, and they ate and drank.

J

12. The LORD said to Moses, "Come up to me on the mountain, and wait there; and I will give you the tablets of stone, with the law and the commandment, which I have written for their

---

5. See Brevard S. Childs, *The Book of Exodus: A Critical, Theological Commentary* (Old Testament Library; Philadelphia: Westminster, 1974), 497–511.

instruction." 13. So Moses set out with his assistant Joshua, and Moses went up into the mountain of God. 14. To the elders he had said, "Wait here for us, until we come to you again; for Aaron and Hur are with you; whoever has a dispute may go to them." 15a. Then Moses went up on the mountain,

P

15b. and the cloud covered the mountain. 16. The glory of the LORD settled on Mount Sinai, and the cloud covered it for six days; on the seventh day he called to Moses out of the cloud. 17. Now the appearance of the glory of the LORD was like a devouring fire on the top of the mountain in the sight of the people of Israel. 18a. Moses entered the cloud, and went up on the mountain

J

18b. for forty days and forty nights.

This division of the chapter into the three sources, with the Elohist tradition being the oldest and the Priestly tradition the latest, is not by any means satisfactory to every Old Testament scholar. General agreement resides only with the attribution of verses 15b–18a to the Priestly tradition (P), the latest of the traditions. Nevertheless, the division of the narrative into its hypothetical source elements does at least suggest why the same idea is repeated with distinct variation. The final compiler of the source materials, who brought the traditions together into one narrative line, treated his sources with pious respect, weaving them together as far as possible rather than merely substituting one tradition for another. By the time the Priestly tradition arose, the anthropomorphic characterization of God as having hands and feet and with whom one could eat and drink, which appears in E (vv. 10–11), was no longer deemed an acceptable way of speaking about God. God's transcendence and majesty, it was thought, preclude anthropomorphic description. Thus in the Priestly tradition God is hidden in a cloud, and what Moses sees and does on the mountain is itself unseen (vv. 15b–18a). The God who makes covenant with Israel remains a hidden God. The most that can be said is that "the *glory* of the LORD"—not the LORD as such—is like a "devouring fire." It is noteworthy that it is this belief in the utter transcendence of God that forms the backdrop to the Johannine concept of incarnation: in the Word made flesh the *deus absconditus* (hidden God) becomes the *deus revelatus* (revealed God) while remaining hidden in the mystery (and foolishness, 1 Cor. 1:18–25) of the cross and resurrection.

However, in their haste to anchor literary sources in historical time and space, source critics ignored the fact that they not only destroyed the narrative structure of the biblical text as it had been known and interpreted over long centuries, they also created a hypothetical story of textual origins so complex, disjointed, and disputed as to be totally inaccessible to all but a handful of incredibly diligent and patient scholars. Whereas the biblical text could easily be deconstructed by source-critical analysis, it could not be effectively or meaningfully reconstructed, however much light might be shed on the development of Israel's cultic traditions and self-understanding, or on its evolving sense of the nature of God and life before God. Another approach to Scripture, called canonical criticism,[6] was devised to address this characteristic inadequacy of source criticism.

Source criticism of the New Testament has been less contentious, centering on the Gospels, Acts, and the book of Revelation. That both Matthew and Luke used Mark and a collection of sayings of Jesus (known by the siglum Q)[7] is all but universally accepted, as is the evidence that both Matthew and Luke employed materials available only to themselves. The question dominating much of New Testament research in the second half of the twentieth century was which of the sayings attributed to Jesus in Q and elsewhere can reasonably be identified as "the very words of Jesus." Once again the canonical picture of Jesus, and the very purpose of the church in acknowledging four Gospels, was set aside in favor of a scholarly re-creation of a hypothetical "historical" Jesus. However theologically germane or ingenious the outcome of such efforts may be, the Jesus thus depicted is inevitably known to few beyond a coterie of academicians and their limited publics.

FORM CRITICISM

Form criticism may be loosely defined "as the analysis of the typical forms by which human existence is expressed linguistically," particularly in their oral, preliterary state.[8] As noted above, such forms are as varied as life itself, from simple greetings (such as "Peace be with you")

---

6. See Soulen and Soulen, *Handbook of Biblical Criticism,* 29–30, "Canonical Criticism."
7. For a proposed reconstruction of Q, see ibid., 151–53, "Q."
8. See ibid., 61–64, "Form Criticism."

to sagas of great length (such as that of Joseph in Genesis or Homer's *Odyssey*). In New Testament form criticism, no genre has received more attention than the parable because it is considered the most illuminating of all the speech forms attributable to Jesus. The literature devoted solely to parable interpretation is vast and ongoing. Hence here we will look instead at the miracle story to illustrate the insights of form-critical analysis.

Few narratives in the Bible have received greater scorn in the modern period than the miracles. Those who told them were allegedly devious fabricators; those who believed them were superstitious simpletons— so Reimarus and Jefferson. Form critics begin, however, by drawing a sharp distinction between a miraculous event and the *story* of a miraculous event. The nature of the event behind the story, even whether there was one, is a question bracketed out of consideration as unanswerable, even though countless interpreters of the Gospel miracles have proffered explanations, ranging from illusions taken as reality (walking on water), to psychosomatic phenomena (healing the lame and the possessed), to pure coincidence (the stilling of the storm), to the power of example (feeding the five thousand), to supernatural intervention, and so on. The form critic is interested solely in the literary form of the miracle story, its structure and function. Who is speaking? Who are the listeners? What is the setting of the miracle story? What is the purpose of the form? (This issue is picked up again in chap. 11 with regard to Hans Frei.)

The structure of the miracle stories in the Gospels follows a set pattern and comprises: (a) a problematic situation, (b) an action directly or indirectly involving Jesus, followed by (c) a resolution of the problem. Consider the following miracle stories in Mark's Gospel:

1:30–31: (a) Now Simon's mother-in-law lay sick with a fever, and they told him about her at once. (b) He came and took her by the hand and lifted her up. (c) Then the fever left her, and she began to serve them.

1:40–42: (a) A leper came to him begging him, and kneeling he said to him, "If you choose, you can make me clean." (b) Moved with pity, Jesus stretched out his hand and touched him, and said, "I do choose. Be made clean." (c) Immediately the leprosy left him, and he was made clean.

4:37–39: (a) A great windstorm arose, and the waves beat into the boat, so that the boat was already being swamped.

But he was in the stern, asleep on the cushion; and
(b) they woke him up and said to him, "Teacher,
do you not care that we are perishing?" He woke up
and rebuked the wind, and said to the sea, "Peace!
Be still!" (c) Then the wind ceased, and there was a
dead calm.

Recognizing the miracle story as a form of speech enables the reader
to distinguish between the plausibility of the story as an actual event
and its function as a story in the evangelistic mission of the early church
to spread the gospel. Note for example Matthew's appended verses:
"And the report of [the miracle] spread throughout that district" (Matt.
9:26), "But [the man previously blind] went away and spread the news
about him throughout that district" (Matt. 9:31), and so on.

The parallel between the function of the Gospel miracle story and
modern television advertising is striking. In both there is the recognition
of a problem, an action, and a resolution of the problem. The problem
may be (a) an allergic reaction to pollen; the action (b) involves acceding
to a proffered remedy, with (c) the resultant (miraculous) state of relief.
The ad is repeated over and over to evoke the intended response: pur-
chase of the remedy. The purpose of the Gospel miracle story is to create
such faith in the salvific power of Jesus and trust in his word as to bring
about discipleship. It is for this reason that the role of faith in healing is
repeatedly emphasized, as in Mark 2:5; 4:40; 5:34; 10:52; etc.).

Luke's expanded version of Mark's narrative of the call of the first
disciples illustrates this function of the miracle story (Mark 1:16–20).
The Markan text, with its parallel in Matthew (4:18–22), is starkly
concise. Jesus is walking by the sea, he sees two pairs of brothers who
are fishermen; he calls them to be "fishers of men" (RSV); they drop
their nets and follow him. Luke fills out this brief narrative by inserting
a miracle story to serve both as revelatory of Jesus' lordship over nature
and as a parabolic extension of the metaphor "fishers of men."

Luke 5:1 sets the stage by the Sea of Galilee, following Mark. The
crowd "was pressing in on [Jesus] *to hear the word of God.*" They listen.
Luke then expands the narrative slightly in order to employ the story of
a miraculous catch of fish. The *problem* is stated by Simon Peter: "Master, we have worked all night long but have caught nothing" (5:5a).
Having anticipated Peter's reply Jesus initiates the *action* with a command: "Put out into the deep water and let down your nets for a catch"
(5:4b). Simon Peter responds, *"If you say so,* I will let down the nets"

(5:5b). The miraculous *resolution* follows: "When they had done this, they caught so many fish . . ." (5:6a). Luke then enlarges the Markan narrative structure again to make explicit his purpose, which is to bring about faith in Jesus, repentance, and discipleship: "When Simon Peter saw it, he fell down at Jesus' knees, saying, 'Go away from me, Lord, for I am a sinful man!' For he and all who were with him were amazed at the catch of fish. . . . Then Jesus said to Simon, 'Do not be afraid; from now on you will be catching people'" (5:8–10). In this example Luke is interested in the miracle as a demonstration of Christ's power, but he is equally interested in *the story's* paradigmatic function: *hear the word*, repent of your sins, and follow Christ.

In this analysis of the structure of the miracle story we have already engaged in what is called redaction criticism.

REDACTION CRITICISM

The motivating concern of redaction (or composition) criticism is "to lay bare the historical and theological perspectives of a biblical writer by analyzing the editorial (redactional) and compositional techniques employed in shaping and framing the written and/or oral tradition at hand."[9] Both source criticism, with its identification of compositional elements, and form criticism, with its attention to the nature and function of literary forms in their oral setting, are necessary prerequisites to redaction criticism. The former two, as noted, are interested in the historical world behind the text, the latter in the narrative world within the text as a whole as it is shaped by the literary techniques and story world of the redactor.

The Theology of St Luke, written by the German scholar Hans Conzelmann, inaugurated the redaction-critical approach to the Gospels in 1953.[10] According to Conzelmann, what we have in the two-volume work of Luke–Acts is the evangelist's *theological reflection* upon the gospel story as it existed in his source materials (Mark and Q), rather than, as generally believed, a simple retelling of that story. Luke is a second-generation Christian. The earlier expectation of the imminent return of the risen Jesus (cf. Mark 16:8), chastened by its nonfulfillment,

---

9. See ibid., 158–60, "Redaction Criticism."

10. Translated from the second edition by Geoffrey Buswell (London: Faber & Faber, 1960). This summary of Conzelmann's work is best followed with a copy of the *Gospel Parallels: A Synopsis of the First Three Gospels*, ed. Burton H. Throckmorton Jr. (New York: Nelson, 1967).

has vanished. To meet the new reality of the delay of Jesus' return (the Parousia), Luke reconfigures the traditions at hand to present a deeschatologized view of the history of salvation. The life, death, and resurrection of Jesus are now conceived as marking the center of history, geographically as well as temporally, rather than its end, and the church is to be understood as a continuation of that ministry into the foreseeable future (the Acts of the Apostles). Conzelmann's critique is based on the assumption that Luke had before him a copy of the Gospel of Mark, a collection of Jesus' sayings (Q), and material unavailable to the other Gospel writers (siglum L). Luke's point of view is thus discovered by how he edits his source materials.

In the Markan tradition, John the Baptist is a type of Elijah whose purpose is to announce the coming of the kingdom of God and of one who, being greater than himself, will baptize with the Holy Spirit. Everyone responds. Pharisees, Sadducees, and the multitudes from Jerusalem, Judea, and the surrounding region go out to the Jordan to be baptized by John. Jesus also goes out to be baptized. A voice from heaven identifies Jesus as God's beloved Son. According to the Q tradition,[11] which is one of Luke's sources but is not found in Mark, Jesus subsequently acknowledges John's special status within the kingdom of God: "From the days of John the Baptist until now the kingdom of heaven has suffered violence and men of violence take it by force. For all the prophets and the law prophesied until John; and if you are willing to accept it, he is Elijah who is to come" (Matt. 11:12–14).

Luke, however, tells the story of John the Baptist and his relationship to Jesus differently (in spite of the Lukan infancy narratives). Luke looks upon the history of salvation as consisting of three distinct epochs; John's ministry marks the end of the first epoch, and the bestowal of the Holy Spirit at Pentecost is the beginning of the third. The central event in the divine economy, falling between these two epochs, is the life, death, and resurrection of Jesus. John is not part of this central event. Accordingly, the passage parallel to the text quoted above (Matt. 11:12–14) is altered by Luke to read: "The law and the prophets were *until* John; *since then* the good news of the kingdom of God is preached, and everyone enters it violently" (Luke 16:16; cf. Matt. 3:2, in which *John* announces the coming of the kingdom of heaven). John is thus part of the old epoch, not of the new.

---

11. Material found in both Matthew and Luke but not in Mark. See Soulen and Soulen, *Handbook of Biblical Criticism*, 151–53, "Q."

Luke indicates this division of roles geographically as well. In Luke's Gospel John's ministry is confined to the Jordan River, while Judea and Jerusalem constitute the domain of Jesus (cf. Mark 1:5); hence Jesus does not, as in the source tradition, go "beyond the Jordan" (cf. Mark 10:1) during his ministry. The multitudes go out to John to receive the baptism of repentance, but the leaders of Judaism, the Pharisees and Sadducees, do not (cf. Matt. 3:7 = Q). They, like the lawyers, reject John's call for repentance (Luke 7:29–30). Most startling of all in his version of the gospel story, Luke obscures John's role as baptizer by placing him in prison (3:19–20) *before* telling of the baptism of Jesus. In the parallel passage Luke reads, "Now when all the people were baptized and when Jesus also had been baptized" (3:21). The reader is left to guess by whom Jesus was baptized. The reason, suggests Conzelmann, is that the continuing existence of the Baptist movement long after Jesus' crucifixion and resurrection challenged the traditional account of John's identity and role with regard to Jesus (see Acts 10:36; 11:18; 13:24; 18:25; 19:4).[12] Subsequent events had thus proved the older tradition to be false or at least questionable. In Luke's account of redemptive history John's ministry ends with his imprisonment. Moreover, John's imprisonment is not the *cause* of Jesus' return to Galilee (see Mark 1:14; Matt. 4:12); Jesus is *led* there by the Spirit following the temptation by Satan in the wilderness (Luke 4:14). The new epoch, the center of time, begins with Jesus' baptism; it is accompanied by a voice from heaven (*Bath Qol*; Heb.: lit., "daughter of a voice"), but that baptism is unattended by John.

The sign that in Luke's mind Jesus is the center of history, Conzelmann suggests, is that Luke tells the story of Jesus' ministry as being free of the activity of Satan. Satan departs after his defeat at the temptation (Luke 4:13) "until an opportune time"; he does not reappear until he "enters into Judas" (Luke 22:3–6) at the end of Jesus' ministry. The familiar words of Jesus, "Get behind me, Satan," said to Peter on the road to Caesarea Philippi (Mark 8:33), are absent from Luke. The temporal dimension of Satan's activity is again indicated by Luke when Jesus, confronted by the chief priests and those who come out against him in the Garden of Gethsemane, says, "When I was with you day after day in the temple you did not lay hands on me. But this is your hour, and the power of darkness" (i.e., Satan's; Luke 22:53).

---

12. An ancient gnostic sect claiming ties to John the Baptist and known as Mandaeans still exists, principally in southern Iraq and Iran, with a few adherents finding refuge in the United States.

In Luke's Christology there is no concept of preexistence. It is at Jesus' baptism that the Spirit descends upon him in bodily form as a dove, designating him the beloved Son. Jesus is now empowered to baptize "with the Holy Spirit and with fire" rather than with water. Jesus' control over demonic forces and over nature, including his acts of healing, is evidence of his authority and proves that in him Scripture (Isa. 61) is being fulfilled (Luke 4:16–30). In Matthew, by contrast, Jesus' authority is demonstrated through his teaching, as in the Sermon on the Mount (Matt. 5–7; cf. "You have heard that it was said, but I say to you . . ."), which is placed at the beginning of Jesus' ministry. Luke's emphasis upon Jesus' deeds is also seen in his account of Jesus' response to John's question whether Jesus was "he who is to come": "Go and tell John what you have seen and heard: the blind receive their sight, the lame walk, . . ." (7:18–23).

Just as the history of salvation is divided into three epochs, so also is the ministry of Jesus, with each phase introduced by a scene of manifestation: baptism, transfiguration, and entry into Jerusalem. The first phase is characterized by Jesus bringing salvation "today" through his acts of healing (4:23, 33–41). The second phase, which follows upon Peter's confession and the first prediction of the passion, is introduced by the transfiguration (9:28–36) during which a voice from heaven again designates Jesus as the chosen Son (v. 35). With this new section, the journey to Jerusalem begins (9:51–56), which follows a second prediction of the passion (9:43b–45) and a dispute about roles in the kingdom. The journey to Jerusalem is destined, "for it cannot be that a prophet should perish away from Jerusalem" (13:31–33). It is to take three days, but there is no trace of progress in the journey; rather, in Luke's christological construction and in contrast to Mark's, the journey is but symbolic of Jesus' full awareness of his passion.[13] Luke alters the tradition in that whereas according to Mark the misunderstanding that accompanies Jesus concerns his messiahship, in Luke the misunderstanding pertains to the suffering accompanying it (see Luke 9:43b–45; 18:34). One also notes that only in Luke is Jesus hailed as king (19:38) upon his triumphal entry; and it is not into Jerusalem as such that he goes, but into the temple (19:45). He does not enter Jerusalem until the supper "as a prelude to the Passion." "We can see a two-fold goal, to which Jesus' journey has been leading: the goal of the journey is Kingship, in other words, the Temple, but the way to glory

13. Conzelmann, *Theology of Saint Luke*, 60–73.

leads on to the Passion, in other words, into the city of Jerusalem." It is a distinction, Conzelmann suggests, that influenced the life of the early church.[14]

The reappearance of Satan (22:3) marks the beginning of the passion and the renewed temptation it entails (22:28, 40, 46). Peter will be "sifted" and the others are instructed "to pray that they may not enter into temptation." According to Conzelmann, there is nothing in Luke to suggest that the crucifixion of Jesus is an atonement for sin.[15] The Markan phrase that the Son of man will die to give his life "as a ransom for many" (10:45b) is omitted by Luke (cf. Luke 2:26–27). Also omitted is the cry of dereliction and the mistaken belief by the crowd that Jesus was calling upon Elijah (Mark 15:34–36). Jesus dies as he commends his spirit back to God. The geographical dimension of the divine economy reemerges in Jesus' directive to his disciples that they remain in Jerusalem. Here Luke knowingly contradicts the tradition found in Mark. Not only is Mark 14:28 ("I will go before you to Galilee") omitted, so also are the words of the risen Lord instructing the women at the tomb to tell the disciples to go to Galilee (Luke 24:6–7). In Luke the disciples on the road to Emmaus return "to Jerusalem" (24:33), where, in an upper room, the risen Lord commands them to preach repentance and forgiveness of sins to all the nations, "beginning from Jerusalem" (24:48). This geographical reference is repeated on the day of ascension: "You shall receive power when the Holy Spirit has come upon you; and you shall be my witnesses in Jerusalem, and in all Judea, and Samaria and to the end of the earth" (Acts 1:8). The center ripples outward from Jerusalem.

The ascension also marks the end of Jesus' "bodily" appearances following the resurrection; thereafter his appearance is "from heaven," where he is seated at the right hand of God (22:69; Acts 2:33–34) and from whence he shall come to judge the world (10:42; 17:30–31), as in Paul's Damascus road experience (Acts 9; 12; 22). And though the risen Christ is made known in the breaking of bread (Luke 24:35), it is the presence of the Holy Spirit, given through baptism, that serves as a substitute for Jesus' bodily presence. This is the role of Pentecost, which, together with the ascension of Jesus into heaven, marks the beginning of the church, the third epoch in the history of redemption. The mission of the church is to proclaim the risen Lord as the "author of life," to warn of his role as the future judge of the earth, to call for

14. Ibid., 198–99.
15. Ibid., 201, 228 n. 1.

repentance and faith in the forgiveness of sins through baptism and for discipleship in the Christian life.

Although Conzelmann sketches out Luke's theology more fully than this, analyzing its development in telling the history of the early church in his Acts of the Apostles, I have here given at least a brief indication of the intent and practice of redaction criticism. Many others have followed in Conzelmann's footsteps, not only with regard to Matthew and John, but also examining the Gospel of Luke further as well. In Old Testament studies one speaks more appropriately of "the history of redaction," because a much greater length of time is involved, with evidence of editing by more than one hand.

SUMMARY

As noted in my opening paragraph, modern biblical criticism turned the perspective of premodern thought inside out. Instead of interpreting the world by way of the Bible, modern biblical criticism interpreted the Bible by way of the world, under the assumption that its findings were objective and neutral, unadulterated by the historical circumstance, social location, and philosophical or theological bias of the modern interpreter. A positive result of this reversal was to bring the human element of Scripture to the fore. Passages once deemed crude and objectionable to Origen, Augustine, and others could now be seen as the work of fallible human beings, rather than as God engaging in deliberate obfuscation to enhance the role of faith. But by treating the Bible as a source book of ancient literature and history, critics overlooked how the Bible was actually used within the life of the community of faith. Its purpose as a sacred text for religious instruction and enlightenment was ignored, and the exegesis of Scripture, once the very essence of Protestant theological thought and training, now became an esoteric science reserved for scholars unrelated to the task of theological reflection. This state of affairs could not change until it was recognized that the distinction between determining what a text meant and what it means is a questionable distinction, and that the notion of neutrality in interpretation is neither an accurate description of the hermeneutical problem nor a goal to be achieved.

Chapter 11
What Is Contemporary Biblical Interpretation?

In recent decades the practice of biblical interpretation has undergone a change so radical as to be described as nothing less than a second revolution, analogous to the introduction of the historical-critical method into biblical studies in the nineteenth century. This revolution has transformed biblical studies from a single discipline to a field of disciplines, each with its own theoretical assumptions and methodologies so diverse and complex (even contradictory) that no one practitioner of biblical criticism can hope to master them all. These methods and approaches include rhetorical criticism, structuralism, ideological criticism, canonical criticism, reader-response criticism, Afrocentric, feminist, African American, Latino, Asian, and postcolonial biblical interpretation, to name but a few.[1]

Since we cannot address all of these, even in the briefest way, we shall focus on three approaches to biblical interpretation that are especially characteristic of the present day. They are postmodern, liberation, and postcritical biblical interpretation. What these three approaches share, as we shall see, is a sense that it is necessary to move beyond the typical assumptions of "modern" biblical criticism, as illustrated in the preceding chapter, at least in certain important ways.

---

1. For definitions of these and other technical terms, see Richard N. Soulen and R. Kendall Soulen, *Handbook of Biblical Criticism*, 3rd ed. (Louisville: Westminster John Knox, 2001).

A POSTMODERN ANALOGY: ON PLAYING BALL
WITH THE TEXT

With the term *postmodern* having as many definitions as *modern*, we can at best depict the postmodern mind-set in a general way with the following, admittedly imperfect, analogy, before offering a brief example.

Let us imagine an automobile stopped at a railway crossing as a passenger train speeds by. Inside the train a boy stands in an aisle bouncing a brightly luminous ball. A curious passenger inside the train (A), oblivious of the train's speed and of the world outside, mentally records the ball traveling its vertical course straight up and down. The driver of the automobile outside (B), aided by magical vision, sees something different. As the speeding railcar enters her vision from the left, she sees the ball leave the boy's hand, hitting the floor only when boy and ball are directly in front of her stopped automobile, bouncing back to the waiting hand when they exit from the driver's view as the train disappears down the track. From the driver's point of view, the ball did not travel in a vertical line up and down, but in a luminous path like a flattened V.

Which observer, one might ask, possesses the *neutral and objective* view of the bouncing ball? It is a question that would never have occurred to anyone prior to the Enlightenment, the beginning of the scientific quest for objectivity in observation. For this reason we call the search for objectivity the modernist's mind-set. The modernist assumes that such a privileged position of neutrality must exist somewhere, even in the interpretation of ancient texts. Reimarus, Schleiermacher, and Jefferson are all modernists in this respect.

From the standpoint of the postmodernist, however, there is no neutral location from which the movement of the ball (or the meaning of a text) can be objectively described in a *universally valid* manner. There are only an infinite number of possible locations, each with its own attendant and relatively valid description, one as valid as another; or, to put the problem in another postmodern way, the shape of the ball's movement, like the meaning of texts, is not something that inheres or subsists in the ball/text itself; shape of movement and the meaning of texts must be said to be indeterminate *until* observed from a *specific* location. Both "shape of movement" and "meaning" are relational concepts. They are judgments made by observers (readers) based on their (social) location.

Changing our metaphors a bit and confining ourselves to texts, one can say the "world" of the text exists "in front of the text" in the interaction between the language of the text and the "location" of the interpreter. Here "location" refers to that complex of attitudes, beliefs, values, knowledge, and so on, which readers bring to the task of interpretation. Location changes *over* time (diachronically: from immaturity to maturity in a single individual, or from one century to another through generations of interpreters) and *at* a given time (synchronically: as for example when a New Testament text is read by a diversity of contemporaneous persons who are rich/poor, Jewish/Christian, male/female, black/white, first world/third world, etc.). At most all one can hope to have, say the postmodernists, is the multiple viewpoints of these observers, each with its own relative validity, analogous to viewing a text from the diverse social locations of feminists, womanists, postcolonialists, African Americans, Marxists, atheists, and so on—all of which make up contemporary biblical interpretation.[2]

The analogy offers still another aspect. According to it, only one person, or class of persons, can "play ball with the boy"—those who are on the train. Is this also true of texts? Is there an "insider's" meaning, from which outsiders are excluded? If so, who then is this "insider"? Contemporary biblical interpretation thinks about these things, as the church has from the beginning.

POSTMODERN BIBLICAL INTERPRETATION:
JOHN FRANK KERMODE

Sir John is not often listed among interpreters of Scripture, or classed among the postmodernists. For many years he held the King Edward VII Chair of English Literature at Cambridge, before holding joint tenure at Columbia University (New York). He was knighted in 1991 for his distinguished life in literary criticism. Kermode did however turn to the narratives and parables of the Gospel of Mark as the focus of his work, *The Genesis of Secrecy: On the Interpretation of Narrative*.[3] The book concludes with the following summation of his postmodern sentiments:

2. For definitions of these and other technical terms, see ibid.
3. Kermode, *The Genesis of Secrecy: On the Interpretation of Narrative* (Cambridge: Harvard University Press, 1979). With Robert Alter, Kermode also edited *The Literary Guide to the Bible* (Cambridge: Harvard University Press, 1987). Using Mark 4:11–12 as his starting point, Kermode devotes his first chapter to "insider" and "outsider" (his spiritual and carnal) interpretation. Who's Who? is one of the questions of this chapter.

World and book, it may be, are hopelessly plural, endlessly disappointing; we stand alone before them, aware of their arbitrariness and impenetrability, knowing that they may be narratives only because of our impudent intervention, and susceptible of interpretation only by our hermetic tricks. Hot for secrets . . . our sole hope and pleasure is in the perception of a momentary radiance, before the door of disappointment is finally shut on us.[4]

Not all postmodernists are as bleak in their outlook as Kermode, but he is representative nonetheless. From Kermode's point of view [sic] texts and their interpretations are "hopelessly plural" because texts do not refer either to a real or possible world that could serve as a measure of their truthfulness. Even an "extended parable" such as the Good Samaritan (Luke 10:25–37) is susceptible to "interminable" interpretations, as the history of exegesis shows. Each interpreter, thinking his or her own sense of the parable's meaning is the natural one, is only "authenticating, or claiming as universal, a habit of thought that is cultural and arbitrary."[5]

The very details of the story (such as the two denarii paid to the innkeeper in the parable), ostensibly provided to clarify intended meaning, have served as invitations to discover a plethora of hidden and secret meanings, suggesting that the process of interpretation need never cease, but also, less hearteningly, that it never comes to resolution or fruition.

This, says Kermode, is Mark's point in quoting Jesus, "To you has been given the secret of the kingdom of God, but for those outside everything is in parables; so that[6] they may indeed see but not perceive, and may indeed hear but not understand" (Mark. 4:11–12). For Mark (according to Kermode), "the parables are about everybody's incapacity to penetrate their sense."[7] From Kermode's postmodern perspective, there are no "insiders" privileged to recognize true meaning. To be an "insider" is to understand that there is no "inside," that *everyone* is an outsider. Not because this is Jesus' intention (an unknowable quantity), but because opaqueness, that is, the ability to hide as well as to reveal, is the nature of narrative, and deliberately so of the parable, best defined as a "dark saying" or "riddle" (cf. Hebrew *mashal*). In this

---

4. *Genesis of Secrecy*, 145.
5. Ibid., 35.
6. Mark uses here the Greek subjunctive *hina*, meaning "in order that" (thus predestining incomprehension); Matthew changes Mark to use the indicative *hoti*, meaning "because" (stating a simple fact). Kermode sees *hina* as original.
7. *Genesis of Secrecy*, 27.

inherent incapacity of the interpreter to divine the true sense lies "disappointment." To seek "the recovery of the real right original thing is," consequently, "an illusory quest."[8]

It is only when the reader intervenes in the text, assigning sense where none preexists, in response to some "momentary radiance," that one may arbitrarily establish meaning—only afterward to discover that such intervention inevitably leads to a dead end from which one must ultimately turn back in disillusionment. Institutions, whether ecclesiastical or academic, maintain their apparently hegemonic interpretations by arbitrarily imposing their own traditional idea of order upon the text. Rightly understood, texts are "treacherous networks," rather than "a continuous and systematic sequence." Order is extrinsic. Even texts that seem to be proclamation "are in fact obscurely oracular."[9]

The ending of Mark's Gospel, a conundrum to even its earliest readers, offers Kermode a case in point. The Gospel, which initially declares with terse and forceful brevity "the beginning of the good news of Jesus Christ, Son of God," ends awkwardly and reticently with the laconic utterance, "And they said nothing to anyone, for they were afraid." Mary Magdalene, Mary the mother of James, and Salome, having found the tomb empty and been informed by an angel that the risen Jesus was going before them to Galilee, are so startled that they are stupefied into silence (Mark 16:1–8). The Gospel that begins with a trumpet call ends, says Kermode, with the whisper of timid women.[10] The reader can make of it anything she or he wills. The Gospel concludes without closure. It is the kind of ambiguity institutional prejudices for order (such as that of the church) do not wish to let stand, as documented by the existence of textual additions to the ending of Mark (16:9–20).

For Kermode, the narrative of the empty tomb is simply a clue to the structure of Mark's Gospel. With its intercalated narratives (see, e.g., the narratives of Jairus's daughter and the woman with a hemorrhage in 5:21–43), the Gospel is a series of interrupted disclosures and concealments that mimics the human predicament of being in the world. What for Kermode the narrative does *not* do, on its literal level, is mean what it says; it does not offer a clue to the world, or to the narrated world, or to a possible world. Like the women, it is silent.

8. Ibid., 125.
9. Ibid.
10. Ibid., 68.

LIBERATION BIBLICAL INTERPRETATION:
JON SOBRINO

In the second half of the twentieth century three dominant cultural forces, particularly in the Americas, caused many Christian and secular scholars alike to turn to Scripture for one of two reasons: either to liberate the culture from the oppressive use of the Bible, or to find within the Bible as sacred Scriptures the theological resources to liberate both the Bible and the culture from forces of oppression.[11] Responding to racial, gender, and socioeconomic forms of injustice, these movements have been called black liberation, women's liberation, and liberation theology, the last more narrowly denoting a movement within both Roman Catholic and Protestant churches in Latin America on behalf of the poor. Diverging somewhat from the path we have taken in the previous chapters, we turn to the Jesuit priest Jon Sobrino to illustrate but one of these, liberation theology.

Born to a Basque family in Barcelona, Spain, Sobrino entered the Jesuit Order in 1957 and was sent to El Salvador the following year. Over a period of thirteen years he furthered his education in engineering and theology in the United States and Germany before returning to San Salvador in 1974 where, he tells us, he "began to wake from the sleep of inhumanity."[12] There he taught at the University of Central America, a Jesuit school he helped establish. In 1989 his outspoken support of the martyred bishop Oscar Romero and his activity on behalf of the poor, along with that of his colleagues, resulted in the murder by the Salvadoran military of six fellow Jesuits as well as his housekeeper and her young daughter in the rectory of the university.[13] By sheer happenstance Sobrino was out of the country and escaped the massacre.

Hermeneutical Location: Thoroughgoing Historicism and the Church of the Poor

Father Sobrino achieved international attention with the 1976 Spanish publication of *Cristología desde américa latina,* translated as *Christology at*

---

11. In general terms these two hermeneutical maneuvers have been called "hermeneutics of suspicion" and "hermeneutics of recovery [or retrieval]."

12. Jon Sobrino, *The Principle of Mercy: Taking the Crucified People from the Cross* (Maryknoll, N.Y.: Orbis, 1994), 3.

13. The martyrs' names are Ignacio Ellacuria, Segundo Montes, Juan Ramón Moreno, Ignacio Martin Baró, Amando López, Joaquin López y López, and Elba and Celina Ramos.

the Crossroads.[14] In this book he stressed the need for a thoroughgoing historical and dialectical approach to the question of Christian faith and praxis. The hermeneutical principle for the interpretation of Scripture, and most particularly the historical Jesus, Sobrino argues, must be derived from the life situation of the church of the poor, not from the high point of doctrinal abstraction. Like Jesus himself, it is the innocent poor who suffer under brutal regimes and systems of injustice and oppression, and it is such suffering that raises the question of God's goodness and love in a manner wholly analogous to what happened on the cross of Jesus of Nazareth. The cross embodies "the problem of love's impotence vis-à-vis sin, of the impotence of good vis-à-vis evil . . . Though it may not always be made explicitly clear, that is the ultimate context in which liberation theology is elaborated. Liberation theology concretizes theodicy"—that is, the task of "reconciling God with what is negative in life and reality (e.g., sin, injustice, oppression, and death)."[15]

By beginning with the life setting of the poor, and finding a parallel between their experience and that of Jesus, it naturally follows in Sobrino's thought that one must also begin with the historical Jesus and not with the Christ of faith in determining who Jesus is and what faith in him requires. In Sobrino's favorite phrase, the *Jesus of history is chronologically and logically prior to the Christ of faith,* and when abstract concepts such as "Son of God" and "Eternal Logos" are used to explain the attitudes and acts of Jesus, such as attributing to him foreknowledge or supernatural power, then Jesus himself is "disfigured" and alienated from the world. Ecclesially and epistemologically speaking, therefore, a hermeneutical circle exists for Sobrino between the Jesus of history and the church of the poor. Each illumines the life of the other. This is Sobrino's interpretive principle.

The Historical Jesus

"By 'historical Jesus' we mean the life of Jesus of Nazareth, his words and actions, his activity and his praxis, his attitudes and his spirit, his fate on the cross (and the resurrection). In other words, and expressed systematically, the history of Jesus."[16] According to Sobrino, the

---

14. The original published: Rio Hondo, Mexico: Centro de Reflexión Teológica, 1976; English translation by John Drury; Maryknoll, N.Y.: Orbis, 1978.

15. Sobrino, *Christology at the Crossroads*, 224, 350.

16. Jon Sobrino, *Jesus the Liberator: A Historical-Theological Reading of Jesus of Nazareth*, trans. Paul Burns and Francis McDonagh (Maryknoll, N.Y.: Orbis, 1993), 50.

history of Jesus is marked by two stages, the first ending in a crisis in Galilee accompanied by a "conversion" in Jesus' self-understanding. In this first stage Jesus appears in the traditional role of the eschatological prophet who preaches the imminent coming of the kingdom of God that will free history from oppression: "This is the time of fulfillment. The reign of God is at hand! Reform your lives and believe in the gospel!" (Mark 1:14b Sobrino). Here Jesus follows in complete continuity with the prophetic tradition. He "called disciples to accompany him on his mission, castigated the sin of oppressors, demanded a faith-trust of the poor and of sinners, prayed in exultation and thanksgiving."[17] In this stage Jesus' teachings are neither about himself nor about God, but about the coming kingdom and its demands (Mark 2:18–20, 22; 9:37 par.; Luke 10:23–24; John 4:35; Matt. 12:38; *et passim*).

The kingdom comes at God's "initiative, gift, and grace," liberating and restructuring human existence at every level. This is the good news, and it is given uniquely to the poor and despised (sinners, prostitutes, publicans, lepers, etc.). In this stage attention is given less to orthodoxy than to orthopraxis. To speak of God as Father, as Jesus does, requires creating communities of brothers and sisters who respond to God in faith and obedience. Sin is perceived to be not just personal but collective. Sin prohibits the utopia of the kingdom of God. Sin is not something merely to be pardoned but to be *taken away* (John 1:29): "The blind receive their sight and the lame walk, lepers are cleansed and the deaf hear, and the dead are raised up, and the poor have good news preached to them" (Matt. 11:5). All the acts of Jesus in this first period are acts of reconciliation, and wherever society, religion, or politics has erected barriers to reconciliation, Jesus uses his power to break down those barriers, whether in the performance of miracles, in table fellowship, or in his proclamation. Such demonstrations of power are perceived by Jesus himself as signs of the kingdom's arrival, the overcoming of the anti-kingdom: "If it is by the finger of God that I cast out demons, then the kingdom of God has come upon you" (Luke 11:20). In these acts of salvation *Utopia* (as something awaited) becomes *topia* (something known).[18] This first stage, however, ends in crisis. Jesus' reconciling acts are insufficient to usher people into the kingdom. "The sin-ridden concrete situation strips Jesus of his power," and he must

---

17. Ibid., 148.
18. Ibid., 78. Here Sobrino is using the terms (*Utopia* and *topia*) of Leonardo Boff, "Salvation in Jesus Christ and the Process of Liberation," *Concilium* 96 (vol. 6, no. 10) (1974): 81.

turn to "the power of truth and of the sacrifice of one's life for others out of love."[19]

This "Galilean crisis," Sobrino asserts, is most clearly recorded in Mark 8. In spite of his activity in the traditional mold of eschatological prophet, the Pharisees still ask for a sign (v. 13); the disciples do not understand him (v. 21), and even Peter must be rebuked, "Get behind me, Satan! For you are setting your mind not on divine things but on human things" (v. 33 Sobrino). Geographically the crisis is symbolized by Jesus leaving Galilee and going to the region of Tyre and Sidon and to Caesarea Philippi (7:24, 31; 8:27). This external crisis leads to an internal conversion on Jesus' part, by which Sobrino means a "turning back" to God, an abandoning of Jesus' "own" place and a turning to "meet God 'there' where God wishes to be met."[20] Jesus abandons the traditional apocalyptic expectation of God's coming kingdom and takes on the role attributed to the Suffering Servant (Mark 8:34).[21] The *person* of Jesus rather than the powerful signs of the kingdom now become normative for Jesus' followers. Jesus himself becomes the way into the kingdom.

Whereas faith and hope were active in the first stage, practical service in the manner of Jesus is demanded in the second. Theologically speaking, the divinity of Jesus (instead of being construed as something divine within Jesus) is seen in relational terms (Luke 11:20; Mark 2:1–12). The Son is the Way to the Father. Discipleship to Jesus is service to the kingdom, which in itself is salvific (Mark 8:19–22, 34–35). From this point on in his ministry Jesus no longer speaks of the closeness of the kingdom; he performs no miracles (and even forbids them), he casts out no demons nor welcomes sinners. The disciples are no longer called into missionary activity. Their lack of comprehension prohibits Jesus from entrusting them with that responsibility. Instruction changes accordingly. From now on the disciples must simply bear their cross. No longer is the sin of the world castigated; it is a reality that has to be borne. In this second stage the prayer life of Jesus also changes; prayer is no longer thankful exultation but the abandonment of the self to the will of God. In a move indicative of his fidelity to God, Jesus sets his face toward Jerusalem (Luke 9:51) fully aware of its consequences in light of the death of John the Baptist (Mark 6:17–29 par.). In this act of obedience the lingering crisis of temptation is overcome.

19. Sobrino, *Christology at the Crossroads*, 359.
20. Sobrino, *Jesus the Liberator*, 148.
21. Sobrino, *Christology at the Crossroads*, 58.

The temptation of Jesus, related by all three Synoptic Gospels (Matt. 4:1–11; Mark 1:12–13; Luke 4:1–13) as well as the Letter to the Hebrews (4:15) and anachronistically placed at the beginning of Jesus' ministry, is to be understood as a theological reflection on the actual temptation Jesus faced. It had to do with the question: With what power shall he serve the kingdom of God? The struggle is not with Satan, but with his own self-identification. It is not a question that arose once but represents "the climate in which his life unfolded."[22] That finally Jesus did not flinch from the temptation to flee from history shows that "he let God be God and that he let himself be carried by God wherever this might lead." "At the end, on the cross, Jesus does not speak of the Kingdom of God, but launches a tortured cry to God. . . . He set out to change history according to the will of God, but history changed him in relation to God."[23]

The Death of Jesus

As noted, the hermeneutical perspective of Sobrino is that of the church of the poor. The explanation for the cross of Jesus, he writes, is readily at hand in the experience of poor people. In the words of the martyred bishop Oscar Romero, Jesus died because "'those who get in the way get killed.' Jesus, surrounded by conflict, got in the way, in the last resort because he got in the way of other gods and he got in their way in the name of God."[24] He did so directly in the religious sphere and indirectly in the social, political, and economic spheres. It is a conflict between the kingdom of God and the anti-kingdom and their mediators (Jesus vs. the Sanhedrin, Herod, Pilate). The Gospels make clear that the chief priests wanted "to put him to death" (Mark 14:55; Matt. 26:59) because "he deserves death" (Mark 14:64; Matt. 26:66). According to Sobrino, the immediate cause, in addition to blasphemy (Mark 14:62 par.) and siding with the devil (Mark 3:19–30 par.), is that Jesus intended to destroy the temple (Matt. 28:59–62 par.), the "structuring core of Jewish society," jeopardizing the very source of power on which the priesthood depended. The priests could not permit Jesus' continuing existence (cf. Luke 6:11; 11:53; 13:31; 19:47; 20:19). The high priest, in the name of "the living God" (Matt. 26:63) sends Jesus to his death; thus "Jesus is

22. Sobrino, *Jesus the Liberator*, 150.
23. Ibid., 148.
24. Ibid., 196.

condemned in the name of a god," the god of worldly, albeit religious, power.[25] However, as representative of Rome, only Pilate has the authority to execute Jesus by crucifixion. The historical context, Sobrino suggests, may be the insurrection in which Barabbas was implicated (Mark 15:7). The religious forces may have wanted, "as is still done today," to associate Jesus with politically subversive groups or actions to make their charges convincing, however unjust or illogical: "We found this man perverting our nation, forbidding us to pay taxes to the emperor, and saying that he himself is the Messiah, a king" (Luke 23:2; cf. John 19:12–15).

Sobrino argues that the theological issue is most clearly presented in John's Gospel (chaps. 18–19). Jesus is a king and has a kingdom, but it is "not of this world." In John's language "this world" is the ideology of the "anti-kingdom." But this (material) world is also the locus of the kingdom of God. The difference lies in the distinction between the world of truth and the world of lies (John 18:37), between the God of Jesus and Caesar, the god of the Roman Empire. Both are "real and historical" and "cannot be contrasted as 'spiritual' and 'material'" as many in the church today are wont to do.[26] For Pilate, who wants to release Jesus, the appearance of setting himself against the emperor (John 19:12) is too grave to let Jesus go (19:16). It is inevitable, then, that Jesus, as mediator of the kingdom of God, should be killed by the mediator of the anti-kingdom. The danger to this kingdom is summed up by Caiaphas: "It is better to have one man to die for the people than to have the whole nation destroyed" (John 11:50; cf. New Century). Jesus represents a greater threat to the existing sociopolitical religious organization than did Barabbas.[27] And so Jesus is crucified. Theologically speaking, says Sobrino, this means that "on the cross God himself is crucified. The Father suffers the death of his Son and takes upon himself all the sorrow and pain of history."[28] This is a truth about history only those engaged in following after Jesus come fully to understand.

The Resurrection of Jesus

The resurrection of Jesus, Sobrino argues, is an eschatological event that has its own distinctive relationship to history. The tradition,

---

25. *The Holy Bible. New Century Version* (Nashville, Tenn.: Thomas Nelson, 1987).
26. Sobrino, *Jesus the Liberator,* 208.
27. Ibid., 209.
28. Sobrino, *Christology at the Crossroads*, 370.

which provides no account of the resurrection as such, takes two forms: accounts of apparitions (the oldest being 1 Cor. 15:3–5, 7) and of the empty tomb (Mark 16:1–8 par.), the latter being a later, perhaps apologetic, tradition—in any case the tradition is not speaking of the revivification of a corpse. What cannot be doubted is that "the disciples had some sort of privileged experience," as its impact on their lives and behavior indicates.[29] Their faith, shattered at the cross, is revived, and it is tied to appearances of the risen Jesus. Equally important are the radical theological assertions that arise from this experience: God is given a new name, as the one "who has raised Jesus from the dead and who brings into being things that have not yet existed." God is now defined as a "liberating power" whose transforming love has become "historicized" in the cross of Jesus. It is understood as a saving action of pardon and revitalization, not one of retribution. "Humanity has been offered a new kind of life based on hope and love. . . . It is a hope *against* death and injustice (the biblical model) rather than simply a hope *above and beyond* death and injustice (the Greek model)."[30] And because it is the Jesus of history who has been raised, it is his way of living, his preaching, his deeds, and his death that have been confirmed. This leads to another characteristic of the resurrection experience: it went hand in hand with a summons to mission. Sobrino concludes: "The meaning of Jesus' resurrection cannot be grasped unless one engages in active service for the transformation of an unredeemed world."[31]

In March 2007 the Vatican's Congregation for the Doctrine of the Faith (formerly the Holy Office of the Inquisition) issued a notification admonishing Sobrino for ideas contained in two works in particular, *Jesus the Liberator* (1991) and *Christ the Liberator* (1999). Although he was neither condemned nor censured in these documents, the congregation did declare that his works contained "propositions which are either erroneous or dangerous and may cause harm to the faithful." Archbishop Fernando Sáenz Lacalle of San Salvador, however, banned Sobrino from teaching at the University of Central America and from lecturing in the archdiocese; the bishop also caused the removal of the Catholic stamp of approval, the *nihil obstat,* from Sobrino's publications.

29. Ibid., 375.
30. Ibid., 377, 380.
31. Ibid.

POSTCRITICAL BIBLICAL INTERPRETATION:
HANS FREI

Postcritical biblical interpretation may be defined as "an approach to scripture undertaken by a community of scholars for whom returning to the biblical text embodies, beyond all scholarship, a living relationship with God and humankind" without which Scripture simply cannot be understood on its own terms.[32] It is postcritical, not in the sense that it rejects the critical methodologies that have arisen in the past three hundred years, but that it judges these methodologies (see chap. 10) to be inadequate to the task of interpreting Scripture because they bracket out Scripture's ultimate subject matter: God's relationship to humanity and humanity's relationship to God. Further, they are inadequate because the practitioners of these methodologies, working in academic autonomy and isolation, often disregard the testimony of the very communities, Jewish and Christian, that hold these Scriptures sacred. We turn to Hans Frei to illustrate but one mode of postcritical interpretation of Scripture, one that has resonated broadly across a wide spectrum of contemporary Christian reflection.

Hans Frei was born in Breslau, Germany, of Jewish parentage in 1922. With the rise of Hitler in 1933, he fled with his family to England, where he attended Anglican public schools before moving to America. He would later recount that a crucifix, confronted each day as he entered his school in England, made a deep and abiding impression on him, accounting perhaps for his Jesus-centered piety and for his attraction to the postcritical theology of the Swiss theologian Karl Barth, the subject of his Yale doctoral dissertation under his influential teacher H. Richard Niebuhr. Frei spent the last thirty-one years of his life on the faculty of Yale University.

Thesis

In 1974 and 1975, respectively, Hans Frei published *The Eclipse of Biblical Narrative* and *The Identity of Jesus Christ*. Although both books are densely written, they have had a significant impact on the development of biblical interpretation in subsequent decades.

---

32. See Soulen and Soulen, *Handbook of Biblical Criticism*, 139–40, "Postcritical Biblical Interpretation."

For this reason, a synopsis of Frei's argument warrants stating: For the past two hundred years and more, Christian theologians have put the cart before the horse. They have tried (sometimes frantically) to prove that God really is *present* in Christ Jesus, before they have taken the time to carefully observe *who Christ Jesus is*. But who Christ is, is something that the Gospels set before us in the form of realistic narratives. Therefore, Christians need to attend first to the way the Gospels use realistic narrative to depict Christ's "unsubstitutable identity" (as Frei puts it), before they then seek to account for God's saving presence in him. But this, in turn, requires that Christians relearn how to appreciate the Gospels as realistic narratives, that is, as stories, not as reports about history or edifying moral truths.

The *Sensus Literalis* of the Text

We noted earlier (chap. 9) that Frei wrote *The Eclipse of Biblical Narrative* to expose how the classical Christian understanding of Scripture as *realistic narrative* had been persistently displaced over the last three centuries by its subordination to ever changing philosophical and anthropological preconceptions of what constituted the meaningfulness of Scripture—be these preconceptions religious, metaphysical, moral, existential, or whatever. Following the lead of Karl Barth, Frei objects to any such preconditions: "There can be no systematic 'pre-understanding,' no single, specific, consistently used conceptual scheme, no independent anthropology, hermeneutics, ontology or whatever, in terms of which Christian language and Christian claims must be cast in order to be meaningful."[33] Of the Gospels in particular, he writes, "There really is an analogy between the Bible and a novel writer who says something like this: I mean what I say whether or not anything took place. I mean what I say. It's as simple as that: the text means what it says."[34]

The problem, Frei says, is that since the nineteenth century and the rise of historical criticism a category error has occurred in which the *meaningfulness* of Scripture is said to be dependent upon the *truth* claims of its historical reference. The error in this conception of truthfulness is that while the Gospel narratives do have historical referents (e.g., the "historical" Jesus, or John the Baptist), they also have a *textual*

---

33. Hans Frei, *Types of Christian Theology*, ed. George Hunsinger and William C. Placher (New Haven: Yale University Press, 1992), 156.
34. Frei, *Theology and Narrative*, 208.

referent (e.g., the "Word of God," which was in the beginning with God [cf. John 1:1]). Frei's point is that from the perspective of the Gospels *as narratives*, the latter cannot be bracketed out of consideration as mythological, symbolic, or whatever, if the text is to be understood as it intends to be understood.

Frei insists that the statement, "God was in Christ reconciling the world to himself," is an adequate account of what the Gospel texts are referring to in a way analogous to whatever historical reference may also be present—"even though we cannot say univocally how." He asks: "Should I really say that the eternal Word made flesh, that is, made fact indeed, is a fact like any other? I can talk about 'Jesus' that way, but can I talk about the eternal Word made flesh in him that way? I don't think so."[35] Historical reference and textual reference are two radically different ways of referring. From Frei's point of view, the "abiding mystery of the union of the divine with the historical," which is the radical claim of the gospel message, is properly (though not exhaustively) conveyed in the Gospels by narratively depicting a realistic series of "miraculous events that are in the nature of the case unique, incomparable, and impenetrable." Taken literally such narratives must be construed to be "the adequate *testimony* to, rather than an accurate *report* of, the reality" to which they refer—that God was in Christ. To set forth this claim is their primary function and their meaning as texts. The hermeneutical and theological task is to restore this *sensus literalis* of Scripture— and therefore Scripture's subject matter—to its rightful role by reading Scripture as realistic narrative, acknowledging that what the stories are about cannot be isolated from the stories themselves.

The Identity of Jesus Christ

The questions of the earliest Christians that we assayed briefly in chapters 1 and 5 are a central project of Frei's, namely, how are we to identify the man who hangs on the cross and how are we to account for the mystery of his presence within the community of faith. Although Frei later expresses qualms about the term *presence*, he suggests that the motivating force behind all Christian, and particularly Protestant, theology has been to set forth how "Jesus Christ is the presence of God in the church to the world."[36] Frei addressed this subject in a series of

35. Ibid., 211.
36. Frei, *Types of Theology*, 8.

essays in the 1960s that later appeared as *The Identity of Jesus Christ* (1975).[37] Simply put, the identity of Jesus Christ is none other than what the narratives of the (Synoptic) Gospels in their *literal, realistic sense* present him to be, irrespective of their historical facticity. The hermeneutical task is "to observe the story itself—its structure, the shape of its movement, and its crucial transitions."[38] It is this narrated Christ who reveals the identity of the singular, unsubstitutable person Jesus of Nazareth behind the text, and it is this narrated Christ who has provided normative continuity to the life of the church despite all the time-conditioned variations in the interpretation of that narrative. The church errs, he argues, when it tries to first make the presence of Christ intelligible philosophically *before* establishing his identity exegetically, which comes from simply reading the Gospels as realistic narratives— the way they are always heard and read in the life of the church.

Concentrating on Luke, Frei sees the structure of the Gospel story as unfolding in three stages. The first, encompassing the birth narratives, is patterned after the cosmic savior figures of pagan mythology. These narratives reveal essentially nothing pertaining to the individual identity of Jesus of Nazareth; but, remarkably, the converse is true: that the historical person Jesus defines the savior figure, not the other way around. In the second stage, beginning either with the infancy narratives as in Matthew or with the baptism as in Mark and Luke, Jesus' identity begins to show forth, though subordinated to his generalized role as representative Israel (e.g., Matt. 1:1–17, 23; 2:6, 13–14, 18, *et passim*) or as the stylized figure of the Son of Man. In this stage, apart from these stylizations, Jesus' identity is manifested as one who is "sent" (Matt. 10:40; 26:53–54; Luke 24:26; John 3:16; 12:27; etc.) to enact the good of humankind in obedience to the will of God (Rom. 5:19; Phil. 2:8; Heb. 5:8). He redeems "guilty men by vicarious identification with their guilt and literal identification with their helplessness" (Isa. 53) out of the sheer quality of his compassion and love.[39] The third stage in the story is marked by the kind of sustained narrative needed to discern the coincidence of Jesus' intention and enactment more clearly. Such enactment is, Frei argues, singularly and unsubstitutably Jesus' own. It opens with Jesus' "turn to Jerusalem" under the shadow of the death of John the Baptist (Luke 9:51; 18:31–34). It is

---

37. Frei, *The Identity of Jesus Christ: The Hermeneutical Basis of Dogmatic Theology* (Philadelphia: Fortress, 1975); presented in serial form in *Crossroads*, 1967.

38. Ibid., 87. For clarity's sake we must bypass here the later nuances he gave to his ideas.

39. Ibid., 102. On the place of Isaiah 53 and the concept of vicarious suffering in Frei's thought, see the "Afterword" by George Hunsinger in *Theology and Narrative*, esp. 248.

most tellingly evident in the scenes of his passion, beginning with the preparation for the Passover and culminating in the Garden of Gethsemane. Here Jesus' inner world and outer world converge in the ineluctable test of his obedience: in prayer ("not my will but yours be done" [Luke 22:42]) and in his arrest ("Do you think that I cannot appeal to my Father, and he will at once send me more than twelve legions of angels? But how then should the scriptures be fulfilled, that it must be so?" [Matt. 26:53–54]). In this decision, Jesus makes "the purpose of God who sent him the very aim of his being." If a man is what he does most uniquely, Frei suggests, then here in this resolve in the garden Jesus "was most of all himself."[40] He freely supplants his own will with the will of God. The temptation to disobedience, enacted here in this crucial stage of the story, is anachronistically placed at the very beginning of the narrative in the temptation story (Luke 4:1–13 par.) to set forth who he is as the one who is obedient.

Each of the three stages, Frei avers, is marked by a discernible transition. The first is dominated by divine activity and human passivity. In the second Jesus himself enacts the power of divine presence ("The Spirit of the Lord is upon me . . ." [Luke 4:18]; "If by the finger of God I cast out demons . . ." [Luke 11:20]). The third stage is marked by the transition from initiative to increasing passivity, from power to powerlessness ("He saved others, he cannot save himself" [Mark 15:31]). It is in the Garden of Gethsemane that Jesus consents to the defeat of the very love whose saving efficacy he had obediently enacted as his specific vocation (Luke 4:18; cf. Isa. 61:1). What had been evidence of divine presence gives way to evidence of absence ("My God, my God, why have you forsaken me?" [Mark 15:34]). Yet what happens on the cross happens only by virtue of the divine will; Pilate would have no power unless it had been given from above (John 19:10). Jesus' intentions and actions are superseded by those of God.[41] Looking at the Gospel narratives as a whole, then, one can say that whereas in the passion and death of Jesus the initiative moves more and more from Jesus to God, in the resurrection God alone is and can be active (Acts 10:40; cf. 2:32; 3:15; 4:10). Even so, in these narratives "the sole identity to mark the presence of [God's] activity is Jesus."[42] "Jesus of Nazareth, he and none other (Lk. 24:36–43; Acts 9:5), marks the presence of the action of God."[43] If before in his ministry it

40. *Theology and Narrative*, 57.
41. *Identity of Jesus Christ*, 120.
42. Ibid., 121.
43. Ibid.

had been Jesus' intent to identify with God, here in the resurrection it is God's intent to identify with Jesus. God raises Jesus; Jesus does not raise himself. By way of resurrection, "the redeemer in need of redemption is in fact redeemed" (Acts 2:24–32, 36; 13:35–37). Jesus' intention to act on behalf of humankind is thus vindicated.

The Resurrection

To differentiate his own view of the resurrection from contemporary alternatives, Frei provides a fourfold typology.[44] The first type argues that the history of Jesus ends with the crucifixion, that the narrated events called "the resurrection" are unknowable and without theological significance; that they are in any case merely a mythological way of saying the cross of Christ possessed saving efficacy.[45] In this view, "the miracle of resurrection is something that happened to the faith of the disciples," not to Jesus (so, e.g., Rudolf Bultmann).[46] On this theme there are multiple variations. Not all are sympathetic to the disciples or place them in a positive light. Reimarus believed that the stories concerning the resurrection of Jesus were fabrications perpetrated by the apostles and that their "faith" was a fraud. Most Deists of the time, like Jefferson, held comparable opinions. According to Schleiermacher Jesus did not die on the cross, but only entered into a coma, being resuscitated by those who attended to his body in the tomb. Since Schleiermacher considered Jesus' whole life of "God-consciousness" to be miraculous, a special "miracle of resurrection" was immaterial to the ultimate estimate of the man. That the disciples confused resuscitation with resurrection was also essentially irrelevant. For other rationalists, the disciples were not being deceptive or fooled by false reasoning; nor were they simply confusing an internal, subjective experience for an external, objective reality; rather, these first adherents of Jesus were led astray by "that intensely heightened condition of spirit whose results were the visions of Christ."[47]

The second type, generally identified with fundamentalists and certain conservative evangelicals, declares that the Gospel accounts are "an absolutely accurate record of the things that actually happened."[48]

---

44. *Theology and Narrative*, 201.
45. Ibid., 202.
46. Ibid., 201. This is most notably the position of the existentialist theologian Rudolf Bultmann.
47. David Strauss, *The Christ of Faith and the Jesus of History: A Critique of Schleiermacher's The Life of Jesus*, translated and with an introduction by Leander E. Keck (Philadelphia: Fortress, 1977), 129.
48. *Theology and Narrative*, 202.

According to this view, the apparent discrepancies in the Gospel accounts of the empty tomb and the resurrection appearances in no wise contradict either one another or Paul's account in 1 Corinthians 15:3–8—for example, it is suggested that the role of women, so prominent in the Synoptic Gospels, was simply removed from the tradition behind 1 Corinthians 15 out of deference to or because of cultural prejudice.[49] Whereas the subject matter of the texts in the first instance refers to the faith of the disciples, here subject matter and reality are said to be one and the same.[50]

A third type falling between the two extremes asserts that the primary subject of the resurrection is Jesus, but that the biblical accounts of the resurrection are not to be taken literally. Rather than being physical in nature, the appearances of Jesus are to be understood spiritually, as a kind of ecstatic vision—not unlike those firsthand accounts of Francis of Assisi or St. Theresa.[51] However, in the case of the resurrection narratives, Frei observes, here the texts and the reality to which they refer "are not that closely related."[52]

The final view, with which Frei is in agreement, is that the subject matter of the texts "is indeed the bodily resurrection of Jesus" and that "the miracle of resurrection" is "a real event" but one "to which human depiction and conception are inadequate, even though the literal description is the best that can be offered."[53] Being fragmentary and confusing in themselves, the narratives "depict a series of miraculous events that are in the nature of the case unique, incomparable, and impenetrable—in short, the abiding mystery of the union of the divine with the historical, for our salvation from sin and death,"[54] It is this divine mystery that the narratives of the empty tomb and the resurrection appearances intend to convey. As such they are not only the adequate but "indeed, the indispensable means for grasping, even though not explaining, the mystery of Christ's resurrection as a real

49. See N. T. Wright, *The Resurrection of the Son of God* (Minneapolis: Augsburg Fortress, 2003); also *The Resurrection of Jesus: John Dominic Crossan and N. T. Wright in Dialogue,* ed. Robert B. Stewart (Minneapolis: Augsburg Fortress, 2005).

50. This position is identified with such persons as Carl F. H. Henry, *God, Revelation, and Authority,* 6 vols. (Waco, Texas: Word, 1976–1983), and Wolfhart Pannenberg, *Jesus God and Man,* trans. Lewis L. Wilkins and Duane A. Priebe (Philadelphia: Westminster Press, 1968), originally published as *Grundzüge der Christologie* (Gütersloh: Gütersloher Verlagshaus Gerd Mohn, 1964). For N. T. Wright, see n. 49. It should not be supposed, however, that the meaning of the resurrection is regarded as the same in each instance.

51. On ecstatic visions see Evelyn Underhill's *Mysticism* (12th ed.; New York: Noonday Press, 1955), 266–97, 358–79.

52. *Theology and Narrative,* 202–03.

53. Ibid., 203.

54. Ibid.

event." "This," Frei insists, "and not their credibility as evidence for the factuality of the event, is their primary function as texts."[55]

To treat the narrative of the empty tomb, for example, as having the status of a factual report and therefore as evidence of Jesus' resurrection as historical, says Frei, is to mistake its function as a text within the total gospel narrative. "It is to turn it from a witness of faith into a report, from testimony to the truth of the mystery that unites the divine and the human into a report of a simply and solely natural-type event that is supposed to demonstrate its divine character by running counter to customary natural experience."[56] Such an argument is unknown to Christian tradition prior to the Enlightenment. Similarly, to interpret the real subject matter of the texts as lying outside the narrative in the interior experience of the disciples, says Frei, is to misunderstand, and even to deny, the actual role of the texts in Christian experience.

The true function of the narratives of the resurrection, Frei contends, is to bear witness to the fact that despite "the real, complete disruption of death," "Jesus, raised from the dead, was the same person, the same identity as before." This is the import of the narrative stress on the physicality of the risen Jesus; it is saying that as in life so in death, "it is Jesus Christ who remains capable of saving us in our mortal condition, who continues to be efficacious on our behalf." Here Frei quotes the great patristic saying, "What he did not assume (i.e., anything less than full humanity), that he could not save." Frei asserts that this must be just as true of Jesus in his resurrection as in his earthly existence. Before and after, Jesus of Nazareth is "God's Word in our midst."[57]

The same testimony is recorded over and over in the Gospels as the experience of those who followed Jesus or came into his presence. Given this identification, Frei writes, it is unthinkable that the tomb not be empty, the crucified Jesus not be raised from the dead. Not only is that, narratively speaking, "logically impossible," it also contradicts the long experience of the Christian community that the Christ of the Gospels is the presence of God in Word and Sacrament. It is in this sense that Jesus' identity as the presence of God "is totally identical with his factual existence."[58] Jesus *is* the resurrection and the life; therefore, he cannot be conceived as not resurrected! This is the significance of the question, "Why do you seek the living among the dead?" (Luke 24:5).

55. Ibid.
56. Ibid.
57. Ibid., 204.
58. *Identity of Jesus Christ*, 146.

Epilogue

All happy families resemble one another; all unhappy families are unhappy in their own way.

Tolstoy, *Anna Karenina*, part 1, chap. 1

This short history of biblical interpretation confirms again Brevard Childs's assertion that discernible within the Christian exegetical tradition are "distinctive characteristic features that constitute and identify a family resemblance."[1] To put it most simply, and to rephrase Tolstoy, one might say that all faithful interpretations of Scripture bear a family resemblance, whereas all other interpretations differ in their own way.[2] I want here briefly to lift up the features that characterize this family resemblance apparent from our own short history of biblical interpretation. While the list is not exhaustive, it is central.

THE AUTHORITY OF SCRIPTURE AND FAITH

The first and most obvious characteristic of faithful interpretation is the affirmation that the ground and source of all being is God, and that Scripture is revelatory of that God. Apart from this faith, all other interpretation of Scripture is simply autopsy. However valuable purely academic approaches to Scripture may be—and they are numerous and indispensable to contemporary faithful interpretation (chap.

---

1. *The Struggle to Understand Isaiah as Christian Scripture* (Grand Rapids: Eerdmans, 2004), 299. Childs provides some of the rubrics employed in this summary.

2. In terms of our analogy given in the preceding chapter, the "family resemblance" would describe those who are "on the train" and "play ball" with the text; all other interpretations would be "outside the train" observing from their own points of view.

191

10)—they cannot understand Scripture on its own terms as the living Word of God. It is this principle of faith that has sought understanding (*fides quarens intellectum*) throughout the centuries of the church's existence.

In chapter 1 we noted that Scripture arose out of the desire to write down the experience of the holy, whether as divine presence, call, or command. Scripture became authoritative (i.e., sacred) not only because it claimed to be a record of that revelation, but because its language was also found to be efficacious in attuning the believing heart to the reality of its origin in God.[3] Counterpart to this experience of the Divine is the corresponding emergence of self-understanding (as John Calvin claimed[4]), as for example that accompanying Isaiah's vision, Jeremiah's call, Augustine's conversion, Abbot Suger's mystical ascent, Luther's "thunderbolt," Francke's rebirth, Schleiermacher's experience of absolute dependence, and so on, each sui generis. Again, whenever Scripture is divorced from this subjective dimension, of God and of the self, it ceases to be the living Word of God and becomes an artifact of antiquity devoid of revelatory authority (so Reimarus, Jefferson, etc.).

THE DIVINE AND HUMAN AUTHORSHIP OF SCRIPTURE

The Christian exegetical tradition has never doubted that Scripture, as a record of the Divine-human relationship expressed in the language of covenant, provides both a human account of the woeful and fallen condition of human beings, with its tales of rape, incest, adultery, fratricide, regicide, suicide, licentiousness, betrayal, and so on, as well as "the Word of the Lord" revelatory of the divine nature and covenantal will. Rather, the questions latent and explicit within the interpretive tradition were how the relationship between the Divine and the human was to be defined, and who was to define it. We have seen these issues, for example, behind canon formation (chap. 2), manuscript transmission (chap. 3), and "authorized" translation (chap. 4). In large measure the easy juxtaposition of the divine and human authorship of Scripture is due to the communal setting in which Scripture is most often heard.[5] There it is incorporated into the liturgy, the language of the

---

3. See Michael Fishbane, *Sacred Attunement: A Jewish Theology* (Chicago: University of Chicago Press, 2008).

4. The classic statement of this correlation is found in Calvin's *Institutes*, 1.1.1–2.

5. Note for example the passages read at the Fifty-Sixth Presidential Inaugural Prayer Service held at the National Cathedral in Washington, D.C., for President Barack Obama, January 21, 2009: Isa. 58:6–12; Rom. 12:9–13, 18; and Matt. 22:36–40.

sacraments, preaching, and catechism, where priest, preacher, or the lectionary itself selects from the total corpus a word for proclamation, exhortation, comfort, or counsel. Marcion (chap. 2) found the combination of the Divine and the human repugnant, and literally cut and pasted his way out of the problem, as did Jefferson (chap. 9). Origen, Augustine, and others (chap. 6) relished the challenge Scripture's crudeness presented to their interpretive ingenuity and found joy in making the rough places plain through allegory.

From the earliest exegetical traditions of the church, beginning with Jesus himself ("You have heard that it was said . . . but I say to you . . ." (Matt. 5:21, 27, passim), it has been assumed that Scripture was of both divine and human origin. This suggested as well that "covenant" was not a univocal concept but a truth whose full implications were yet to be discerned in the evolution of moral consciousness. In chapter 5 we noted how both Judaism and the early church of the New Testament period continually reinterpreted the tradition in order to save it, from irrelevance and error—an implicit acknowledgment that human elements had obscured or misrepresented the divine will. From time to time, particularly since the beginning of the Protestant Reformation and its focus on the centrality of Scripture for faith and practice, interpretive extremes have arisen, such as the doctrine of inerrancy among fundamentalists on the one side and purely secularist approaches to interpretation on the other. But these have been extreme positions and not representative of the heart of the exegetical tradition.

A SCRIPTURE OF TWO TESTAMENTS

It is to Irenaeus in the second century that we are indebted for establishing the indispensable place of the Old Testament in telling the metanarrative that overarches the story of the Christ and in affirming that the Father to whom Jesus prayed is none other than the God of Abraham, Isaac, and Jacob (chap. 6). Irenaeus's Rule of Faith bound Old Covenant and New Covenant together into one continuous story with a beginning, middle, and end, threaded by the guiding telos of the consummation of creation through the coming of the kingdom of God. It is this feature that roots Christian faith in (Jewish) history and wards off the gnostic temptation of making belief a disincarnate system of philosophical abstractions removed from the Gethsemanes and Calvaries, indeed, the holocausts, of the world. Although, as Childs

observes, there is no one definitive interpretation of the relationship of
the New Covenant to the Old, commitment to that relationship has
repeatedly drawn the church back from sin and error. This conviction,
though still debated, has at no time been more strongly supported than
in the twenty-first century.

THE LITERAL AND SPIRITUAL SENSES OF SCRIPTURE

If Scripture had but one meaning, and that resident in its literal sense,
there would be no history of biblical interpretation. As we saw in our
discussion of typology (chap. 5), the interpretation of Scripture begins
within Scripture itself. Our short history describes a variety of ways by
which Christian interpreters have gone behind the literal sense of texts
in search of Scripture's deeper meaning, the experience of the church
being that the Word of God, particularly as moral imperative (e.g.,
Mic. 6:8; Luke 10:25–28 par.), is relevant not just to the past but to the
present. Since human being is as diverse as life itself, the Word of God
must a fortiori speak to the whole human condition, as the Quadriga
of the Middle Ages affirmed (chap. 7): to faith (via *allegoria*), to hope
(via *anagogia*), and to love (via *tropology*).

For Paul, Augustine, Luther, and others, Scripture's inspiration
is a result of the work of the Holy Spirit in the act of hearing with
understanding. This meant for Augustine (and in a modified way for
Protestant translation theory since) not only that one translation could
be as valid as another (since the Holy Spirit was at work in the act of
translation as much as in the text's original inspiration), it also meant
that a given text could have more than one meaning, since understanding was also the work of the Spirit. Warning against any single, literal
interpretation of the opening verses of Genesis, for example, Augustine
presciently wrote, "We should not rush in headlong and so firmly take
our stand on one side that, if further progress in the search of truth
justly undermines [our] position, we too fall with it."[6]

While enormous theological and exegetical energy has gone into
the question of the relationship of the spiritual to the literal sense of
Scripture, it is likely to continue as our understanding of the human
condition, the hermeneutical setting of biblical interpretation, and the

---

6. *Saint Augustine: The Literal Interpretation of Genesis*, trans. and annotated by John Hammond Taylor, S.J.,
(Ancient Christian Writers 41; New York: Newman, 1982), 1.18.37.

nature of divine presence deepens (see especially chaps. 7 and 11).[7] For time has shown that the same text has given voice to a fresh Word of God in ever new contexts (Childs), revealing the power to author (i.e., "inspire") a new life of obedience. It is my conviction that in the modern period Hans Frei has addressed this issue most provocatively, so far as it relates to Jesus and the Synoptic narratives.

THE CHRISTOLOGICAL CONTENT OF SCRIPTURE

Although belief in multiple senses of Scripture contributed to the diminution of the centrality of Christ in favor of an ecclesiastical emphasis on church doctrine (first by Roman Catholicism, leading to the Protestant Reformation, and later by Lutheran scholasticism, leading to both biblical literalism and to Pietism), that the Scriptures themselves (including Old Testament Scriptures) were directly or indirectly about Christ was never in question. If, as Scripture and faith assert, the Word that became flesh in Jesus Christ was "in the beginning with God and was God," then what the Old Testament, properly interpreted, said about God could not contradict what is revealed of God in Christ (so, e.g., Abelard, chap. 7). Nevertheless, it is characteristic of the Christian exegetical tradition that this feature of the family resemblance also continues to be debated.

With multiculturalism increasingly characterizing life in the twenty-first century, the church would do well to meet the future with a firm knowledge of its own exegetical traditions. To that end I hope this work is a modest contribution.

---

7. See, for example, Francis S. Collins, *The Language of God: A Scientist Presents Evidence for Belief* (New York: Free Press, 2006). Collins served as head of the Human Genome Project in the United States.

Bibliography

Abbott, Walter M., ed. *The Documents of Vatican II*. New York: Guild, 1966.

Abelard, Peter. *Ethical Writings: Ethics and Dialogue between a Philosopher and a Jew and a Christian*. Translated by Paul Vincent Spade. Introduction by Marilyn McCord Adams. Indianapolis: Hackett, 1995.

————. *The Story of My Misfortune*. Translated by Henry Adams Bellows. Introduction by Ralph Adams Cram. Mineola, N.Y.: Dover, 2005.

————. *The Letters of Abelard and Heloise*. Translated with an introduction by Betty Radice. New York: Penguin, 1974.

Ackroyd, P. R., and C. F. Evans, eds. *From the Beginnings to Jerome*. Vol. 1 of *The Cambridge History of the Bible*. Cambridge: Cambridge University Press, 1970.

Adam, A. K. M. *Faithful Interpretation: Reading the Bible in a Postmodern World*. Minneapolis: Fortress, 2006.

————. *Making Sense of New Testament Theology*. Eugene, Or: Wipf & Stock, 2005.

————, ed. *Handbook of Postmodern Biblical Interpretation*. St. Louis: Chalice, 2000.

————, et al., eds. *Reading Scripture with the Church: Toward a Hermeneutic for Theological Interpretation*. Grand Rapids: Baker Academic, 2006.

Adams, Dickinson W., ed. *Jefferson's Extracts from the Gospels: "The Philosophy of Jesus" and "The Life and Morals of Jesus."* Princeton: Princeton University Press, 1983.

Andresen, Carl. *Logos und Nomos: Die Polemik des Kelsos wider das Christentum*. Arbeiten zur Kirchengeschichte 30. Berlin: De Gruyter, 1955.

Arndt, Johann. *True Christianity*. Classics of Western Spirituality. Translated with an introduction by Peter Erb. New York: Paulist Press, 1979.

Auerbach, Eric. *Mimesis: The Representation of Reality in Western Literature*. Princeton: Princeton University Press, 1953.

Augustine. *On Christian Doctrine*. Translated by D. W. Robertson. Indianapolis: Bobbs-Merrill, 1958.

————. *The City of God against the Pagans*. Edited and translated by R. W. Dyson. Cambridge: Cambridge University Press, 1997.

————. *The Confessions*. Translated by Maria Boulding. Hyde Park, N.Y.: New City Press, 1997.

————. *The Confessions of Saint Augustine.* Translated with an introduction and notes by John K. Ryan. Garden City, N.Y.: Image Books, 1960.

————. *The Literal Meaning of Genesis,* vol. 1. Translated and annotated by John Hammond Taylor, S.J. Ancient Christian Writers 41. New York: Newman, 1982.

————. *Saint Augustine: Earlier Writings.* Edited by J. H. S. Burleigh. Library of Christian Classics 6. Philadelphia: Westminster, 1953.

Bailey, Lloyd R., ed. *The Word of God: A Guide to English Versions of the Bible.* Atlanta: John Knox, 1982.

Bailie, Gil. *Violence Unveiled: Humanity at the Crossroads.* New York: Crossroad, 1995.

Bainton, Roland. *Here I Stand: A Life of Martin Luther.* New York: Abingdon-Cokesbury, 1950.

Baird, William. *History of New Testament Research.* 2 vols. Minneapolis: Augsburg Fortress, 1992–2002.

Barth, Karl. *From Rousseau to Ritschl.* London: SCM, 1959.

Barzun, Jacques. *From Dawn to Decadence: 500 Years of Western Cultural Life.* New York: HarperCollins, 2000.

Bayer, Oswald. *Martin Luthers Theologie: Eine Vergegenwärtigung,* 2nd ed. Tübingen: Mohr Siebeck, 2004.

Bernard of Clairvaux. *Five Books on Consideration: Advice to a Pope.* Translated by John D. Anderson and Elizabeth T. Kennan. Kalamazoo, Mich.: Cistercian Publications, 1976.

————. *The Letters of St Bernard of Clairvaux.* Translated by Bruno Scott James. Introduction by Beverly Mayne Kienzle. Great Britain: Cistercian Publications, 1998.

————. *On the Song of Songs I.* Works of Bernard of Clairvaux 2. Translated by Kilian Walsh. Spenser, Mass.: Cistercian Publications, 1971.

————. *Selected Works.* Translated by G. R. Evans. New York: Paulist Press, 1987.

————, and Amadeus of Lausanne. *Magnificat: Homilies in Praise of the Blessed Virgin Mary.* Translated by Marie-Bernard Saïd and Grace Perigo. Introduction by Chrysogonus Waddell. Kalamazoo, Mich.: Cistercian Publications, 1979.

Betz, Hans Dieter, et al. *Die Religion in Geschichte und Gegenwart,* 4th ed. 9 vols. Tübingen: Mohr/Siebeck, 1998–2007.

Beyreuther, Erich. *August Hermann Francke (1663–1727): Zeuge des lebendigen Gottes.* Marburg an der Lahn: Francke-Buchhandlung, 1956.

Black, Matthew, and William A. Smalley, eds. *On Language, Culture, and Religion: In Honor of Eugene A. Nida.* The Hague: Mouton, 1974.

Blowers, Paul M., ed. *The Bible in Greek Christian Antiquity.* Notre Dame: University of Notre Dame Press, 1997.

Bluhm, Heinz. *Martin Luther: Creative Translator.* St. Louis: Concordia, 1965.

Bodem, Anton. *Das Wesen der Kirche nach Kardinal Cajetan: Ein Beitrag zur Ekkesiologie im Zeitalter der Reformation.* Trierer theologische Studien 25. Trier: Paulinus-Verlag, 1971.

Boehme, Jakob. *The Way of Christ.* Translated by William Law. Repr. Goodyear, Az.: Diggory, 2007.

Bray, Gerald, ed. *Romans.* Ancient Christian Commentary on Scripture: New Testament 6. Downers Grove, Ill.: InterVarsity Press, 1998.

Brecht, Martin. *Martin Luther.* Vol. 1: *His Road to Reformation, 1483–1521.* Translated by James L. Schaaf. Minneapolis: Fortress, 1985.

Brower, Jeffrey E., and Kevin Guilfoy, eds. *The Cambridge Companion to Abelard.* Cambridge: Cambridge University Press, 2004.

Brown, Peter. *Augustine of Hippo: A Biography.* A new edition with an epilogue. Berkeley: University of California Press, 2000.

Brown, Raymond E. *The Birth of the Messiah.* Garden City, N.Y.: Image Books, 1977.

———. *The Gospel According to John.* 2 vols. Anchor Bible 29–29A. Garden City, N.Y.: Doubleday, 1966–1970.

Bruce, F. F. *History of the Bible: From the Earliest Versions.* 3rd ed. New York: Oxford University Press, 1978.

Bruns, Gerald L. *Hermeneutics Ancient and Modern.* New Haven: Yale University Press, 1992.

Cassian, John. *Conferences.* Translated by Colm Luibheid. Classics of Western Spirituality. New York: Paulist Press, 1985.

Castelli, Elizabeth A., et al., eds. *The Postmodern Bible: The Bible and Culture Collective.* New Haven: Yale University Press, 1995.

Childs, Brevard S. *The Book of Exodus: A Critical, Theological Commentary.* Old Testament Library. Philadelphia: Westminster, 1974.

———. *The Struggle to Understand Isaiah as Christian Scripture.* Grand Rapids: Eerdmans, 2004.

Chadwick, Henry. *History and Thought of the Early Church.* London: Variorum, 1982.

Clanchy, M. T. *Abelard: A Medieval Life.* Oxford: Blackwell, 1997.

Colish, Marcia L. *Medieval Foundations of the Western Intellectual Tradition: 400–1400.* New Haven: Yale University Press, 1997.

Conzelmann, Hans. *The Theology of St. Luke.* Translated by Geoffrey Buswell. London: Faber & Faber, 1960.

Crapanzano, Vincent. *Serving the Word: Literalism in America from the Pulpit to the Bench.* New York: New Press, 2000.

Daniell, David. *The Bible in English.* New Haven: Yale University Press, 2003.

Daniélou, Jean. *Origen.* Translated by Walter Mitchell. New York: Sheed & Ward, 1955.

Deanesly, Margaret. *The Significance of the Lollard Bible.* London: Athlone, 1951.

De Lubac, Henry. *The Four Senses of Scripture.* Vol. 1 of *Medieval Exegesis.* Translated by Mark Sebane. Grand Rapids: Eerdmans, 1998.

Dinzelbacher, Peter. *Angst im Mittelalter: Teufels-, Tods- und Gotteserfahrung: Mentalitätsgeschichte und Ikonographie.* Paderborn: Ferdinand Schöningh, 1996.

Dodd, C. H. *The Parables of the Kingdom.* Welwyn: James Nisbet, 1958.

Donner, Herbert, et al., eds. *Beiträge zur alttestamentlichen Theologie: Festschrift für Walther Zimmerli.* Göttingen: Vandenhoeck & Ruprecht, 1977.

Dudden, F. Homes. *Gregory the Great: His Place in History and Thought.* London: Longmans, 1905.

Ebeling, Gerhard. *Luther: An Introduction to His Thought.* Philadelphia: Fortress, 1970.

———. *Lutherstudien.* Vol. 3. Tübingen: Mohr (Siebeck), 1985.

Eck, Johannes. *Enchiridion of Commonplaces.* Translated by Ford Lewis Battles. Grand Rapids: Baker, 1979.

Evans, C. A., and J. A. Sanders, eds. *Paul and the Scriptures of Israel.* Sheffield: JSOT Press, 1993.

Fishbane, Michael. *Biblical Interpretation in Ancient Israel.* Oxford: Clarendon, 1985.

———. *Sacred Attunement: A Jewish Theology.* Chicago: University of Chicago Press, 2008.

Fowl, Stephen E., ed. *The Theological Interpretation of Scripture.* London: Blackwell, 1997.

Frei, Hans. *The Eclipse of Biblical Narrative: A Study of Eighteenth and Nineteenth Century Hermeneutics.* New Haven: Yale University Press, 1974.

———. *The Identity of Jesus Christ: The Hermeneutical Bases of Dogmatic Theology.* Philadelphia: Fortress, 1975.

———. *Theology and Narrative: Selected Essays.* Edited by George Hunsinger and William C. Placher. Oxford: Oxford University Press, 1993.

———. *Types of Christian Theology.* New Haven: Yale University Press, 1992.

Froehlich, Karlfried, trans. and ed. *Biblical Interpretation in the Early Church.* Philadelphia: Fortress, 1984.

Galling, Kurt, et al., eds. *Die Religion in Geschichte und Gegenwart.* 3rd ed. 7 vols. Tübingen: Mohr (Siebeck), 1956–1965.

Geneva Bible. Facsimile of the 1599 edition. Ozark, Mo.: L. L. Brown, 1990.

Gierl, Martin. *Pietismus und Aufklärung.* Göttingen: Vandenhoeck & Ruprecht, 1997.

Gögler, Rolf. *Zur Theologie des biblischen Wortes bei Origenes.* Dusseldorf: Patmos, 1963.

Goppelt, Leonhard. *Typos: The Typological Interpretation of the Old Testament in the New.* Translated by D. H. Madvig. Grand Rapids: Eerdmans, 1982.

Grant, Robert. *A Short History of the Interpretation of the Bible.* 2nd ed. with David Tracy. Philadelphia: Fortress, 1984.

Greenslade, S. L., ed. *The West from the Reformation to the Present Day*. Vol. 3 of *The Cambridge History of the Bible*. Cambridge: Cambridge University Press, 1963.

Gregory of Nyssa. *The Life of Moses*. Translation with introduction and notes by Abraham J. Malherbe and Everett Ferguson. New York: Paulist Press, 1978.

Gregory the Great. *The Letters of Gregory the Great, Books 1–4*. Translated with introduction and notes by John Martyn. Toronto: Pontifical Institute of Medieval Studies, 2004.

Greschat, Martin, ed. *Zur neueren Pietismusforschung*. Darmstadt: Wissenschaftliche Buchgesellschaft, 1977.

Hall, Christopher. *Reading Scripture with the Church Fathers*. Downers Grove, Ill.: InterVarsity Press, 1998.

Halliday, E. M. *Understanding Thomas Jefferson*. New York: HarperCollins, 2001.

Harnack, Adolf von. *What Is Christianity?* Introduction by Rudolf Bultmann. Reprint Philadelphia: Fortress, 1986.

Hart, David Bentley. *The Beauty of the Infinite: The Aesthetics of Christian Truth*. Grand Rapids: Eerdmans, 2003.

Hartt, Julian N., et al. *The Critique of Modernity: Theological Reflections on Contemporary Culture*. Charlottesville: University Press of Virginia, 1986.

Hennecke, Edgar. *New Testament Apocrypha*. Vol. 1: *Gospels and Related Writings*. Rev. ed. Wilhelm Schneemelcher. English translation edited by R. McL. Wilson. Philadelphia: Westminster, 1964.

Holmes, Michael W., ed. *The Apostolic Fathers*. Translated by J. B. Lightfoot and J. R. Harmer. 2nd ed. Grand Rapids: Baker, 1989.

Irenaeus. *Against the Heresies, I*. Ancient Christian Writers 55. Translated and annotated by Dominic J. Unger. New York: Newman, 1992.

Jedin, Herbert, ed. *History of the Church*. 7 vols. New York: Crossroad, 1981–1986.

Jefferson, Thomas. *The Jefferson Bible: The Life and Morals of Jesus of Nazareth*. Introduction by Forrest Church. Afterword by Jaroslav Pelikan. Boston: Beacon, 1989.

Jellicoe, Sydney. *The Septuagint and Modern Study*. Oxford: Oxford University Press, 1968.

Jerome. *Jerome's Hebrew Questions on Genesis*. Translated with introduction and commentary by C. T. R. Hayward. Oxford: Oxford University Press, 1995.

Johnson, Paul. *Cathedrals of England, Scotland, and Wales*. New York: Harper & Row, 1990.

Justin Martyr. *Dialogue with Trypho*. Ante-Nicene Fathers 1. Reprint Grand Rapids: Eerdmans, 1987.

Kehl, Medard, and Werner Löser. *The von Balthasar Reader*. Translated by Robert J. Daly and Fred Lawrence. New York: Crossroad, 1985.

Kermode, Frank. *The Genesis of Secrecy: On the Interpretation of Narrative*. Cambridge: Harvard University Press, 1979.

Kraus, Hans-Joachim. *Geschichte der historisch-kritisch Erforschung des Alten Testaments von der Reformation bis zur Gegenwart.* 2nd ed. Neukirchen-Vluyn: Neukirchener Verlag, 1969.

Kugel, James L., and Rowan A. Greer. *Early Biblical Interpretation.* Philadelphia: Westminster, 1989.

Levenson, Jon. *Hebrew Bible, Old Testament, and Historical Criticism.* New York: Blackwell, 1998.

Levi, Anthony. *Renaissance and Reformation: The Intellectual Genesis.* New Haven: Yale University Press, 2002.

Lindberg, Carter, ed. *The Pietist Theologians: An Introduction to Theology in the Seventeenth and Eighteenth Centuries.* Oxford: Blackwell, 2005.

Longenecker, Richard N. *Biblical Exegesis in the Apostolic Period.* 2nd ed. Grand Rapids: Eerdmans, 1999.

Lull, Timothy F., ed. *Martin Luther's Basic Theological Writings.* 2nd ed. Minneapolis: Fortress, 2005.

MacKenzie, Ian. *Irenaeus's "Demonstration of the Apostolic Preaching": A Theological Commentary and Translation.* Burlington, Va.: Ashgate, 2002.

Maier, Paul L. *Eusebius—The Church History: A New Translation with Commentary.* Grand Rapids: Kregel, 1999.

Mâle, Emile. *The Gothic Image: Religious Art in France of the Thirteenth Century.* Translated by Dora Nussey. 1913. Reprint New York: Harper & Brothers, 1958.

McCracken, George E., ed. *Early Medieval Theology.* Library of Christian Classics 9. Philadelphia: Westminster, 1957.

McGuckin, John Anthony. *Patristic Theology.* Louisville: Westminster John Knox, 2004.

———, ed. *The Westminster Handbook to Origen.* Louisville: Westminster John Knox, 2004.

McKenzie, Steven L., and Stephen R. Haynes, eds. *To Each Its Own Meaning: An Introduction to Biblical Criticism and Their Application.* Revised and expanded. Louisville: Westminster John Knox, 1999.

Meeks, Wayne A., ed. *Early Biblical Interpretation.* Philadelphia: Westminster, 1986.

Metzger, Bruce M. *The Bible in Translation: Ancient and English Versions.* Grand Rapids: Baker Academic, 2001.

Mondésert, C. *The Bible in Greek Christian Antiquity.* Translated and edited by Paul M. Blowers. Notre Dame: University of Notre Dame Press, 1997.

Muller, Richard H., and John L. Thompson. *Biblical Interpretation in the Era of the Reformation.* Grand Rapids: Eerdmans, 1996.

Nida, Eugene. *Toward a Science of Translating.* Leiden: Brill, 1964.

Niebuhr, Richard R. *Schleiermacher on Christ and Religion: A New Introduction.* New York: Charles Scribner's Sons, 1964.

Oberman, Heiko A. *Luther: Man Between God and the Devil.* Translated by Eileen Walliser-Schwartzbart. New York: Image Books, 1992.

O'Keefe, John J., and R. R. Reno. *Sanctified Vision: An Introduction to Early Christian Interpretation of the Bible.* Baltimore: Johns Hopkins University Press, 2005.

Origen. *Commentary on the Gospel according to John, Books 1–10.* Translated by Ronald E. Heine. *Fathers of the Church: A New Translation* 80. Washington, D.C.: Catholic University Press, 1989.

———. *Contra Celsum.* Ante-Nicene Christian Library 25. 1872. Reprint Peabody, Mass.: Hendrickson, 1994.

———. *On First Principles.* Gloucester, Mass.: Peter Smith, 1973.

———. *The Song of Songs, Commentary and Homilies.* Translated by R. P. Lawson. London: Longmans, Green, 1957.

Orlinsky, Harry M., and Robert G. Bratcher. *A History of Bible Translation and the North American Contribution.* Atlanta: Scholars Press, 1991.

Pagels, Elaine. *Beyond Belief: The Secret Gospel of Thomas.* New York: Vintage Press, 2003.

Panofsky, Erwin. *Abbot Suger on the Abbey Church of St.-Denis and Its Art Treasures.* 2nd ed. by Gerda Panofsky-Soergel. Princeton: Princeton University Press, 1979.

———. *Gothic Architecture and Scholasticism.* 1951. Reprint Latrobe, Penn.: Archabbey Publications, 2005.

Pelikan, Jaroslav. *Christianity and Classical Culture: The Metamorphosis of Natural Theology in the Christian Encounter with Hellenism.* New Haven: Yale University Press, 1993.

———. *Credo: Historical and Theological Guide to Creeds and Confessions of Faith in the Christian Tradition.* New Haven: Yale University Press, 2003.

———. *The Emergence of the Catholic Tradition (100–600).* Vol. 1 of *The Christian Tradition: A History of the Development of Doctrine.* Chicago: University of Chicago Press, 1971.

———. *Interpreting the Bible and the Constitution.* New Haven: Yale University Press, 2004.

———. *The Melody of Theology: A Philosophical Dictionary.* Cambridge: Harvard University Press, 1988.

Peschke, Erhard. *Studien zur Theologie August Hermann Francke.* Berlin: Evangelische Verlagsanstalt, 1964.

Pope, Marvin H. *Job: Translated with an Introduction and Notes.* Anchor Bible 15. Garden City, N.Y.: Doubleday, 1965.

Pragai, Michael J. *Faith and Fulfillment: Christians and the Return to the Promised Land.* London: Valentine, Mitchell, 1985.

Preus, James Samuel. *From Shadow to Promise: Old Testament Interpretation from Augustine to the Young Luther.* Cambridge: Harvard University Press, 1969.

Pseudo-Dionysius. *Pseudo-Dionysius: The Complete Works.* Translated by Colm Luibheid. New York: Paulist Press, 1987.

Quasten, Johannes. *Patrology.* Westminster, Md.: Newman, 1962.

Rad, Gerhard von. *Old Testament Theology.* Translated by D. M. G. Stalker. 2 vols. New York: Harper & Row, 1962–1965.

Redeker, Martin. *Schleiermacher: Life and Thought.* Translated by John Wallhausser. Philadelphia: Fortress, 1973.

Reimarus, Hermann Samuel. *The Goal of Jesus and His Disciples.* Translated with an introduction by George Wesley Buchanan. Leiden: Brill, 1970.

Ricoeur, Paul. *Essays on Biblical Interpretation.* Edited with an introduction by Lewis S. Mudge. Philadelphia: Fortress, 1980.

Roberts, Alexander, and James Donaldson, eds. *The Ante-Nicene Fathers.* 1885–1887. 10 vols. Reprint Peabody, Mass.: Hendrickson, 1994.

Robinson, James M. *The Secrets of Judas: The Story of the Misunderstood Disciple and His Lost Gospel.* New York: HarperSanFrancisco, 2006.

Russell, D. A. *Criticism in Antiquity.* London: Duckworth, 1981.

Sanneh, Lamin. *Whose Religion Is Christianity?* Grand Rapids: Eerdmans, 2003.

Schleiermacher, F. D. E. *The Christian Faith.* Philadelphia: Fortress, 1976.

———. *Hermeneutics and Criticism: And Other Writings.* Translated and edited by Andrew Bowie. Cambridge: Cambridge University Press, 1998.

———. *The Life of Jesus.* Edited by Jack C. Verheyden. Philadelphia: Fortress, 1975.

———. *On Religion: Speeches to Its Cultured Despisers.* Translated by John Omann; Foreword by Jack Forstman. Louisville: Westminster John Knox, 1994.

———. *Schleiermacher's Soliloquies.* Translated with an introduction by Horace Leland Friess. Eugene, Or.: Wipf & Stock, 2001.

Schnackenberg, Rudolf. *The Gospel According to St. John.* 3 vols. New York: Crossroad, 1990.

Schweitzer, Albert. *The Quest of the Historical Jesus.* New York: Macmillan, 1956.

Seeligmann, Isaac Leo. *The Septuagint Version of Isaiah and Cognate Studies.* Forschugen zum Alten Testament 40. Tübingen: Mohr Siebeck, 2004.

Simson, Otto von. *The Gothic Cathedral: Origins of Gothic Architecture and the Medieval Concept of Order.* 3rd ed. Princeton: Princeton University Press, 1988.

Sobrino, Jon. *Christ the Liberator.* Translated by Paul Burns. Maryknoll, N.Y.: Orbis, 2001.

———. *Jesus the Liberator: A Historical-Theological Reading of Jesus of Nazareth.* Translated by Paul Burns and Francis McDonagh. Maryknoll, N.Y.: Orbis, 1993.

———. *The Principle of Mercy: Taking the Crucified People from the Cross.* Maryknoll, N.Y.: Orbis, 1994.

Soulen, R. Kendall. *The God of Israel and Christian Theology.* Minneapolis: Fortress, 1996.

Soulen, Richard N., and R. Kendall Soulen. *Handbook of Biblical Criticism.* 3rd ed. Louisville: Westminster John Knox, 2001.

Spener, Philipp Jakob. *Pia Desideria.* Translated, edited, and with an introduction by Theodore G. Tappert. Eugene, Or.: Wipf & Stock, 2002.

Stein, K. James. *Philipp Jakob Spener: Pietist Patriarch.* Chicago: Covenant, 1986.

Stendahl, Krister. *Paul Among Jews and Gentiles.* Philadelphia: Fortress, 1976.

Storrs, Richard S. *Bernard of Clairvaux and His Relation to General European Affairs.* Reprint Kessinger, 2005.

Terrien, Samuel. *The Elusive Presence.* San Francisco: Harper & Row, 1978.

Thomas, Rudolf, et al., eds. *Petrus Abaelardus (1079–1142): Person, Werk, und Wirkung.* Trierer theologische Studien 38. Trier: Paulinus-Verlag, 1980.

Tov, Emanuel. *The Greek and Hebrew Bible: Collected Essays on the Septuagint.* Supplement to Vetus Testamentum 72. Leiden: Brill, 1999.

Tyndale, William. *The Works of William Tyndale.* Edited and introduced by G. E. Duffield. Courtney Library of Reformation Classics 1. Appleford: Sutton Courtenay Press, 1964.

Vincent of Lérins. *The Commonitory.* In *Early Medieval Theology.* Translated and edited by George E. McCracken. Library of Christian Classics 9. Philadelphia: Westminster, 1957.

Wilder, Amos. *Jesus' Parables and the War of Myths: Essays on Imagination in the Scriptures.* Philadelphia: Fortress, 1982.

———. *Theopoetic: Theology and the Religious Imagination.* Philadelphia: Fortress, 1976.

Wyclif, John. *The Obedience of the Christian Man.* Edited with an introduction by David Daniell. London: Penguin, 2000.

———. *On the Truth of Holy Scripture.* Translated with and introduction and notes by Ian Christopher Levy. Kalamazoo, Mich.: Western Michigan University Press, 2001.

Wyschogrod, Michael, and Clemens Thoma, eds. *Understanding Scripture: Explorations of Jewish and Christian Traditions of Interpretation.* New York: Paulist Press, 1987.

Young, Frances M. *Biblical Exegesis and the Formation of Christian Culture.* Cambridge: Cambridge University Press, 1997.

Index

Abelard, Peter, 100, 105–12, 112
  on God as love, 110–11
  on reason drawing out faith's deeper
    meaning, 109
Abraham, as archetype of responsive
    obedience, 69–70
Adam (abbot of St.-Denis), 107
Against Celsus (*Contra Celsum*) (Origen),
    82, 85
Aland, Kurt, 127
allegorical sense, for reading Scripture,
    98, 99, 105–12
American Standard Version, 31, 54
anagogical sense, for reading Scripture,
    98, 99, 100–102
Anselm of Laon, 107, 116n8
Apocrypha, 20, 26, 32
Apocryphal New Testament, 25–26
Aquinas, misunderstanding Aristotle,
    118n14
Arndt, Johann, 122
Athanasius, 113
atonement, Abelard's account of,
    109–10
Augustine, 32–33
  conversion experience of, 88
  on interpreting Scripture, 89–94
  life of, 86–87
  representing the birth of the modern
    mind, 87–88
Augustine of Dacia, 99
author
  determining mind or intent of, 138
  emphasis on, 142

Babylonian Captivity of the Churches, The
    (Luther), 118
Bacon, Francis, 148
Baird, William, 121
baptism, significance of, 15
Barth, Karl, 138, 183, 184
Beatty (Chester A.) papyri, 39
Bernard of Clairvaux, 100, 102–5, 107,
    109, 112
Beza, Theodore, 50
Bible. *See also* New Testament; Old
    Testament; Scriptures
  humanity of, 156
  Latin translations of, 32
  mirroring God's perfect truthfulness,
    120
  new era for translation of, 34–35
  not translated into vernacular
    versions for an extended
    period, 48
  perceived as a book of teaching,
    120
  stimulating ambiguity of, 56
  translations, variety of, 45, 58
  understanding of, influence of
    modern biblical criticism on, 156
  vernacular translation of, desire for,
    48–49
biblical criticism, modern
  different approaches and methods of,
    156
  identifying, 155–56
biblical fundamentalism, 51–52
biblical inerrancy, 121

biblical interpretation
 liberation, 171, 176–82
 Luther's early approach to, 116
 postcritical, 171, 183–90
 postmodern, 171, 173–75
 premodern, 155
 radical changes in, 171
Biblical Interpretation in Ancient Israel
  (Fishbane), 62–63
biblical studies, Francke's influence on,
 126–27
biblical thinking, linear, historical, and
 cyclical, 65
biographical correlations, 62
biographical typologies
 in the New Testament, 74–75
 in the Old Testament, 69–70
Bishops' Bible, 50
black liberation theology, 176
Bodmer papyri, 39
Book on Consideration (Bernard of Clairvaux), 103
Bratcher, Robert, 35
British Revised Version, 54
Bruns, Gerald, 105, 116
Bultmann, Rudolf, 188
burning bush, 4
Byzantine family of text types, 35–36

Calvin, John, 50
canon
 contentious feelings surrounding, 26
 fluid sense of, in the early church,
  22–26
 formation of, 17, 21
 representing continuity amid change,
  78
 varieties of, in first century, 37
canonical criticism, 161
Cassian, John, 97–98
Celestial Hierarchy, The (Dionysius the
 Areopagite), 100–101
charity, 90, 92

Childs, Brevard, 131, 191, 193–94, 195
Christ. *See also* Jesus
 as center of Christian's life, 124–25
 climactic place of, in Irenaeus's
  writings, 80
 depiction of, in Synoptic Gospels vs.
  Gospel of John, 143–45
 humanity and deity of, 113
 as second Adam, 140–41
 self-consciousness of, 144–46
 two natures of, 83n18
Christian faith, rooted in Jewish history,
 193–94
Christian Faith, The (Schleiermacher),
 140
Christianity
 claiming the unfolding of a new revelation, 9
 no sacred language for, 46
 profoundly different forms of, and
  influence on Scripture, 23–26
 as translated religion, 46
Christians
 first-century sect of, 19, 37, 38
 life of, related to life of Christ, 75
 meaning of Old Testament to, 5
Christ the Liberator (Sobrino), 182
christophanies, 12–15
church architecture, Suger's influence
 on, 100–102
church fathers. *See* Augustine; early
 church, leaders of; Irenaeus; Origen
Clement of Alexandria, 80
codex, 22, 24
Codex Bezae Cantabrigiensis, 34
Codex Sinaiticus, 31, 34, 39
Codex Vaticanus, 31, 34, 39
cognitio literalis, 128
cognitio spiritualis, 128
Collegium Pietatis, 123
Complutensian Polyglot Bible, 33
composition criticism. *See* redaction
 criticism

Confessions, The (Augustine), 87–88
Congregation for the Doctrine of the Faith (Vatican), 182
Constantine, 24
Contemporary English Version, 58
Conzelmann, Hans, 164–69
cosmological-historical typologies, 62, 63–65, 70–71
cosmology, Origen's, 82–83
Council of Javneh (Jamnia), 21
Council of Sens, 107
Council of Trent, 33
covenantal law, 6
Covenants, Old and New, linked, 193–94
Coverdale, Miles, 48, 50
creation
    as God's self-revelation, 2–3
    linked with redemption, 79–80
Cristología desde américa latina (*Christology at the Crossroads*) (Sobrino), 176–77
critical text, 35, 39–43
cupidity, 90, 92
Cyrus II, 61

Damascus, road to, 14–15
Damasus, 32
Daniell, David, 50, 51, 57, 58
Dead Sea Scrolls, 36–38
De heretico comburendo, 48
Deism, 147, 148
Demonstration of the Apostolic Preaching (Irenaeus), 79
dependence, absolute, feeling of, 140
Deuteronomist, 158
Dialogue with Trypho (Justin), 136
Diaspora Judaism, 38
Dionysius the Areopagite, 100–101, 106
disciples, call of, 11
Divine Comedy (Dante), 103
divine name, as God's self-revelation, 4–5

dualists, 26
dynamic equivalence translation, 52–58

ear, as proper medium of revelation, 3, 15
early church
    leaders of, representing change and continuity, 77–78
    sacred Scriptures of, 22–27
Eck, Johann, 118
Eclipse of Biblical Narrative (Frei), 131–32, 153–54, 183, 184
Eden, as spatial symbol, 68–69
Editio octava critica maior (Tischendorf), 34
eisegesis, 90
Elohist, 158
Emmaus, road to, 13–14
enculturalization, 48
Epicurus, 149
epiphanies
    divine, occurring at God's choosing, 3
    relating to Jesus, as sacred Scripture, 11–13
Epiphanius of Salamis, 81
Erasmus of Rotterdam, 33
Essenes, 18, 19, 38
Eusebius, 24
events, correlation of, to prototypes of divine activity, 64
experience, concern for centrality of, 139
external witness, in textual criticism, 42

faith
    hearing of, 15
    linked to God's Word, 117
    related to understanding, 94
    seeking understanding, 192
Fishbane, Michael, 3, 62–70
formal equivalence translation, 52, 53–58, 59
form criticism, 157, 161–64

Francke, August Hermann, 122, 125–29
Franckesche Stiftungen, 125
Franklin, Benjamin, 123
free association, 124–25
Frei, Hans, 131–32, 146, 183–90
fundamentalist movement, 121

Gemara, 6
Genesis of Secrecy, The: On the Interpretation of Narrative (Kermode), 173–75
Geneva Bible, 49–51, 59
genre criticism, 157
Gerl, Martin, 124
Glossa Interlinearis, 116n8
Glossa Ordinaria, 116n8
Gnosticism, 24, 26, 78–79
Goal of Jesus and His Disciples, The (Reimarus), 132–33
God
  acting in history, 75
  anthropomorphic characterization of, 160
  etymology of term, in English, 55
  experiencing the love of, 103
  as ground and source of all being, 191
  as love, Abelard's explanation of, 110–11
  righteousness of, Luther struggling with phrase, 114–15
  self-revelation of, 1–9
Good News Bible, 58
gospel
  as center of Scripture, 115
  distinguished from law, 119
Gospels, containing two different points of view, 134–38
Gospel of Thomas, 26, 38
Great Bible (1539), 50
Gregory the Great, 98–99
Griesbach, J. J., 34, 35

Hagiographa, 19–20
Hebrew Bible
  resulting from defensive reaction to Christianity's rise, 21
  Scripture interpreting Scripture in, 63–70
Heloise, 106, 107
Hemings, Sally, 150
hermeneutical circle, and art of interpretation, 141–42
hermeneutics, 116, 142
Hexapla (Origen), 31, 81
historical Jesus, 176–80
historical typologies, 62
  in the New Testament, 71–73
  in the Old Testament, 65–70
history
  God acting in, 75
  as sense for reading Scripture, 98
History of Calamities, A (Abelard), 106
Hodge, Charles, 121
holiness movement, 129
Holman Christian Standard Bible, 46n2
Holy, experience of, 6n7
Hort, F. J. A., 34

Identity of Jesus Christ, The (Frei), 183
indigenous myths, merged with biblical stories, 48
interlinear translations, 54
internal considerations, in textual criticism, 42
interpretation, art of, 141–42
intertextuality, 142
intuition, 142
Irenaeus, 24, 78–80, 113, 193
Isaiah, commissioned by the Lord, 7–8
Islam, role of Scripture in, 1
Israel, salvation for, history of, 5

James, M. R., 25, 26
James I, 50–51

Jefferson, Thomas, 147–53, 158, 172, 188
Jeremiah, commissioned by the Lord, 8
Jerome (Eusebius Hieronymous), 26, 31, 32, 33, 81
Jerusalem, identified with Eden and Zion, 68
Jesus
    associated with forgiveness of sins, 9
    attempting to arouse God-consciousness in others, 146
    death of, liberation biblical interpretation of, 180–81
    divinity of, seen in relational terms, 179
    historical, 134, 176–80
    identification of, 71–73, 74–75, 185–88
    interpreting identity of, 9–10
    introducing higher standard of righteousness, 135
    Jefferson valuing, in world of ideas, 147–48
    resurrection of, interpreting, 181–82, 188–90
    sayings of, as sacred Scripture, 10–11
    teachings of, made subordinate to story of, 10–11
    typological correspondence with Suffering Servant, 72–73
Jesus the Liberator (Sobrino), 182
Jewish life, importance of law in, 6–7
John, apostle, 78
John, Gospel of, Prologue to, 56–57, 70–71
Judaism
    Diaspora, 38
    first-century diversity of, 18–19, 37–38
    emergence of, 21–22
    following the Hellenistic period, 3n3
    Orthodox, reverence for Scripture's Hebrew text, 46
    sacred Scripture of, 18–22

justification, gospel of, 115
justification by faith alone, seed of concept, 117
Justinian, 81

Kermode, John Frank, 173–75
King, Martin Luther, Jr., 66, 69
King James Version, 30, 31, 33, 34, 54, 58–59
    compared to Geneva Bible, 51
    popularity of, 52
Knox, John, 50
Koine text, 35–36

Lacalle, Fernando Sáenz, 182
Latin, 48
law, distinguished from gospel, 119
the Law, 19
lectio historica, 128
legal sayings, as divine revelation, 6
Lessing, G. E., 133, 134
liberation biblical interpretation, 176–82
liberation theology, 176–77
Life of Jesus (Schleiermacher), 146
Life and Morals of Jesus of Nazareth extracted textually from the Gospels in Greek, Latin, French & English (Jefferson), 152–53
living knowledge, 128
Locke, John, 148
Lord, etymology of term, in English, 55
Lord's Prayer, 4
Lubac, Henri de, 99
Luke, Gospel of
    redaction criticism applied to, 164–69
    three stages of, 186–87
Luther, Martin, 33, 113–20
    on the authority of Scripture, 117–19
    early approach of, to biblical interpretation, 116
    New Testament translation of, 119–20

Luther, Martin (*continued*)
  setting special value of portions of
    Scripture, 119
  struggling with "righteousness of
    God," 114–15
  understanding of the canon as a
    whole, 119–20
  understanding of the center of faith,
    115

Mandaeans, 166n12
manuscripts
  copies of, 29
  determining which are the best, 31
Marcion, 23–24, 150
Masoretic Text, 37
Matthias, Markus, 128
meaning-for-meaning translation, 52.
    See also dynamic equivalence
    translation
Message, The, 56–57
Metzger, Bruce, 40
miracles, indicative of Jesus' transcen-
    dent holiness, 11–12
miracle stories, form critical approach
    to, 162–64
Mishnah, 6, 21–22
Moses
  calling of, 4
  later biblical figures related to, 69
  response of, to the burning bush, 4
mouth, symbolic purification of, 8
mystery, as essence of sacred narrative, 7
mysticism, 3n4
myth, historicization of, 64

Nag Hammadi Library, 38
National Council of Churches of the
    United States, 29
New American Bible, 54
New English Bible, 57
New International Version, 30–31, 54
New Revised Standard Version, 57

New Testament
  Apocryphal, 25–26
  authorship of, disputed for certain
    books, 25
  early, without limitations, 24
  Luther's translation of, 119–20
  Reimarus's outlook on, 134–38
  as sacred Scripture, 9–15
  viewed in light of natural reason, 133
New Testament in the Original Greek
    (Westcott and Hort), 34
Newton, Isaac, 148
Nicene Creed, 77–78
Niceno-Constantinopolitan Creed, 78
Nicholas of Lyra, 99
Nida, Eugene, 54–55
Niebuhr, H. Richard, 183
Niebuhr, Richard R., 140
numbers, importance of, for
    Augustine, 93

Old Testament
  conclusion of, 7n9
  literal reading of, 133
  as sacred Scripture, 1–9
On Christian Doctrine (Augustine),
    88–89
On First Principles (*De principiis*)
    (Origen), 82, 83
*On Religion: Speeches to Its Cultured
    Despisers* (Schleiermacher), 139–40
Oral Torah, 6
ordinary people, lives of, as subject of
    sacred Scripture, 12
Origen, 31
  approach of, to Scripture, 90
  cosmology of, 82–83
  interpretation of Scripture, 83–86
  legacy of, 85–86
  life of, 80–82, 86–87
  on purpose of translation and
    necessity of study, 59
original languages, difficulties with, 53

Orlinsky, Harry, 34–35
Otto, Rudolf, 6n7

parables, subject to form criticism, 162
past
    as prototype for the future, 67
    recent, linked with prototypical
        events, 65–66
Paul, called into Christ's ministry,
    14–15
Pelikan, Jaroslav, 77
Pentateuch, not set, at time of Dead Sea
    Scrolls, 37
Pentecost, 45
Peter the Venerable of Cluny, 107, 112
Peterson, Eugene H., 57
Pharisees, 18, 19, 37
Philosophy of Jesus, The (Jefferson), 151
Pia Desideria ("Pious Wishes") (Spener),
    122, 123
Pietism, center of Scripture and, 121–29
Plato, 142–43, 148–49
plenary inspiration, 120
poetry, 3
Polycarp, 78
Pope, Marvin, 53
postcritical biblical interpretation,
    183–90
postmodern biblical interpretation,
    173–75
postmodernism, 172–73
prehistory, relating, to the present, 63
present, interpreting, by way of the
    past, 66
Preus, James, 117
Priestley, Joseph, 149
Priestly tradition, 158
Princeton Theological Seminary, 121
projective cosmological-historical
    typology, 71
projective typologies, in the Old
    Testament, 67–68
prophecy, cessation of, 8–9

prophetic oracle, reflecting God's
    self-revelation, 7–9
prophets, sacred revelations attributed
    to, 2
Prophets, the, 19
Protestant Reformation, 26
Protestant scholasticism, and center of
    Scripture, 120–21
proto-Septuagint text, 37
Psalms
    book of, development of, 18
    Luther's interpretation of, 116–17
Pseudepigrapha, 20

Q, 10, 161
Quadriga, 97–100, 107–9, 112, 116
Quenstedt, Johannes, 120–21
Qumran community, 36
    canon of, 37–38
    writings of, 19, 21
Qur'an
    on Jesus' death, 71–72
    sacred only in Arabic, 45–46

Rabbi Judah, 57
rabbinic Judaism, 21
reason, used to draw out faith, 109–10
rebirth, spiritual, as basis for true biblical
    interpretation, 125
Received Text, 33–34
reception theory, 54
reconciliation, as Christ's work, 110–11
redaction criticism, 157–58, 164–69
redemption
    linked with creation, 79–80
    traditional schema of, reversed, 67
redemptive history, 75
Reformation, renewal of search for
    Scripture's thematic center, 113–20
Reimarus, Hermann Samuel, 132–38,
    149, 158, 172, 188
reiteration, role of, in typological
    thinking, 64–65, 67, 69

repetition, role of, in typological think-
    ing, 64–65
retrojective cosmological-historical
    typology, 70–71
retrojective typologies, in the Old Testa-
    ment, 65–66
Revised English Bible, 57
Revised Good News Bible, 58
Revised Standard Version, 29–31, 35,
    36, 57
Revised Today's English Version, 58
Revised Version, 31
risen Lord, encounters with, 12–15
Romero, Oscar, 176, 180
rule of faith, 79, 113, 193
Rush, Benjamin, 149

Sadducees, 18, 19, 37, 38
Salvation Army, 129
Samaritan Pentateuch, 37
Sanneh, Lamin, 46
Schleiermacher, Friedrich D. E.,
    138–47, 129, 143, 157, 172, 188
scholastics, 120–21
Schweitzer, Albert, 123, 132, 134, 138,
    146
scopus, 127–28
Scripture
    Augustine's approach to interpreting,
        89–94
    authority of, 117–19
    Bernard of Clairvaux's approach to,
        103–5
    centers of, 113
    christological content of, 195
    determining literal sense of, 131–32
    divine and human authorship of,
        192–93
    employing typology, 62
    establishing authority of, 120–21
    four senses of (Quadriga), 97–100
    holiness of, inseparable from Law's
        holiness, 7

intentional difficulty of, 90
interpreting from the situation of the
    church of the poor, 177
interpreting Scripture, 92
leading to experience of God's love,
    103
literal meaning of, laying in biblical
    narrative itself, 154
literal and spiritual senses of, 194–95
multiple senses of, 97
not taking literally, 84–85
Origen's interpretation of, 83–86, 90
as part of every Christian's daily life,
    123
Protestant scholasticism and center of,
    120–21
refocusing center of, in Christ's pres-
    ence in life of the believer, 122–23
Reimarus investigating real world
    behind the text, 132–38
revelatory of God, 191
rooted in time and space, 62
sensus literalis of, 184–85
Suger's interpretation of, in architec-
    ture, 100–103
thematic center of, and Luther's Ref-
    ormation, 114–20
three senses of (Gregory the Great),
    98–99
tracing back to individual authors,
    142
translatability of, 45–46
translating into architecture, 100–102
as the Word become words, 15
Second Council of Constantinople, 81
Second Ecumenical Council, 78
semiotics, 89–90
Semler, J., 34
sensus literae, 128
sensus literalem, 128
sensus literalis, 128, 131
sensus mysticus, 128
Septuagint, 20, 21, 31, 32–33, 38

compared to Dead Sea Scrolls and
  Masoretic Text, 47–48
Spirit at work in translation of, 93
Shepherd, Geoffrey, 48
Sic et Non (*Yes and No*) (Abelard), 107,
  109
Sobrino, Jon, 176–82
Song of Songs, Bernard of Clairvaux's
  sermons on, 103–5
source criticism, 156–57, 158–61, 164
spatial correlations, 62
spatial typology
  in the New Testament, 74
  in the Old Testament, 68–69
Spener, Philipp Jakob, concepts of,
  on the center of Scripture, 122,
  123–25
spiritual formation, 123–24
spiritual reading (*lectio divina*), 99
Strabo, Walafried, 116n8
study Bible, 59
Suger of St.-Denis, 100–103, 105,
  112
*Syllabus of an Estimate of the merit of the
  doctrines of Jesus* (Jefferson), 150
Synoptic Gospels
  four-source hypothesis related to, 157
  Schleiermacher preferring John's
  Gospel over, 143–44
systema, 134

Talmudic traditions, dating of, 6n8
Talmuds, 21–22
target audience, 55, 57–58
target language, 55–56
Targums, 37, 38
Ten Commandments
  giving of, 4
  as God's self-revelation, 6–7
text, placing in context, to determine its
  literal sense, 139, 142
*Textual Commentary on the Greek New
  Testament* (Metzger), 40

textual criticism
  current state of, 35–36
  effect on, of the Dead Sea Scrolls
    discovery, 36–37
  emergence of, 34–35
  illustrations of, 39–43
Textus Receptus, 33–34
Theodosius I, 77–78
Theologia Summi Boni (Abelard),
  107
Theology of St Luke, The (Conzelmann),
  164–69
theophany, as God's self-revelation,
  3–4, 7
theoretical knowledge, 128
Tischendorf, Constantin von, 34, 39
Today's English Version, 58
Torah, meaning of, 6
TR. *See* Textus Receptus
translation
  challenge of, 46–48
  deciding on the best, 52
  dynamic equivalence, 52–58
  formal equivalence, 52, 53–58, 59
  incompatible goals of, 55
  interlinear, 54
  involving textual interpretation, 42
  linguistic impact of, 55
  modern, aims of, 52–58
  range of, from most to least
    formal, 58
  target audience for, 55, 57–58
  used to contemporize text, 47
  vernacular, desire for, 48–49
translational considerations, in textual
  criticism, 42
tropological sense, for reading Scripture,
  98, 99, 102–5
True Christianity (Arndt), 122–23
Truman, Harry S., 61
Twelfth-Century Renaissance, 100
twelve-step programs, 129
Tyndale, William, 33, 48

typology, 61–62
  in the New Testament, 70–75
  in the Old Testament, 63–70
  types of, 62–70

Underhill, Evelyn, 103–4
understanding, as the reward of faith, 94
United Bible Societies, 39
United Societies, 124n28

verbal inspiration, 120
vernacular translations, desire for, 48–49
von Balthasar, Hans Urs, 81
Vulgate, 26, 33

Wesley, John, 124n28, 129
Westcott, B. F., 34

William of St. Thierry, 109
wisdom, Augustine's seven steps toward,
  94
women's liberation theology, 176
the Word, as proper method for
  referring to Christianity's sacred
  Scriptures, 9
Word of God, 1, 2
word-for-word translation, 52.
  See also formal equivalence
  translation
Writings, the, 19–20
Wyclif, John, 48

Yahwist, 158

Zinzendorf, Nicholas Count von, 129